CHARLES BUKOWSKI'S

Scarlet

A Memoir by
Pamela "Cupcakes" Wood

2010   SUN DOG PRESS   NORTHVILLE, MICHIGAN

Charles Bukowski's Scarlet
A Memoir by Pamela "Cupcakes" Wood

Copyright © 2010 by Pamela Wood

Cover design by Grey Christian

Book design by Judy Berlinski

For information, address:

Sun Dog Press
22058 Cumberland Drive
Northville, MI 48167

arberlin@twmi.rr.com
info@sundogpress.net

Library of Congress Control Number: 2010920817

ISBN: 978-0-941543-58-3   Trade paper

ISBN: 978-0-941543-59-0   50 paper copies numbered & signed by the author .

ISBN: 978-0-941543-60-6   26 lettered copies signed by the author and hand bound in boards by Bill Roberts of Bottle of Smoke Press

Printed in the United States of America   First Edition

This book is dedicated to the two most important people in my life: my sister, Tracey and my daughter, Stacey.

ONE

"Bukowski is the best fucking writer alive," she yelled out to anyone who would listen, which was nobody except me.

It began as a whim. It would end the same way. In between, I would spend almost two years with Charles Bukowski and find myself both celebrated and castigated in his writing. He would exalt me as his muse and his missing piece. I would inspire volumes of prose and poetry affirming his love and passion for me, including his rare book of love poems written as a paean to me, titled *Scarlet*. He would then excoriate me as elusive, vicious and unfeeling. He would fall madly in love with me and I would drive him mad.

It was November 10, 1975. It was a gorgeous autumn evening in Los Angeles, and I'd spent most of it barhopping with my friend, Georgia. It was her thirty-second birthday, and she wanted to go out in classic Bukowski-esque style by hitting every dive bar in Hollywood: two unruly, fun-loving, charm school dropouts—slumming with the slummiest—starting from the east side of town and heading west.

Pleasure seeking was one of the few things I excelled in. At twenty-three, I was working a dead-end job as a waitress with few options of finding a better way to make a living. As a single parent with a six-year-old daughter to support, finding the time and money to further my education was out of the question. Like many young people at that time, I was lost and adrift, but I never lost hope that something exciting was in store for me. I didn't know what it was or where to find it, but I knew it was out there.

1

But until I found it, or it found me, I would continue my daily quest for immediate gratification. Forget that five-year plan, I was too busy living in the moment. I didn't take myself, or life, too seriously and most of the time was easily pleased. I had youth and good looks on my side—as long as I had a full pack of cigarettes, good music to listen to, and a cheap bottle of champagne, it was a good day.

Like Alice in Wonderland, my impulsive, venturesome nature would often lead me down winding trails, full of twists and turns, which sometimes caused me to lose my way.

Tonight my wanderlust would take me on a life–altering journey down a road named Carlton Way, where I would make a left turn and meet Charles Bukowski.

Georgia and I were now at our last stop—a rowdy, rock 'n' roll nightclub called Barney's Beanery in West Hollywood. She had insisted we go there because that's where her idol Janis Joplin used to hang out. Legend has it that Janis spent her last evening at this very spot the day she died five years earlier.

We were seated at the bar and it was getting close to last call. I'd had more than a few Stingers, while Georgia, like her idol Janis, was getting wasted on Southern Comfort. While we waited for another round, she began blathering loudly about her latest hero—a writer by the name of Charles Bukowski. With each shot of whiskey, she would raise her glass to the Poet Laureate of Skid Row.

"Bukowski is the best fucking writer alive," she yelled out to anyone who would listen, which was nobody except me.

"To Bukowski!" she said, then tilted her head back and poured the shot down her throat.

"Isn't that the guy who writes a column in the *Freep* called 'Notes of a Dirty Old Man'?" I asked.

"Yep, that's him. I'm telling you, Pam, the guy's a fuckin' genius."

With the exception of his weekly column in the *Los Angeles Free Press*, I knew virtually nothing about the man, his work or his growing literary reputation. I had read a couple of his columns and wasn't impressed. His writing seemed common and vulgar, full of gratuitous profanity, designed merely for shock value. I wasn't a prude—I appreciated the ribald, nonconformist works of Henry Miller and Hubert Selby, Jr. But from what little I had read of Bukowski, I found it difficult to understand my friend's overwhelming enthusiasm for him.

"I don't know, George . . . his writing seems so simple and . . . crude," I ventured, as the bartender set down another drink.

"Oh, pa-lease, St. Abdela," she said, skewering me with her green cat's-eyes. "You just don't get it. He does it all—prose—poetry—the guy's fucking amazing. Try reading one of his books."

Though I was young and my education was limited at the time, I loved to read and would rely on my older, more intellectual friends for referrals. Georgia was one of my more eccentric friends, but also one of the most literate people I knew. I figured I didn't know enough about his work to debate the subject. I assumed if she liked him, he must be good.

"Bukowski is out-of-sight. His stuff is so raw and real—and he's so fucking hilarious. I love that son of a bitch!" she said, getting louder with each shot.

"You'll have to loan me one of his books."

"Shee-it—every time I buy one, some bastard steals it from me."

This came as no surprise since Georgia's Hollywood bungalow was a magnet for oddballs and quirky, bohemian characters who could have stepped out of an Andy Warhol flick. There was always a crazy party going on at her place, usually involving drugs and alcohol. Sometimes she'd add strobe lights or a fog machine to the mix. Stealing a Bukowski book would be one of the tamer activities that occurred under her roof.

"Frankly, George, I'm having trouble understanding your excitement for this Bukowski guy. I guess I will have to try reading one of his books—his column just doesn't do it for me," I said, draining my glass.

"Listen . . . read one of his books, and then tell me he's not the best fucking writer around. There's no one like him." She downed another shot, then said, "I'd love to meet that motherfucker."

An idea flashed into my head, and if there's such a thing as fate, this was it. I knew I couldn't bring Janis back from the dead, but thought I might be able to do the next best thing.

"Let's go," I told her, jumping off my barstool.

I was feeling kind of woozy and couldn't remember how many drinks I'd had. I reached into Georgia's purse and rummaged around until I found a Dexi. I threw it in my mouth and swallowed.

Georgia was a walking pharmacy. As long as we were friends, there would be an endless supply. It was a different climate then—it was considered fashionable to experiment with various mind-altering drugs. But my drug of choice was amphetamines. The habit began innocently enough. I'd just wanted to lose a few pounds. But, after losing the weight, I continued taking the pills. I loved the way they made me feel fearless and in control. I figured I could stop anytime I wanted—there was no physical withdrawal to worry about, other than sleeping for a couple of days—right?

Georgia's head was dipping closer and closer to the bar. I yanked her by the arm.

"Come on, George, wake up—it's time to go."

"It's not even last call," she mumbled.

I turned to the guy behind me and looked at his watch. It was almost two in the morning. I turned back to Georgia, but the guy with the watch had other ideas. He put his hands in the back pockets of my jeans and pulled me closer.

"What's your name, gorgeous?" he whispered in my ear. Then he pulled his hands out of my pockets and ran them through my hair. "I'm a sucker for redheads," he said.

"Well, I'm a sucker for gentlemen," I said. Then I looked him in the eye and added, "Let me know if you see one."

He narrowed his eyes, wondering if he should be offended. But then he gave me the once-over and smiled. He couldn't resist the redheaded magic, even if the redhead had just flipped him off.

I didn't consider myself a classic beauty, but, over the years, had come to take for granted the effect I had on men. Maybe it was my long, auburn hair. Maybe it was my petite, 38-24-36 figure. People often told me I looked like a cross between Ann-Margret and Susan Sarandon. It was some sort of inherent, powerful sex appeal, and it could get me into, as well as out of, a lot of trouble.

When I turned back to Georgia, she had her head on the bar. By now she had guzzled about a quart of Southern Comfort, so I wasn't surprised if she was passed out. But I had a mission to accomplish. I was going to make this a night she'd never forget.

"Please, George, wake up," I said, shaking her shoulder. "I'm going to give you the best birthday present of your life."

She opened her eyes, but kept her head on the bar.

"I'll take a knockout face and tits to match," she slurred.

Georgia was obsessed with her looks. She wanted to be beautiful and thin. She had recently lost over a hundred pounds, so she had half of what she wanted. But she was not a pretty woman. Her face was long and horsy, and her features appeared exaggerated. She had a prominent ski-sloped nose, topped off with large, flaring nostrils. Her mouth was unusually wide, accented by deep laugh lines. Though she had just turned thirty-two, she was beginning to show signs of aging—possibly from her considerable weight loss and frequent drug use. Not that her looks, or lack of them, prevented her from getting her own share of male attention. She did have beautiful green eyes and long, silky, jet-black hair. Men loved her out-there personality, her quick wit, and her don't-give-a-damn attitude. She was a connoisseur of the male species, and only the best looking would do—and she usually got what she wanted.

"Come onnn, George—I mean it," I said. "You are going to die when you see what I'm going to do!"

"Listen, Bubbles McGee—or whatever it is your boyfriend used to call you. We're all going to die someday—none of us are going to get out of here alive," she groaned.

"It's Cupcakes O'Brien," I said, correcting her. "Now let's go!"

Somehow I managed to get Georgia outside the bar and navigated her toward the payphone next to the parking lot. I propped her against the phone booth and reached into my jeans pocket to extract a dime.

"If you're calling Bill [not his real name], don't bother," Georgia said, referring to her live-in boyfriend. "I told him I wouldn't be back till dawn."

I dropped the dime in the phone and put my finger in the "0" and dialed.

"How do you spell Bukowski?" I asked Georgia, poking my head out the booth.

"If you're calling the library," she said, "they're fucking closed."

"Just spell it for me," I told her.

"It's spelled like it sounds," she said, then sauntered away to bum a cigarette from a good-looking guy leaving the bar.

I couldn't even remember how to pronounce Bukowski, let alone spell it. Was it BU-kowski? BOO-kowski? BUCK-owski?

When the operator finally came on the line, I said, "Charles Bukowski in Los Angeles, please."

She didn't ask me to spell the name or give her a street address. She just rattled off a phone number.

"Could you please repeat that?" I asked, as I searched through my purse for something to write with. I found a Maybelline eyebrow pencil and scrolled the number on my left palm.

After I hung up, I ran over to Georgia who was still engaged in picking up her young victim.

"I've got it!" I squealed, flashing my hand in front of her face.

She squinted at the number for a second, struggling to keep her balance. Then she turned to the young man and said, "Excuse me, Baby," then turned back to me and said, "if you're calling AA, leave me out."

"It's Bukowski's number," I said, as I guided her back to the phone booth. I propped her back up, dropped a dime in the slot, and dialed the number on my palm.

"Hello?" whispered the male voice on the other end.

"Hellooo," I said, trying to sound sexy. "Is this Charles Bukowski?"

"Yeah," he said as though he was bored by the question.

"Oh, hi . . . umm, it's my girlfriend's birthday and she's a big fan of yours. We're at Barney's Beanery and we were just wondering if we could come by to meet you?"

"Yeah, okay," he said in the same bored tone, "bring it on over."

"Oh . . . okay," I said, not expecting it to be that easy. "What's your address?"

"I'm at 5437 Carlton Way—it's between Hollywood and Sunset, off Western. I'm in the front bungalow on the right."

I wrote the address next to his phone number.

"We'll find it," I said, glancing at Georgia as she slid down the side of the booth.

"Bring a six-pack," he said, then added: "Oh, it's after two," alluding to the cut-off time for buying liquor in L.A.

"You'd be amazed what a little cleavage can do," I said.

"Not really," he said.

After I hung up, I turned and looked at Georgia, who was now sitting on the pavement. She had a silly grin on her face and her green eyes were glowing. She looked up at me with her mouth hanging open.

"Out-o-sight! We're going to meet your lover boy!" I whooped, extending my hand to help her up.

"Far fuckin' out," she said sarcastically, brushing the dirt off her mini-skirt. Then she stopped for a moment and said, "Are you shittin' me? You better not be bull-shitting, Pam."

"I'm not shitting you. You just heard me talking to him."

We wobbled off down Santa Monica Boulevard to find my 1967 red Camaro—Georgia in her thick platform shoes and me in my spiked heels.

"What'd he sound like?" Georgia asked.

"He has a strange voice . . . soft-spoken . . . almost feminine. He sounds kind of like that cartoon character, Snagglepuss—only depressed. I can't believe he's still up at this hour."

"Who isn't?"

As we wandered down the street, Georgia began singing to the tune of Joplin's hit song, "Mercedes Benz."

"Oh Lord, won't you help me find my red Ca-mer-o,
my friend is a loony with re-ed hair-o."

Actually, it was my mom's Camaro. At twenty-three, I still didn't own a car and didn't even have a driver's license. My mother let me take the car whenever I needed it. I think she was glad to get rid of me—or on a subconscious level hoped I'd have a fatal accident, delivering her from all the hell I was putting her through with my constant thrill seeking. We were always fighting, and she never missed an opportunity to tell me how disappointed she was in me. But I couldn't really blame her. Though I was working and had a place of my own, I would find any excuse to get out for a night of hell raising. If I didn't need her for her car, babysitting, frequent loans and an occasional place to stay, I wouldn't have had anything to do with her. Tonight she was with my six-year-old daughter, Stacey. I had Stacey at sixteen. I knew I should be home taking care her, but my need to escape overwhelmed the guilt I felt. I'd had too many responsibilities at a very young age and I was now in desperate search of my lost adolescence.

Georgia elbowed me in the ribs. "Hey, Lucy—there's the red bomber," she said pointing up the street.

"Good job, Ethel!"

We hopped in the car, cranked up the radio and drove to the all-night Safeway on Sunset Boulevard. Georgia waited in the car so I could work my redheaded magic getting the six-pack after cut-off time.

I did my best to charm the clerk, flashing a smile and offering a few glimpses of my 38Ds. I was dressed in my typical class-trash outfit—tight jeans, high heels, low-cut crop top, and preppy tweed jacket with patches on the elbows. While the clerk's eyes said "yes," his head shook "no."

"Can't do it," he said.

"Oh, please," I said in my best sex-kitten purr.

I shook my red mane and looked him in the eyes. He was a young kid, maybe still a teenager, and I could see how conflicted he felt. He wanted to be the cool guy and help out the cute gal, but something wouldn't let him go there.

"I'd like to," he said, and I could see he meant it. "But I just can't."

"Oh, come on, pleease," I cooed, leaning into him.

"Well . . . okay," he whispered, "but I can't do it now because my boss is standing right behind us. I get off in an hour. Meet me out front in the parking lot. I'll stick a bunch under my jacket. How 'bout it?"

"No, that won't work. I really need it now," I said with a pout.

"Okay, I'll tell you what . . . meet me in the dairy section in five minutes . . ."

Just then his boss yelled, "Steven, can I see you for a minute?"

"Sure, Mr. Phillips. I'll be right there."

This assignment was becoming too complicated. I decided to give up on the poor kid and left empty-handed.

When I got back to the car, Georgia was nodding off. I poked her in the ribs, and she jolted straight up, glancing around with her big eyes.

"Are we there yet?" she asked.

I peeled away, speeding down Sunset Boulevard. Fleetwood Mac's "Rhiannon" was blaring on the radio. Georgia was singing along, slurring all the wrong words as she drowned out Stevie Nick's dulcet tones. Her head rocked back and forth and from side to side like a bobble-head doll, as we rumbled along. I wondered if she had taken more pills while I was in the market.

When I first met Georgia, five years earlier, she was extremely overweight and looked like a frumpy, suburban housewife. She was experimenting with drugs at the time, but only recreationally. She would smoke marijuana, have a few drinks, and occasionally take a barbiturate, or two.

I hadn't seen or heard from her since she left Los Angeles over three years before to move back to her hometown, Bradford, Pennsylvania—the same town my mother and father were from. So when she walked into the restaurant where I worked to surprise me, I didn't recognize her. She had changed drastically from the last time I had seen her. Yet she still had that irrepressible, anything-goes style and sardonic wit that I found wildly entertaining.

But now I suspected she had graduated to the hard stuff. I didn't know how often she was using heroin, but I was certain she had crossed that line into dangerous territory. I figured the less I knew the better. We were complete opposites in many ways, including our preference when it came to altering our state of mind; I wanted to be alert and in control, and she wanted to be anesthetized.

We were now racing along on the nearly deserted streets. But when I approached Western Avenue, there was more traffic—in every respect. We were in the heart of the red light district. Cars cruised the parade of hookers, male and female—deals were made—people hopped in and out of cars.

I made a left on Western and drove a few blocks up toward Hollywood Boulevard. Sex shops, strip clubs, and massage parlors announced their wares with signs framed in bright, flashing bulbs. The sexual revolution was at its peak. The morality pendulum had now swung to the other extreme from that of the repressed attitudes of the 1950s. The boundaries of censorship were being pushed to the limit.

As we approached Hollywood Boulevard, I realized I must have passed Bukowski's street. I made a U-turn in the middle of Western Avenue and headed back toward Sunset. Georgia was now butchering the words to the Eagle's song, "Lyin' Eyes," adding to my frustration.

"Maybe he gave you a fake address," Georgia said.

"Nobody gives you a fake address and asks you to bring a six-pack."

Georgia was now fiddling with her black nylons that bagged around her knees. Since she'd lost so much weight, she couldn't seem to find anything that fit properly. After years of muumuus and elastic-waist pants, she was finally dressing up. Only she didn't know what was in style, so she created her own. She thought the fashionable woman dressed as a street-walker—mini skirts, fishnet stockings (held up with a garter belt), skimpy halter-tops, and platform shoes. Sometimes she added a feather boa or saloon girl choker to the mix, because that's what Janis had worn.

Georgia would later enjoy some minor celebrity when she was photographed with Charles Bukowski in front of his refrigerator. In the famous photo, she looks like a wasted hooker. That's pretty much the way she looked this night.

As we headed south on Western Avenue, I began to wonder if Georgia had been right about the fake address. It felt as though we were driving in circles.

"Where the hell are we?" Georgia whined.

"Dammit, I know he's gotta be somewhere around here. We're going to find this genius of yours, if it takes all night!"

Then, as if on cue, I spotted the street sign for Carlton Way. I turned left and found a parking space right across the street from Bukowski's complex.

Georgia adjusted her garters and then tumbled out of the car. I ran my hands through my hair and straightened myself up in preparation to meet the great writer.

2 TWO

Georgia looked up and noticed Bukowski watching her. Since she was a fan of his writing, she probably knew how he felt about women's legs. That may be why she was all spread out like that on the couch, or she was too stoned to care.

$\mathcal{W}e$ were standing in front of two rows of plain, box-like, beige bunga-lows facing each other—three on the left side and one on the right. There was a small courtyard in-between with a sidewalk down the middle leading to a two-story building at the back of the lot, consisting of four units—one on top of the other, facing the street. The front bungalow on the right was set back much further from the curb than the others—that's where Bukowski lived. There were a total of eight units in the bread-and-butter complex.

As we approached his bungalow, there was a galley-type porch with an old davenport taking up most the space. I had to lean over it to ring the doorbell.

On the top half of his front door was a small window covered with ratty looking Venetian blinds. The blinds parted, and I saw an eyeball staring out at us.

"Who is it?" a voice growled.

"It's us," I said, "Pam and Georgia—the birthday girls."

The door opened a crack. "Are you alone?" he asked, looking beyond us.

"It's just us chick-a-dees," Georgia said.

Convinced we were alone, he opened the door and invited us in. He was fairly tall and fairly old, with a large head and ravaged face. After one glance, I averted my eyes. I didn't want to hurt his feelings by staring at his scarred, pockmarked skin. *Wow,* I thought, *this guy has had a rough life.* It looked like a road map to hell imprinted on his face.

Bukowski made a slight turn, and I could see a knife behind his back. I didn't feel threatened. I understood right away that the knife was for his own protection in case we were there to roll him. Considering the neighborhood, it didn't surprise me at all. Georgia and I glanced at each other, but said nothing about it.

His eyes moved from my face, to my chest, to my empty hands.

"You've got the cleavage, but you don't got the six-pack," he said.

"Sorry," I said. "I tried, but I didn't want to get the kid fired."

Georgia held out her hand. She had on three-inch platforms, so she was close to Bukowski's height—about six feet tall. She looked him straight in the eyes.

"I'm Georgia," she said, extending her hand.

"Call me Hank," he replied in that same tired, Snagglepuss drawl.

The phrase—"Exit stage left"—flashed through my mind. I quickly shook the silly thought and introduced myself.

"I'm Pam, but my friends call me Cupcakes—Cupcakes O'Brien."

It was a pet name given to me by my last boyfriend—a creative thinking screenplay writer—and it never failed to elicit the desired response.

Bukowski half smirked and half smiled, then glanced again at my chest and nodded.

"Have a seat, ladies," he said gesturing toward the sofa.

Georgia flopped down and lit a cigarette. She gazed around the room with an awestruck look on her face—as if she were in the Sistine Chapel. She was sitting in her hero's apartment.

I took a seat next to her on the sofa. I tried to see the place through Georgia's eyes, but the charm escaped me. It was the most rundown-looking dump I'd ever seen: An old sofa with a faded red blanket thrown over it; across from the sofa sat an overstuffed, worn-out, mustard and brown striped chair with blotchy stains; in-between was a round coffee table, which was too big for the room and covered with debris, including overflowing ashtrays and

Interior of Buk's Carlton Way apartment (courtesy of Thomas Schmitt)

empty beer bottles; the rug was stained and covered in lint—dust was everywhere, and newspapers were strewn about. To my right was the entrance to the kitchen. The wall connecting the two was partially painted in a chocolate brown. It looked as though someone got too tired to finish the job. To my left was the entrance to the bedroom. From what I could see of both, they looked just as bad. The entire place was approximately five hundred square feet and a hundred miles from bohemian. It was just plain seedy.

"Would you ladies like something to drink?" he asked.

"Do you have any champagne?" I said.

"Jeezus," he said with a hint of a lisp. "What do you think this is—a nightclub?"

"We don't care," Georgia said, shooting death rays at me with her eyes, "whatever you have, man."

He shuffled into the kitchen and we heard him yell, "Hey, ladies, you're in luck."

He came back into the living room holding a bottle of champagne and three jelly glasses.

"I forgot I had this," he said, "must be left over from my last lovely."

While he opened the bottle, I took my first good look at him. He was wearing a white T-shirt that was two sizes too small, so that a bit of his beer belly peeked out. He had on baggy blue jeans that came up well above his ankles. He wore old black socks with no shoes. His thick, wavy, salt and pepper hair was on the long side, slicked back with water or maybe Brylcreem ("A little dab'll do ya!")—apparently, the only thing he'd done to get ready for our visit.

On his ravaged face was a large, bulbous nose. He had a funny mouth that made him look a little like a Muppet, covered by a well-trimmed beard. From what I could see of his eyes, which were always at half-mast, they appeared to be a beautiful, pale greenish-blue. Aside from a slight beer gut, he had a strong looking physique. He looked to be in very good shape for a man his age.

He poured the champagne, and we clinked our glasses together.

"Happy birthday, Georgia," Bukowski said.

"It's not my birthday anymore," she said. "It was on the 9th. What is today—November 11th?"

"This was a day I always looked forward to when I worked for the post office," Bukowski said. "Veterans Day—it's a holiday."

Georgia laughed. "I read that book, *Post Office*," she said. "Did all that shit really happen to you?"

"Unfortunately, yes," he said.

Georgia asked Bukowski some more questions about his writing. I was afraid he would ask me about one of his books or columns—and find out I knew almost nothing about his work.

While they talked, I ambled over to the kitchen, which was right off the living room. A 1950s-style kitchen table with chrome legs and Formica top was pushed up against the wall. Sitting on the table was an old, black, manual typewriter, with a transistor radio beside it. One small, armless, chrome chair with a vinyl seat was pushed underneath the table in front of the old Royal. On the left side of the table sat a two-foot trash can full of empty beer bottles and wadded papers.

I must have been really deep in thought, because the next thing I knew Bukowski was standing by the open refrigerator retrieving some beers. He looked around the room and grinned.

"Not what you expected, huh?"

"I don't know how you can write in here," I said. "It doesn't look very comfortable."

"You thought maybe I'd have a cozy writing den with a blazing fire?"

"Something between that and this," I told him.

He handed me a beer, but I held up my still-full glass of champagne.

"Better drink up," he said, "before your friend and I finish it all."

He turned his weary eyes on me and seemed to see right into me. From the look on his face, it didn't appear as if he liked what he saw.

I was confused. I couldn't remember the last time a man hadn't been immediately attracted to me. And this one actually seemed to *dislike* me. He acted guarded and aloof toward me. It was a shock to my self-image.

We walked back into the living room. He sat in his striped throne and I sat on the sofa next to Georgia. She was looking at herself in the big silver mirror she kept in her over-sized purse. Knowing Georgia, she'd probably opened her purse to get some pills, and had then become distracted and started gazing at herself. When she saw us watching her, she grabbed an eyebrow pencil and began to touch up her eyebrows. Bukowski and I stared at her as though she was an artist painting an interesting piece of sculpture.

Her legs were now splayed out on the couch. Her skirt was hiked up, with her garters in full view. I would soon learn that he was a leg man par excellence. Never before, or since, have I met a man who adored women's legs the way Bukowski did. He just went gaga over them. Someone once told me that "leg men" were often momma's boys when they were young, deriving great comfort and security from holding onto their mother's calves. Georgia's legs were long and skinny and her nylons were bagging around her knees. The effect was more sluttish than sexy. But Bukowski didn't seem to mind.

Georgia looked up and noticed Bukowski watching her. Since she was a fan of his writing, she probably knew how he felt about women's legs. That may be why she was all spread out like that on the couch, or she was too stoned to care.

"I hate pantyhose," she said. "The motherfucker who invented those should be strung up by the balls—probably some female-loathing homo."

"Couldn't agree with you more," he said.

Georgia continued penciling her eyebrows as she continued her rant, "With those fucking pantyhose, your twat can't breathe, so you end up with a vat of buttermilk in your crotch."

Bukowski laughed, throwing his head back. I could see the gaps on both sides of his mouth where he was missing teeth.

"Pam wears pantyhose," Georgia said, putting away her mirror and eyebrow pencil.

Even though Georgia and I were friends, I never completely trusted her. Every time she had the chance, she slung a barb or two my way. I guess she figured I could take it. I admired Georgia's acerbic, irreverent wit, but sometimes the barbs stung, though I never let on. I assumed she was envious of all the attention I got from the opposite sex. Though right now, she was the one getting most of it.

"I have to wear them at work," I explained. "It's part of my uniform."

"Uniform?" Bukowski said. "Don't tell me you work at the post office."

Georgia let out a horsy laugh, complete with a couple of snorts.

I tried to think of a witty retort, but figured anything I said would fall flat with these two.

"I'm a waitress at the Alpine Inn on Hollywood Boulevard," I said, hoping to close the subject.

15

"She wears a girdle," Georgia said.

"A dirndl," I corrected.

"I was born in the land of dirndls," Bukowski said, "though I don't remember much about it."

"Maybe you should come over to the Alpine Inn," I said, "and refresh your memory. You can wear your lederhosen."

Georgia curled her lip at me. It was as if we were both vying for Bukowski's attention. I wasn't really interested in him, and didn't think she was either—at least not in a romantic way. But I figured this was her night, so I was fine with giving her the limelight.

Georgia tugged again at her black stockings. Her skirt was hiked up exposing the garters. She was now attempting to tighten up her nylons.

"Need some help with that?" Bukowski asked, as he stood up and headed for the sofa.

He sat down between us. I decided to move to the floor. Georgia flopped her legs over Bukowski's and he began to gently smooth out her stockings.

"That tickles," she said, laughing.

I smiled. I had definitely given Georgia the best birthday of her life.

More drinks followed. Now we were all lying on the floor, with Bukowski in-between, and he was playfully stroking Georgia's legs and mine. Somehow his right foot ended up in Georgia's purse, which was also on the floor. He rolled it over and her pill bottles spilled onto the carpet.

"What are you holding, woman? Looks like you robbed a drugstore." He sat up and grabbed a couple of bottles, shaking them like maracas.

"You name it, Baby—I've got it," she said. "Want some?"

"Sure, why not?" he said in that cool, slow drawl.

I would later learn that he would try anything once. He never really listened to anyone's advice, never had any preconceived judgments, and had to figure out everything for himself. He had a high tolerance for trial and error. But when it came to pills or any kind of drug, Bukowski usually ended up sick and sorry for the experiment.

He swallowed a pill and said, "Okay, girls—let's celebrate!"

I was surprised at how much his mood had changed. He'd shifted from the wary, defensive, sad man with the knife behind his back to the fun guy who was ready for anything. We were all in pretty good spirits by now.

Bukowski was now back in his striped chair. Georgia was sprawled out on the couch and I stayed on the floor, seated beside him. He pointed to Georgia and said, "You've got the soul." Then he looked down at me and said, "You've got the looks."

He took a long pull on his beer and his eyes rolled toward the ceiling, as if he were deep in thought.

"I'd like to combine the two of you into one person," he told us. "The looks and the soul. I would then have the perfect woman."

I glanced at Georgia, wondering if she was as insulted as I was. It was a bizarre, back-handed compliment and/or insult.

"Hey, Baby, beauty's only sin deep," Georgia quipped.

"Yah, yah, yah," I sang, hoping to lighten the sting.

I began putting the pill bottles back in Georgia's purse. She had given Bukowski a Dexi.

"You're not going to get any sleep tonight, Mr. Bukowski," I said.

"Why? Are we going to have a threesome?"

I looked over at Georgia for some help, but she was beginning to pass out from the booze and downers.

Pleasantly buzzed and feeling rather playful, I said, "You want me—it'll cost ya."

"How much?"

"Oh . . . at least a hundred," I teased.

"Okay," he said.

Worried that he thought I was serious, I laughed and said, "Hey, I was just kidding."

"Well, what will it cost?" he asked.

By this time, his ravaged face was beginning to look less intimidating. He was gruff on the outside, but underneath it he had a vulnerability that I found appealing. I wasn't sure if it was the booze taking over, but I began to find him strangely sexy, in a rugged sort of way.

I looked into his eyes, and with a "come hither" look and flashed him a coy smile.

"Oh, no, Cupcakes," he said, "I don't think I can ever pay that price again."

I took a dramatic puff on my cigarette and slowly blew out the smoke. Then I said in my best Lauren Bacall, "Sure you can."

He studied me with his head tilted to one side, then said, "You're dangerous, Red."

We both broke out in laughter. His guard was coming down, and I felt relieved. It had been a while since any man had held out so long against the redheaded charm.

"I like your earrings," he said, pointing to the big gold hoops I was wearing.

"You want them?" I said, starting to take one off.

"They look a lot better on you," he said.

We continued with our silly banter and laughed and drank some more. I was having a good time with him. He didn't act as if all of this was just a prelude to a bedroom romp.

After a while, Georgia woke up. It was close to five a.m.

As we were standing at his door ready to leave, Bukowski said, "Thanks, girls. Come back anytime."

As we started down the courtyard sidewalk, I could hear a typewriter clicking away inside Bukowski's bungalow.

"Now that's a fucking writer," Georgia said, as she piled into the Camaro.

I dropped Georgia off at her apartment in Hollywood, where she lived on welfare with her boyfriend Bill and her two little girls. Then I drove to my rented guesthouse about ten minutes away in Los Feliz. My daughter was spending the night with my mom. Since it was Veterans Day, they both had the day off. I would pick her up that afternoon.

When I crawled into bed, I thought about what an interesting night it had been, never imagining that I'd see the old man again.

"What a trip," I said to myself before I fell asleep.

THREE

I'd see him glancing at my chest, then his eyes would linger on my legs, even my feet, but not in a lecherous way. It was as though he was appraising a piece of art and found it aesthetically pleasing.

During 1975, I worked as a barmaid at the Alpine Inn on Hollywood Boulevard, an authentic German restaurant catering to German immigrants. My hours were from six p.m. till two a.m., Tuesday through Saturday. It would sometimes take hours for me to unwind after my shift and I usually didn't feel like going straight home. One Saturday night, about two weeks after I'd first met Bukowski, I'd had a rough night at the bar and was feeling tense. I decided to stop by to pay him a visit on my way home. His place was located about a mile from my work. He had mentioned that he kept strange hours, so I was fairly confident he'd still be up at 2:30 a.m.

When I knocked on his door, he barked out, "Who is it?"

"It's the redheaded floozy," I said and giggled.

I felt nervous and shy—probably because I was completely sober.

Bukowski opened the door—this time without a knife behind his back. He seemed pleased to see me—even if I didn't have a soul.

He looked at me with those weary, blue-green eyes and said, "No place else to go, Kid?"

"Is that the only reason women visit you?" I asked as I walked into the living room.

"That—and I usually have something to drink," he said, shutting the door.

I followed him into the kitchen as he grabbed two bottles of Michelob from his ancient refrigerator. The place was as grungy-looking as I remembered. He was wearing his usual too-tight T-shirt and belly-hugging jeans. It was not a great look, but his hospitality made up for it.

It was my first drink of the day. I could go for days like that, living the straight life—no pills, no alcohol, no partying—just going to work and taking care of my daughter. But then something would pull me, and I would be back to that other life.

Bukowski seemed almost bashful as he led me to his worn-out sofa. This was not a scene for seduction. But I was intrigued by his mind, and I wanted to get to know him better.

I sat down beside him and kicked off my white Minnie Mouse pumps and curled my legs under my barmaid uniform. I was wearing a dirndl, which was a green floral dress, with a short, full skirt, tight fitting bodice, and a low-cut, white, peasant blouse underneath. I liked it because it had a sexy, but sweet, milkmaid look about it.

I raised my bottle and clinked his.

"Here's to ya, Mr. Bukowski," I said.

"Here's to you, Red," he said, taking a long pull from his beer.

"So—did you just get off work, or do you always dress like Heidi?"

I laughed and went on to tell him about the argument I had with one of the regulars at the bar. He was a nice enough guy, but after a few drinks would often bring up the Holocaust. Apparently he felt guilty about it and would go off on rants denying it happened. Not wanting to insult a good paying customer and possibly get fired, I'd bite my tongue and try to change the subject. But this evening, I'd had enough. I told him that it certainly did happen and he should be ashamed of himself for implying otherwise. *How dare he attempt to dismiss the existence of millions of Jews put to death by a madman that he hoped to defend?* I was so upset, I left the bar and walked around the block. I returned fifteen minutes later expecting to be fired on the spot. Surprisingly, the owner, who witnessed the confrontation, was apologetic to me, but did suggest that in the future I try to keep my opinions to myself.

Bukowski, though he did agree it was a dark period in history, seemed more interested in my customers than discussing the topic of my argument.

"I imagine you have to put up with a lot of crazy, drunken bastards," he said.

I told him about some of the regulars, like the young Marine that came in every night and just stared at me. It was a little creepy, but he always left a huge tip. There was the young Austrian man who would come in, put a dime in the jukebox and play, "The too Fat Polka." Then he would jump behind the bar, grab me by the waist and take me for a polka romp across the floor. Luckily the owner would intervene and save me from the pie-eyed Lawrence Welk. But the guy that always got to me was the old widower who had lost his wife years ago and still mourned for her. He played the same song over and over, and talked about her incessantly. The song was called, "Du Du Liegst Mir Im Herzen" (You, You, Weigh on My Heart). It was the only song I actually liked on the German playlist, but my heart broke for the old man, and I never knew what to say.

Bukowski sat politely listening to me ramble on about the characters in the bar. The mood between us was much different than our first meeting. I was more coherent and down to earth. Not the capricious, smart-aleck he met two weeks ago.

I found myself wanting to know more about him. He was an enigma. His lifestyle seemed to belie his almost regal manner. Of course, I had yet to see the dark side of this complicated man.

"Okay," I said, "enough about my dead-end job. Tell me about you. Are you from L.A.?"

"I was born in Germany," he began. "My father was a soldier with the U.S. Army and stationed there during World War I—that's where he met my mother. They married, had me, then two years later he moved us back to the States. We settled in Los Angeles and, except for a few dark years, I've been here most of my life. I've lived in this place for about a year. The rent's cheap and this is where it's happenin', Baby. There's no place I'd rather be than L.A. This is the pulse of the universe—where the blood is the brightest."

"And I'm sure you see it flow frequently in these streets. Must be good for material," I said.

"Especially when people like you come to visit."

"Do you meet a lot of people like me?"

"Let's say people come over—can't say they're like you."

I could tell he liked me—mostly by the way he avoided looking in my eyes. He was like a shy little kid at his first dance. He also had a nervous habit of peeling the labels off his beer bottle when he spoke. After a couple drinks, I decided to loosen him up.

I stood up and walked over to the kitchen table where he kept the radio. "Mind if I play some music?" I asked.

"Make yourself at home, Red," he said, following me to grab a couple more beers from the fridge. He handed one to me as we walked back into the living room. I set the radio on the coffee table and turned it on. Classical music began playing.

"Oh, no, that won't do," I said. "This will put us to sleep."

"You don't like classical music?"

"Not really—except for the *William Tell Overture*. I'm a 'rock 'n' roll' baby. That's all I listen to."

"Longhaired stuff is all I can listen to. It gets the juice flowing. Besides, I hate the sound of the human voice. It ruins the beauty of the music. In fact, it usually ruins everything."

"Jeez, you're quite the cynic, Hank. You need to loosen up, mister."

I think by now he realized he was dealing with a "Bukowski" virgin. Knowing almost nothing about him, I had no preconceived notions. He didn't have to worry about living up to an image. I was like a child who had no idea she was in a room with a madman—reminiscent of the scene in the Boris Karloff version of Frankenstein, when the little girl meets the monster by the lake.

I found a rock station that was playing top 40 tunes. Linda Ronstadt was singing her version of "Heat Wave." I jumped up and grabbed him by both hands, pulling him from the couch.

"Come on, Hank—let's dance!"

"No thanks, Kid. You dance, I'll watch."

"Like a heat wave, burning in my heart," I crooned. "Like a heat wave, tearing me apart—yah, yah, yah, yah, yah."

Bukowski watched me, sitting and smiling through my impromptu act. I danced around the room like a fool, pretending my beer bottle was a microphone. Being the frustrated entertainer that I was, I loved having a captive audience. When the song was over, I bowed and he clapped.

"Now didn't you like that song?"

"I like your voice," he said. "It's sexy."

"You like my voice or Linda Ronstadt's?"

"What's her name?"

"You've never heard of Linda Ronstadt?"

Bukowski shook his head. "I told you, I only listen to classical stuff. It helps me write. Sometimes I don't mind listening to the female voice, but I can't stand hearing a man sing."

Just then, Paul Simon's "50 Ways to Leave Your Lover" began playing. I danced and sang along to all the words.

"Just slip out the back, Jack—make a

new plan, Stan—you don't need to be coy, Roy—

just get yourself free," I crooned.

When the song ended, I asked, "Now didn't you like that one?"

"Yeah, I did," he said chuckling. "That guy's got some style—some sparkle. What were those lyrics—just jump out the back, Jack? Yeah, that was okay, Kid."

When the DJ came on and began his puke-like spiel, Bukowski quickly turned off the radio.

"Sorry, Cupcakes—that voice is sickening. It offends my delicate sensibilities. Listening to it makes me want to heave."

We sat for a while on the sofa, sipping our beers and talking. For the first time since I'd arrived, he looked me right in the eyes. His eyes were quite beautiful. They seemed out of place in his ravaged head. I wasn't sure what I wanted from him, but he intrigued me. I needed some direction in my life and felt he may be a good friend and mentor.

After a while, I found myself strangely attracted to him. I've always had an affinity for writers. Maybe it was the combination of intellect and self-destruction that I found so attractive. I was just ending a five-year relationship with a well-known screenplay writer. My father was also a writer. He left when I was five-years old—maybe there was some Freudian draw at work.

I could tell he was attracted to me too. He kept gazing at my hair. Every so often, I'd see him glancing at my chest, then his eyes would linger on my legs, even my feet, but not in a lecherous way. It was as though he was appraising a piece of art and found it aesthetically pleasing. I felt admired and appreciated, not at all uncomfortable or threatened.

We continued talking, moving from the kitchen to the living room and back again. We went nowhere near the bedroom. Bukowski was respectful, even courtly.

I told him I was twenty-three and asked his age. He was fifty-five. Though he was thirty-two years my senior, he seemed much younger, as though he had been locked away somewhere for years.

I told him about my six-year-old daughter. He mentioned that he also had a daughter. She was eleven-years-old and lived with her mother near the beach. He would visit her often.

I also told him that I admired him for being able to make a living writing (though it appeared sales were rather slow) and wished I had a talent for it. I mentioned the many writers in my life: the screenplay writer; my brother Larry, who had majored in journalism while attending UCLA; and my father, who had been a newspaper reporter and had his first novel published a year earlier.

"I'd love to write, but I just don't know where to begin," I said.

"You begin at the beginning. You can learn how to write if you work at it," he said.

"But how do you make a living from it?" I asked. "People actually buy what you write."

"I make more money at the racetrack than I do from my writing."

I laughed. Judging by his surroundings, I believed him.

"Let that be a lesson to you, Red. Most people who think they can write are better off finding a real occupation. Like anything you want in life, if you're not driven by it, or willing to sacrifice for it, don't waste your time." Then he raised his beer and added, "That includes your liver too."

Then I finally admitted I knew nothing about his writing.

He grabbed a copy of *Notes of a Dirty Old Man* from the makeshift bookshelf, picked up a pen and wrote something inside. Then he handed the book to me.

"This is one of my earlier books. Don't want you to leave empty-handed."

"Am I leaving?"

I looked at the clock. It was going on four a.m.

"Only if you want to."

As I flipped through the paperback, Bukowski told me how he came to write his first novel, *Post Office*. John Martin, his publisher, had offered to give him a hundred dollars a month—whether he ever wrote anything or not. The money allowed Bukowski to quit his job and write full time. Three weeks after he left the post office, he called Martin and told him to come over and pick it up. Martin was incredulous when he realized that Bukowski had written a novel in three weeks.

"I thank the gods every day for John," Bukowski said. "Without him, I'd still be a sniveling, red-ass monkey working for the government. Or maybe I'd be dead."

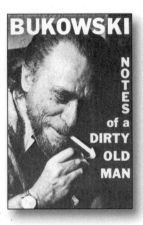

The inscription inside read: "For Pamela Brandes—Who brought me the knife of laughter. Charles Bukowski." On one side, he had drawn his signature man smoking a cigarette with the sun shining above his head; on the other side he had drawn a side view of the same little man with a bird flying above with a dog at his feet. I guess I should have been more impressed with the book. But it just looked like a small press paperback to me and not very professional. Even my father was published in hard-cover.

"Thank you, Hank. That's very nice of you. I'll read it in bed tonight," I promised, as I slipped it in my purse.

Around five a.m., I stood up to leave.

"Let me walk you to your car," Bukowski said, slipping on his old black loafers.

After I got in the car, he leaned through the open window and kissed me gently on the lips.

"Can I have your phone number?" he whispered.

I smiled and began to dig through the litter on the passenger seat. Somehow I managed to extract a pen. I tore off a piece of a McDonald's bag and wrote my name and number on it.

He took the paper from me and slipped it into the pocket of his jeans.

"Goodnight, Cupcakes," he said, then stood up and waved.

At the end of the block, I looked in my rearview mirror. He was still waving.

FOUR

"And I was 'Miss Pussycat of 1973," I said.

Two days later, Bukowski called. It was around nine on a Monday evening.

"Can I come over?" he asked.

I was putting my daughter to bed, so I asked him to wait an hour.

I gave him my address. He was happy that I lived only five minutes or so from him. In L.A., many romances end before they begin because one person lives near the ocean and the other person lives on the east side—a commute of at least several hours. But Bukowski and I were a great match, at least geographically.

After tucking Stacey into bed and kissing her goodnight, I straightened up my place. I lived in a guesthouse behind a "real" dirty old man who was always trying to corner me the minute his wife left the house. I hated always having to avoid the pervert, but the place was a cute one-bedroom in a fairly decent neighborhood. (Stacey slept in the bedroom and I slept on the sofa bed in the living room.) The rent was cheap and it was close to my mom and my job.

I picked up Stacey's toys and put away the dishes. My place wasn't the neatest or most stylish in the world, but next to Bukowski's it belonged in *House and Garden* magazine. I just had time to put on a clean T-shirt over my miniskirt and run a comb through my hair when I heard a faint rapping.

I closed the door to Stacey's room, then tiptoed in my bare feet to the front door. I started to get nervous. I felt comfortable with Bukowski, but I didn't know what he expected during his visit. I rarely invited men to my place when my daughter was there—and I certainly never slept with anyone while she was home. As far as I was concerned, we were just going to talk for a while and then he was going back to Carlton Way.

When I opened the door, Bukowski was standing there in a polyester shirt with a hideous green pattern that included birds, canoes, and mountains. He was smiling and holding a six-pack of beer in each hand. He handed one to me as he walked in the door.

"What? No roses?" I kidded.

"My rose garden is bare till spring—so I brought the next best thing," he said in an unintentional rhyme.

"Wow, you really are a poet."

He laughed and I put my finger up to my lips and pointed to the bedroom door. Like Bukowski's place, there were no hallways—one door led into another room.

"She's asleep," I said.

"I understand," he said. "I have a daughter too."

He followed me to the kitchen. I pulled out two beers and put the rest in the refrigerator. We sat with our beer and cigarettes at the small ice-cream style table in my kitchen. I couldn't take my eyes off his shirt.

"So you got all dressed up for me tonight," I said.

He blushed, looked at the floor, then smiled. He seemed pleased that I'd noticed. It looked like a brand new shirt. Somehow I knew he'd purchased it earlier in the day so he'd have something special to wear tonight. I was flattered.

The table was small and the kitchen light was bright. He looked a little uncomfortable, so I began the conversation.

"Tell me more about your daughter," I said.

"Her name is Marina, she's eleven years old and lives with her mom near the beach. I see her when I can. She knows her dad is different, but she knows I love her and do the best I can. It's so strange to see her becoming this beautiful female creature—and she's already smarter than her old man." He looked away as though he were in deep thought, then said, "Okay . . . that's all."

"Were you married to her mom?"

"Frances didn't want to get married. She's a free spirit and a very good soul."

"How did you meet?"

"She was a fan. She liked my writing and we corresponded for a while. She said she wanted to meet me. I guess she thought I was a sensitive guy," he said with a chuckle. "She is a poet too. We ended up living together, and she got pregnant. She didn't want to get married—she knew better. She's a smart woman."

"So do you have a lot of female admirers?" I asked.

"Some women read my books and think they want to meet me."

"Maybe it's a good thing I haven't read any of your books." Though from what little I had read, "sensitive" was not an adjective I would assign to him.

He laughed. The sound came out louder than he'd expected. He looked toward the living room and covered his mouth with his hand.

"Sorry," he whispered.

"She's a pretty heavy sleeper," I said. "Anyway, if she wakes up, she's not going to see anything she's not supposed to see."

I looked in his eyes to see if he knew what I meant. He did.

"When I phoned you tonight," Bukowski said, "it's the first time I've called a woman in years. They usually come to me."

"I should be flattered," I said.

"Aren't you?"

"Half the time," I said, "I think you're pulling my leg."

"I would never do that," he said. "I hate clichés."

He took a sip of beer, and then peeked under the table to get a look at my crossed legs.

"I'd like to push your leg sometime," he said.

Suddenly he furrowed his brow and looked very sad. He set down his beer and closed his eyes. His shoulders hunched over. His entire demeanor seemed to change in an instant.

"What's wrong?" I asked.

"Sorry, it's nothing. I'm fine," he said, heaving a sigh.

"Tell me—what is it—something I said?"

"No, no, it's nothing. Your legs reminded me of someone, that's all."

"Frances?"

"No, Jane . . . I guess you could say she was my first love. She had great legs too. She's dead. She liked the wine too much. Okay . . . that's all. Let's change the subject—sorry I brought it up," he said wistfully.

I brought him another beer. After I opened it, I put my hand on his shoulder. He looked so incredibly sad. By the way his eyes welled up, I could tell the memory of this woman was extremely painful. If this was an act to endear him to me, it was working. As we began to know each other better, he would tell me more about Jane. But tonight, I left it alone.

"I'm sorry," I said.

His pain was palpable. I could feel what he was feeling—overwhelming grief and guilt. I hadn't met too many men who felt anything so deeply—especially when it came to women. I was beginning to realize why so many of his female fans wanted to meet him. A sensitive man was hard to find.

He drank the rest of his beer in silence. After a while, he looked up at me.

"What about you?" he said.

"Me?"

"Husbands? Boyfriends?"

"I was married to Stacey's father," I said. "But it only lasted a year or so. We were too young to get married. Actually, I was too young. I was fifteen and a virgin when I met him—he was twenty-two. A year later I became pregnant. After much pressure from his Mormon parents and my 'Dear God, what will the neighbors think' mother, I married him. I left him shortly after Stacey was born."

With Bob

I then went on to tell him about my last two ex-boyfriends—starting with the screenwriter, Bob, who left me for the actress, Cindy Williams. Bob lived in the guesthouse behind Georgia when she first arrived in Hollywood five years earlier. He wrote during the day and worked the late shift as a forklift driver. He would join the party at Georgia's once he got off work after midnight. I was seventeen and he was twenty-five. It was love at first sight. We would stay together until he had some luck with his writing. A few years after we met, his screenplay was optioned by MGM. They also asked him to write a screenplay as a vehicle for Dean Martin. It was called, *Mr. Ricco*. It starred Dino and Cindy Williams, who would go on to fame as "Shirley" in the hit TV show Laverne and Shirley. Bob and Cindy met on the set while filming *Mr. Ricco* and hit it off immediately. That was the end of Bob and me, at least romantically. Shortly thereafter, I began dating the vice-president of Pussycat Theaters, where I was working at the time. It ended up getting me fired. I violated the "no dating coworkers" policy.

"What did you do at Pussycat?" Bukowski asked. All of a sudden, he didn't look so sad. The subject of an adult movie theater chain can make anybody perk up.

"I started at the candy counter . . ." I began.

"They sell candy at skin flicks?" he asked.

"Don't tell me you've never been to one."

"Not my style, Kid," he said. "They're like watching open heart surgery to me. I don't want to see it all. I prefer to imagine what's behind the curtain."

Bukowski was probably the first man I'd met who had never seen an adult film. I would never see any pornography in his home the entire time we were together.

"You're a romantic, eh?" I said.

"Just an old-fashioned motherfuck underneath it all, Baby. So finish telling me what happened after you handed out the Raisinets?"

I explained that I was nineteen and looking for a job. I answered an ad in the *Los Angeles Times* classifieds advertising for a candy girl at a movie theatre. It didn't give the theatre name in the ad, only the address on Western Avenue in Hollywood. When I showed up to fill out an application I was surprised to find it was an adult theatre. But I didn't really care because I needed a job and wasn't going to watch the movies, or star in them, just sell Milk Duds. A few weeks later the owner of the conglomerate stopped by with his hair on fire, looking for someone to help out temporarily in the main office, which was located right around the corner on Sunset Boulevard. His receptionist had walked out and he needed someone immediately to answer the phones. He was a flamboyant gay man named Vince Miranda. He saw me behind the counter and asked if I'd mind coming with him to the main office for the day. He ended up offering the position to me full time. My job was to answer phones, file, call all the theaters to get the receipts, then calculate the daily box-office for each one.

"And I was Miss Pussycat of 1973," I said. "I took over when the actual Miss Pussycat got married. I think she was pregnant."

That was another stroke of fate, when the actual Miss Pussycat called Vince to tell him she was resigning, effective immediately. Again, Vince was in a tizzy because she was to appear that weekend at one of the legitimate theatres he owned in San Diego to have her picture taken with the troops.

Vince Miranda at the Pussycat Theater

Bukowski laughed again. He had a nice laugh that sent out waves and let me know how much he enjoyed my company.

While he chuckled, I told him how I would go to openings of new theaters and officiate at the ribbon-cutting ceremonies. I was even interviewed once by Johnny Grant, the honorary mayor of Hollywood. My name would occasionally appear in show business publications, like the *Daily Variety* and *The Hollywood Reporter*, linking me with male celebrities who were in reality gay. Their publicists would call and ask my permission. I didn't mind—anything for a good cause.

"Sounds like a great job," he said.

"It was fun while it lasted," I told him.

I brought him another beer. Then he asked if I would mind moving to the living room. We sat on the couch, and I turned on the radio so it played at low volume. Linda Ronstadt was singing "Tracks of My Tears."

"I like that singer," he said. "What's her name?"

"Linda Ronstadt. You heard her singing the other night, remember?"

"Linda, right," he said, and a cloud seemed to drift across his eyes. "I just broke up with a woman named Linda."

I found it strange that this was the first I was hearing about her. After some coaxing, Bukowski told me about his five-year relationship with Linda King. He said there were a lot of good times and a lot of bad times and that he had been very much in love with her. At the end, there were more bad times than good. He just found her too volatile. He needed to get away from all the drama.

"When did you break up?" I asked.

"I don't know if she knows that it's really over," he said. "She keeps calling, but I just don't want anymore to do with her."

"Don't you think you ought to let her know?" I said.

He just sighed. He was getting that same furrowed-brow sad look again. He looked at me and then put his hand over mine. We stayed like that for a while. I glanced at the clock. It was three in the morning. He saw me checking the time, but didn't seem to be in a hurry to leave. It was getting late and I was tired.

"Could we lie down next to each other?" he asked. "Could I just hold you for a while?"

I looked at him, not sure what to think about what he'd just asked. I was beginning to feel nervous. Was he going to make a move? Then I looked in those sad eyes. He looked so sweet and vulnerable. I couldn't say no. But just for a little insurance, I embellished the truth.

"Okay, but no kissing. Sorry, but I have a bad tooth and I wouldn't want to offend you," I said as a defense mechanism.

"You should see a dentist," he said.

"I will," I said, as I pulled the cushions off the sofa. "There's a dentist in the same building as my doctor. I have an appointment to get a B-12 shot next week. I'll do it then."

We pulled out the sofa bed and turned down the lights. I switched off the radio, but left the television on without sound. We stretched out next to each other. I faced the TV and he faced my back, with his arms around me. We fit together like spoons in a drawer. He held me gently and stroked my hair. We stayed like that for a while until we both dozed off. It was achingly sweet. I could sense his feelings for me. I felt safe and protected.

When I woke up, it was after five a.m. I turned and looked at him in the darkness.

"Hank," I whispered nudging him. "You're going to have to leave before Stacey wakes up."

"I will."

"When?"

"Soon."

"Now, Hank. I don't want my daughter waking up seeing some strange man in her mom's bed."

We both swung our legs over the side of the mattress. He stood up slowly and followed me to the front door. As he stood in the doorway half asleep, I touched him on the cheek and gave him a peck on the lips.

"Can I see you again, Cups?" he asked.

I was having difficulty assessing this man in front of me. There seemed to be so many fascinating incongruities about him. Like meeting an elegant bum, I did want to know more about him. He was clearly interested in a romantic relationship with me. I wasn't sure at this point that I wanted to take things to the next level. But not wanting to hurt this shy, vulnerable, sensitive man, I said the only thing I could say. *Yes.*

The Whole "Fam Damily"

Top left to right: *Maternal Grandma; Mom's brother, Gino; Mom; Grandpa behind counter—all in family general store.* Insert: *Maternal Grandparents*
Center left to right: *Mother, Parents, Dad.*
Bottom left to right: *Tracey, Me, Larry*
Insert left to right: *Tracey, Me, Larry, Stacey*
(photos courtesy of Pamela Wood)

FIVE

I remember many a night sitting in the dark by candlelight because she couldn't afford to pay the electric bill, or unable to take a warm bath because she couldn't pay the gas bill, or the phone didn't work for the same reason—I don't think we ever had all three utilities on at the same time. But Mom did the best she could.

After my third meeting with Bukowski, I now realized that he was smitten with me. He began leaving notes, poems, even trinkets at my house while I was gone. He was infatuated with what appeared to be a pretty, vibrant, young woman with a charming sense of humor, some brainpower, and the potential to be or do anything she set her mind to. It was a very seductive package, but the attractive appearance belied the true nature of the turmoil brewing beneath the appealing surface.

Though my childhood was less than idyllic, the first eleven years of my life were not too bad. I was the middle child born to Rose and Lauritz Miller. My father was of Irish, Danish and German descent. He was born in a small town called Bradford, Pennsylvania, but raised in Detroit, Michigan. He came from a dysfunctional family, consisting of six boys and one girl. His father was a raging alcoholic who left his wife and seven young children to fend for themselves. My mother would lovingly refer to Grandma Miller as "Ma Barker."

Dad was an intelligent, good-looking, charming playboy who considered himself a man's-man, a la Ernest Hemmingway. He was a career Army man and served during the Korean War, but saw no combat. He spent most of his service time stationed in Japan working as a journalist for the *Stars and Stripes* newspaper.

My mother was a sweet, naïve, small-town girl also from Bradford, Pennsylvania. Her mother and father were proud immigrants from Central Italy. They were from a small, well-heeled, medieval town called Sarnano, just east of Tuscany, near the coast of the Adriatic Sea. They were good, decent, hardworking people who placed much emphasis on appearance, integrity, nobility and the Catholic Church. Mom met my father while he was visiting relatives in Bradford. He stopped to have lunch in the diner owned by my mother's Uncle Nunzio. She was a waitress there and he was struck by her exotic good looks and shy, good-girl demeanor. She was entranced by the handsome bad-boy and they married soon afterward.

My brother Larry was the first child, and then I followed four years later. My sister Tracey was born two years after me. My parents divorced when I was five years old. We lived in Tokyo at the time. My father was stationed there. And just like his father before him, ended up leaving us—this time for a Japanese concubine.

Crushed, but not defeated, Mom took the next Flying Tiger back to the States, eventually settling in the San Fernando Valley in California. Mom, being a proud woman, and no doubt just plain scared, would make sure we lived in the nicest middle-class neighborhoods in the Valley. We would often end up in guesthouses built with the hired help in mind or a small, one bedroom apartment.

Living on a secretary's wage and sometimes supplementing her income by working as a maid for the pampered, suburban housewives on the block, she still couldn't seem to make ends meet. We were underprivileged and I knew it. I always felt an undercurrent of shame and inferiority. Though Mom made sure we dressed well, never went hungry and had a roof over our heads, I would worry that the rich kids I went to school with would discover there was no meat between my mayonnaise sandwich, or afraid my shoe would come off exposing the cardboard inside, inserted to protect my feet from the holes on the bottom.

I remember many a night sitting in the dark by candlelight because she couldn't afford to pay the electric bill, or unable to take a warm bath because she couldn't pay the gas bill, or the phone didn't work for the same reason—I don't think we ever had all three utilities on at the same time. But Mom did the best she could.

From a very young age, I was acutely aware that I was different from the other kids and soon developed a minor complex. Fortunately, I was an attractive child, and the other kids would gravitate to me, making me very popular in school. I also compensated for my perceived deficits by becoming a stellar athlete. I was always team captain and often nominated for class president. But I worried my classmates would find out where I lived, asking their moms to drop me off a block away from where my house was located. And, of course, my friends were never allowed to spend the night.

But it wasn't all bad. One happy memory I have of my childhood is the constant sound of music in the house. Mom loved pop music and was especially fond of Broadway musicals.

I would lock myself in the bedroom for hours with the record player, singing show tunes. By nine years old, I developed a technique of turning out the lights and propping a flashlight on the bed, so the beam would hit the bare wall just right, creating a circular spotlight. I would pretend I was performing in front of thousands of adoring fans while I belted out "Wouldn't it be Loverly" from *My Fair Lady*. By the time I was eleven, I knew every word to every song from *My Fair Lady, West Side Story, The Flower Drum Song*, etc. I joined the drama club at the local park. My finest achievement was portraying Amy in Louisa May Alcott's *Little Women*. I became the kid in the apartment complex that would gather the others together and say, "Hey, let's put on a show!" Then, when I saw Ann-Margret at age eleven in *Bye, Bye Birdie*, my fate was sealed. She even had long, red hair, almost identical to mine. I knew from then on I had found my calling. Sadly, all those dreams would disappear in the following year, shortly after my twelfth birthday.

I was now in my first year of junior high school, or middle school, as it's now referred to. I felt lost and wasn't sure where I fit in. I had also developed ample breasts at a very young age, and the attention it garnered made me feel shy and self-conscious—it was confusing.

My best friend, Janet, from elementary school decided she liked the greasers and joined that clique. But I wasn't comfortable with the greasy-haired boys in leather jackets or the tough looking girls with their teased, bouffant hairdos. The socially elite rich girls invited me to become part of their sorority, but that made me nervous because I knew it was just a matter of time before they found out I was not "to the manner born" and would reject me. The Surfers liked me, too, but I wasn't quite the Gidget type either.

I began to develop a social phobia. My identity crisis turned to feelings of alienation. I found myself not wanting to go to school. My poor mother, who was overwhelmed just trying to keep three children and herself alive, didn't know how to deal with this. It manifested into some sort of depression and some days I just didn't want to get out of bed and would refuse to go to school. Not everyday, but enough so that the school system eventually intervened. Mom would beg and plead with me to get up, but some mornings I just couldn't. She would write excuses for me, but the school soon got wise. They issued a warning to my mother and explained that there would be significant consequences if she couldn't control her daughter—and they weren't kidding.

The school would ultimately get an order from the court to make me a ward of the state. (All I did was stay home once in a while and watch soap operas for crying out loud!) Long-story-short, I ended up being taken out of my home and transported to Juvenile Hall until they could figure out where to place me.

My father and his new wife offered to take me in, but that soon ended in disaster (I'll save the gory details for another book). I eventually landed in a foster home for girls located in Santa Monica. I lived there until I was sixteen.

The girls' home is where I met my first husband, Pete. I was a virgin and barely fifteen—he was twenty-two, but I was allowed to spend time off campus with him during the day. We dated for over a year before I ended up getting pregnant. After much pressure, I married him—I was sixteen years old and seven months pregnant.

Six months after my daughter Stacey was born, I left her father and the two of us moved in with my mother. It was during this time when I met Georgia.

Georgia was new to L.A. and dating my cousin Butch. Georgia grew up in the same small town in Pennsylvania as my mother and father. She met Butch while she worked as a hairdresser in my aunt's Bradford hair salon. Shortly after they began dating, Butch decided to move to Los Angeles to find his fame and fortune as an actor.

Heartbroken and lonely, Georgia decided to pack up her two little girls and drove cross country to be with him in Hollywood, California. My brother Larry and Butch were good friends. They would spend every weekend together at Georgia's small Hollywood home, attending her crazy parties full of eccentric, artistic types. One weekend they invited me to come along. This is when I began experimenting with drugs and alcohol.

It was a revolutionary time in the country, a time of much social change. Most of my generation considered themselves members of the disillusioned counterculture born out of the turbulent 1960s. I thought of myself as very cool and jaded while hanging out with all of my older literati outlaws. We had no concept of the havoc our reckless behavior could wreak on our lives. We were just having a good time expanding our minds while we searched for the meaning of life.

By the time I met Charles Bukowski, I had experienced a lot of trauma in my short life. I had many undigested psychological issues I hadn't dealt with and was still trying to make sense of it all—exacerbated by drug and alcohol use. I wasn't sure who I really was, what I wanted to be, or where I belonged.

Though I may have lacked personal insight at the time, Bukowski was surely sage enough to realize that a meaningful relationship with an alluring, young redhead known as Cupcakes O'Brien had to be a long shot.

SIX

He wasn't cheap, just careful.

$\mathcal{T}wo$ days after Bukowski spent the evening at my house, I found a note from him wedged in my front door. Judging from the message, he sounded as though he was now in love with me. My unresponsiveness seemed to cause him to accelerate the chase. During the next few days, I found more notes from him. He'd leave them on the door or  in my mailbox. He'd been trying to phone me, but I was never home when he called. He said he was worried about me, wondered if I was okay, and wanted me to call him. One day I came home to find a German Iron Cross medal hanging from my door. It was flattering, but also a little unsettling. There was an inappropriate, desperate tone to it all.

I was taking Stacey to school every morning, and then going back home and sleeping until noon. I would often spend several consecutive days drying out at my mother's apartment, after days or weeks of using drugs and alcohol. I still had a schism in my personality creating a pattern of three or fours days on, then three or four days off. I was leading a double life, which would make Bukowski crazy. I would run errands in the afternoon, often searching for a new doctor to write an amphetamine prescription. I would pick up Stacey after school, grab some take-out food, and then head to my mom's apartment. When mom got home around 5:45, I left for work at the Alpine Inn.

I usually found Bukowski's notes when I got home from work about 2:30 in the morning. I stuck the notes in my kitchen drawer and didn't

41

think much about him during the week. I was mostly worried about getting kicked out of my guesthouse for owing back rent.

After I got home from work, it would take me hours to fall asleep. Sometimes, I just stayed awake until it was time to pick up Stacey at my mom's and take her to school. This was no kind of life for a child, and I knew it. But the worse I felt about our situation, the more anxious I would become and the more I wanted to escape to take the edge off. I knew if I quit my pleasure seeking, I would not only be a better person and a better mother, I would also save a lot more money—and be able to pay my bills, including the rent.

I wasn't receiving any child support, not that I wasn't supposed to. Stacey's dad just never paid me anything, even when I called and begged. He was now remarried, and told me he had expenses of his own to worry about. He claimed he wasn't working and had nothing to give me at that time.

I knew I had to find a better paying job. These days, every time I went into the guesthouse, I felt like a criminal because I was behind on the rent. Every time there was a knock on the door, my heart jumped. Every time I left the house, the landlord was watching me through his front window.

Over the weekend, I found more poems and messages from Bukowski. Most of them said he couldn't stop thinking about me. I had a lot on my mind and, frankly, wasn't sure what to make of them. He seemed obsessed with me. I thought it would be best to put some time between us to cool him off.

On Monday, my day off, I decided to stop by his place around one in the afternoon. It had been a week since his visit to my place. When he opened the door, his face beamed.

"Where in the hell have you been, Little Reds?" he said, ushering me excitedly into his living room.

"Working," I said, "and taking care of Stacey."

"Nothing else?"

"That's pretty much it."

"No boyfriends to monopolize your time?"

"Not recently."

Bukowski grabbed two bottles of Michelob from his refrigerator and set them on the kitchen table. There was a piece of paper in the typewriter and a stack of papers next to the machine.

"Hope I'm not interrupting anything," I said, flicking my finger against the typewriter.

"That's last night's haul," he said, nodding toward the papers on the table.

"You make it sound like fishing," I said.

"It is, in a way," he said. "You just throw out the net and see what you get."

"So you don't plan anything out? You just start writing and see what you get?"

"Pretty much," he said. "If it's good it should come out like a sweet, hot, beer shit."

"Lovely image," I said.

"A true one, My Dear," he said.

He took me in his arms and hugged me tight. Then he began to kiss me. Bukowski really adored kissing, I would soon learn. He could kiss all night. He had told me he was a "kiss fiend." His aggressiveness on this day caught me off guard. He was really happy to see me.

He nudged me toward the bedroom. When we were standing in the doorway, I looked around at

(courtesy of Thomas Schmitt)

the dark blue walls and then took in the dilapidated bed. Even from across the room, the bed smelled like sex.

He pulled me closer and I could feel him hard against my stomach. I pulled back, glanced at the bed, and then stared up at him.

"When you get a new mattress, let me know," I said. "Until then, I wouldn't even consider it."

He took a step backward so he could see me better. He was farsighted and needed a little distance to focus his eyes. He was studying me, trying to figure out whether I was kidding.

"You're serious?" he said.

"Absolutely, positively, completely," I said, taking him by the hand and leading him back to the living room.

We sat on his old sofa drinking our beers in silence for a while. I could tell he was trying to digest what I had just told him.

"It seems a shame to get rid of a perfectly good mattress," he said.

He wasn't cheap, just careful. He would never spend a dime unless he absolutely had to. His wardrobe was virtually nonexistent. When he did have to buy, say, a new shirt, it was usually something cheap from a discount store on Sunset called Zody's. His furnishings looked like things he'd dragged in from the alley. He lived mostly on cold cuts, eggs and bread. He drank, yes, but it was usually cheap beer and wine. Sometimes he even rolled his own cigarettes. When he bought anything, including his beloved '67 Volkswagen, he paid for it in cash. Even with me he wasn't what you'd call overly generous. He thought the old mattress still had years of life, so he was loath to get rid of it. I never discussed money with him, but assumed he was bordering on poverty. I couldn't imagine he lived this way by choice and not by necessity.

"I hope you and your mattress will be very happy together," I said.

We sat in the living room drinking our beer.

"You're different, Cups," he said. "You never mention my writing at all. With most of the other women, that's all they want to talk about."

"So there are lots of other women?" I asked.

"Women call me and write me letters and show up at my poetry readings," he said. "I guess they think I know something that other men don't."

"What do they think you know?"

"Maybe they think I'm sensitive and know how to please a woman," he said.

He tried to read my expression to see whether or not I'd ever had the pleasure. He was testing me. This was not a subject we had discussed previously. I felt he was trying to gauge my attitude toward sex, more specifically, sex with him. I wasn't about to let on one way or the other.

"You're more of a philosopher—a dirty-minded philosopher—but still a philosopher," I said.

He laughed, the gap from his missing teeth appearing at the corner of his mouth.

"I have a hunch," he said, "that maybe you have read more of my writing than you claim."

I still hadn't tackled the _Notes of a Dirty Old Man_ book he had given me our second night together. I felt conflicted. It was nice that he'd given me the compilation of his work, but now I would have to address it. He was sure to ask some questions the next time I saw him. I had flipped through some of the pages and still wasn't convinced he had superior talent. I'd have to read more of it. I was certain I could find something positive to say, if the subject came up.

The phone rang and Bukowski got up to answer it. I assumed it was one of his female fans, someone more than willing to come over and do anything he wanted on the icky mattress.

I got up and waved while he listened on the phone. He held up a hand to say, "Don't go," but I was already gone.

SEVEN

... it felt peaceful and safe in the dark blue bedroom, with just the two of us like shipwrecked misfits floating along the ocean on a raft. He was so sweet and gentle that I let go and floated away with him.

The next day, Bukowski called me around noon. I had just woken up.

"Hey, Cups, get yourself over here," he said. "I have a surprise for you."

"I haven't even taken a shower," I said.

"You can take a shower later," he said. "You need to come over now."

He sounded so excited and insistent, that I threw on jeans and a T-shirt, ran a comb through my hair, grabbed my purse, and headed for the car.

When I was halfway down the walk, my landlord Mr. Walters jumped out through his backdoor. He was a creepy guy in his mid-sixties. He reminded me of a balding Bela Lugosi with a bad comb-over. Rather than wait for the obvious, I said what I guessed he was thinking.

"I know I'm late with the rent," I offered. "But I still haven't caught up on the wages I lost after the accident."

In September, I'd been rear-ended on Hollywood Boulevard and had taken a few weeks off from work. My employer continued paying me, but minus the tips. And now that my hours were cut back because they kept the woman they hired while I was on leave, I was having a tough time catching up financially. The December payment was now due and I was two months behind in the rent.

"Come inside for a minute," Mr. Walters said, holding the backdoor open.

I knew Bukowski was waiting for me, but figured I had no choice but to see what the landlord wanted. I expected he was going to hand me an eviction notice.

When I got inside, everything was quiet—no TV, no radio, no wife. I had a hunch about what was going to happen next, but didn't know how to prevent it.

The place looked like a waiting room in a funeral parlor—dark and garishly decorated. It smelled like garlic. He led me to the red velveteen sofa. I sat down, and he slid right next to me. He picked up a magazine from the coffee table, opened it, and began to flip from page to page.

He reached over and pushed my hair behind my shoulders. I felt nauseated, with chills running up and down my back.

Mr. Walters looked down at one of the photos, a naked woman getting it from behind.

"Do you like this?" he asked, holding the photo in front of me.

I wanted to kick him in the gonads and run, but didn't want to get arrested for assault, ending up in jail, or, at the very least, out on the street. Instead, I jumped up as if I'd just remembered something urgent.

"Oh," I said, "I've got to go or I'll be late for my appointment."

I ran out the backdoor, leaving Mr. Walters with the porn rag hanging limply in his hand.

I smoked four cigarettes on the way to Bukowski's, and he only lived about ten minutes away. Every time I thought about the landlord, the same two words came to mind—"sick fuck." God, I was so tired of this kind of abuse. No matter what their age or level of attractiveness, men thought they could make a move on a young, single woman—especially a single mother. It was so disgusting. I felt like vomiting.

When I pulled up in front of Bukowski's place, two men were hauling out his disgusting mattress. Bukowski was out front and opened the car door for me. He was smiling like a little kid who'd just gotten a new bike. When he looked at my scowl, the smile disappeared.

"Hey, smile, Cups. You look like you just ran over a drunken nun."

I lit another cigarette and gave him the short version of what had just happened with the landlord.

"Want me to go over and beat his ass?" he asked.

"No . . . I need to live someplace," I said.

"Move in with me," he said.

"I've got a daughter, remember?" I said, not certain if he was serious.

"We'll figure something out," he said.

I threw down my cigarette and ground it out.

"Come on inside, Kid, I've got a surprise for you," he said, putting his hand behind my elbow and gently guiding me into his place. He led me right to the bedroom.

On the bed sat a mattress wrapped in cellophane. I moved closer to the bed, bent down, and gazed at the mattress. It was covered in a pattern of roses and vines.

"It's so pretty," I said. "How considerate of you. Did you to do this just for me?" I asked, while thinking, "Uh oh."

"So, what do you say?" he said.

"I say we're going to need some champagne to christen it."

He took out his wallet and extracted a twenty-dollar bill.

"Why don't you go and get the champagne while I remove the cellophane," he said. "Hurry back," he added.

I drove over to the Safeway at Hillhurst and Sunset where they knew me and I didn't have to worry about being carded. I didn't have a driver's license, but did have a fake ID I had purchased at the Hollywood Ranch Market when I was nineteen and needed it to work as a cocktail waitress at a nightclub in West Hollywood called P.J.'s. (That gig lasted two hours. I was so nervous my first day on the job I spilled an entire tray of cocktails on half a dozen businessmen at one of my tables then ran out the front door before they could fire me.) Instead of one good bottle of champagne, I decided to buy two cheap ones—one for each of us.

When I got back about fifteen minutes later, I handed Bukowski the change and the champagne.

He looked tired and pained.

"Now what's wrong?" I asked.

"I told her you'd come back with the champagne and the change," he said.

"Told who?"

"Linda called," he said, referring to his ex-girlfriend, Linda King. "She sounded crazy, ranting and raving. She thinks she might be pregnant."

I tried to read his expression, and he saw me studying him. He opened the champagne, while I looked for two clean glasses in the kitchen.

"Don't worry, it's not mine," he said. "She rattled off the names of five different guys who might have the honor."

"Why'd she call?"

"Who knows?" he said. "I told you—she's crazy. She likes to torture me."

I wondered if she had called him, or if he had called her to brag about his latest soon-to-be, tender-aged conquest. He didn't seem like a mean person—but I wondered if their relationship involved sick tormenting games. The thought made me feel a little uncomfortable, but I quickly erased it from my mind. He convinced me it was completely over and, after all, he'd actually bought a new mattress just for me.

Now that the champagne was poured, Bukowski looked a lot more relaxed. We clinked glasses. I really needed a couple of drinks to get in the mood.

"To roses and vines!" he toasted.

"To roses and vines!" I echoed, then added, "To stems without thorns!"

I took a shower, then stepped into the bedroom, dripping wet. He was lying on the bed on top of a clean sheet, with another sheet over him. Soon enough, the sheet started to rise. I walked over to the mirror and looked at myself. I sucked in my already flat stomach. No matter how much weight I lost, I always thought I was too fat. But in retrospect, I had a beautiful, almost flawless, voluptuous body. Though I was only 5'3", at 38-24-36, I was perfectly proportioned—and it was all natural. Around that same time, I had been approached by a well-known photographer from *Penthouse* magazine to do a photo shoot—which I turned down. My physical attributes would be a great source of inspiration to the poet lying beside me.

The sun was shining through the window. It was about three in the afternoon. I didn't have to worry about Stacey because she was going to spend the afternoon at her best friend Nina's house, where my mom would pick her up.

No, I had nothing to worry about until it was time to go to work in a couple of hours.

I got in bed and moved close to Bukowski. He gently approached one of my breasts with his hand. I looked down at his hands while he caressed me. I noticed his fingernails were long and ragged. I pulled back.

"You're going to have to do something about those nails," I said.

"Be right back," he said.

He quickly jumped out of bed. He was wearing boxer shorts and a white T-shirt. Soon, I heard the sound of nail clipping coming from the bathroom. I've always felt the length of a man's fingernails says a lot about his sex life, or lack thereof. The longer they are, the less sex they're getting. It appeared to have been a long time for Bukowski.

While he was in the bathroom I noticed a bottle of Oil of Olay on his nightstand. I figured one of his older girlfriends had left it. I never used creams or lotions but figured I'd try it while I was waiting. When he came back I was rubbing lotion on my arms. He showed me his hands. They were clean and the nails were cut down to the nubs. He was a man who would do just about anything to please a woman. It was endearing—but scary at the same time. Sometimes it seemed too intense.

I was in a silly mood and a little nervous. I continued to nonchalantly rub the lotion on my arms after he got back under the covers. He tried out his clean hands on other parts of my body. He looked up to see my expression. I didn't respond and continued to rub the lotion on my arms, pretending to be bored.

"Hey, can I get you a nail file . . . or maybe you'd like an apple to eat?" he said.

I laughed, then relaxed into it. It was a noisy afternoon in East Hollywood, with police sirens, fire engines, buses, traffic, and general street noise outside the window. But it felt peaceful and safe in the dark blue bedroom, with just the two of us like shipwrecked misfits floating along the ocean on a raft. He was so sweet and gentle that I let go and floated away with him. His approach was a little awkward at first, but he eventually managed to hit all the right buttons. He was a much better lover than I anticipated. This was special, and we both knew it.

Afterward, we leisurely smoked our cigarettes and engaged in a little pillow talk. He then got dressed and went to Pioneer Chicken and picked up some food. When he came back, his arms were loaded with bags.

"Are you that hungry?" I asked.

"I wasn't sure what you wanted," he said. "So I got everything."

EIGHT

Years later I would discover this wouldn't be his last attempt to defame me.

When I came home from work that night, another note from Bukowski was wedged in the door. After I got inside, I opened the envelope. It was a page filled with the word "Yes!" He signed it and asked me to call him.

I put the note in the kitchen drawer with the others he'd left. I looked at the notes surrounded by twine and felt guilty. This was no way to treat a man's tender messages. I found a shoebox and put them inside, then set the box in the bedroom closet.

After enjoying such a lovely afternoon with Bukowski, I'd more than paid for it with the lousy evening I was about to spend at work.

Roz Kelly, the new barmaid, was making my life miserable. She had been hired to fill in for me while I was out recuperating from my car accident. She was a brassy New Yorker with a bad attitude. I didn't know what her problem was with me. I would try to be friendly and talk with her, but she would make some sarcastic comment and basically flip me off. I didn't understand where all her hostility was coming from. She was just plain mean. On the nights we worked together, we barely spoke. She would stay at the other end of the bar and flash dirty looks my way all night. But the owner and the customers seemed to like her, so they kept her on and cut my hours back. She was an aspiring actress and would land a job on the popular sitcom *Happy Days* as Fonzie's girlfriend, Pinky Tuscadero. *Type-casting*, I thought.

But now I knew I had to find another job. Exhausted, I collapsed in a kitchen chair and popped open a beer. I needed a couple of beers to help me sleep for a few hours before the alarm clock rang at seven, when I had to run over to Mom's and take Stacey to school.

I kept asking myself, "What am I going to do?" as I drank the beer and smoked cigarette after cigarette.

I really wanted to go back to school, but that wasn't a possibility. I couldn't even type. I needed to work and support Stacey. It seemed that the only option was to look for another waitress job. The thought made me depressed as hell.

I almost wished I'd get laid off. After a few minutes, I convinced myself that may be the best thing that could happen to me. That way, I could collect unemployment, stay out of work for a while, and get myself together. *Thank you, Roz,* I thought as I snuffed out my cigarette and made my way to bed.

A few days had gone by since Bukowski and I had consummated our relationship. He had made attempts to contact me with more written correspondence left at my door while I was out. I was preoccupied with other things and, frankly, I still felt that he was moving too quickly, so I wasn't anxious to get back to him immediately.

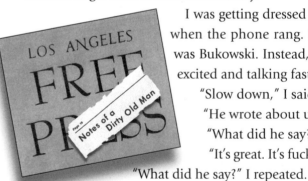

I was getting dressed to pick up my daughter, when the phone rang. I answered, assuming it was Bukowski. Instead, it was Georgia. She was excited and talking faster than usual.

"Slow down," I said.

"He wrote about us in the *Freep*," she said.

"What did he say?"

"It's great. It's fucking great," she squealed.

"What did he say?" I repeated.

"Let me fucking read it to you."

"Just tell me what it's about. I've got the shower running."

"It's a fucking poem. I can't tell you about it. I have to read it to you."

"What's it called?"

"'The Price'," she told me, then began reading the poem.

I stopped her after the first sentence.

"He called us *hookers*?!"

"Just listen," she said.

Then she read the entire poem.

After Georgia finished reading, I said, "That butt-head, he even used our real names."

"Just think if he had used our last names. We could have been famous," she said.

"Infamous is more like it."

"Lighten up, Pam. He says he was just kidding in the end. I love it. I think it's fuckin' great."

The poem first appeared in the _Los Angeles Free Press_ on December 5, 1975. In it, Bukowski describes some of the actual events that took place the first night we met, but refers to Georgia and me as hookers. It would later appear in his book of poetry published in 1977, titled _Love is a Dog from Hell_. In that book, his poems appear in four sections. In section three titled, "Scarlet," all the poems were inspired by, and are about, me. However, "The Price" does not appear in that section.

At the time this poem appeared in his newspaper column, I wasn't too upset because I figured he didn't really know us when he wrote it and assumed he'd never see us again. He would write other poems about me that appeared in his weekly column, but I wasn't aware of them. During the entire time Bukowski and I were together, I rarely read the _Free Press_. Years later I would discover this wouldn't be his last attempt to defame me.

Later that day I stopped by Bukowski's. When he opened the door he was thrilled to see me. He had been trying to contact me all week and was getting worried.

He was worked up into a frenzy over an incident that had taken place the day following our mattress christening.

"Where have you been, Cups? You missed all the excitement around here. I've tried calling you. I stopped by your place several times. I even called Georgia and she hadn't heard from you, either."

"Forget about me, just tell me what happened," I said.

He went on to tell me about the disastrous episode that took place the day after our new mattress session. He'd come home from the racetrack and found the front door window broken and his place was trashed. He caught Linda King hiding in the bushes with shopping bags full of his books and paintings. When she saw him coming toward her, she began to rip up his books and paintings and hurl them into the street. Then she took his typewriter from under the bushes, ran back into the middle of the street and smashed it to the ground. While she's destroying everything, she's screaming, "DON'T EVER TELL ME ABOUT YOUR FUCKIN' WOMEN—I DON'T EVER WANT TO HEAR ABOUT YOUR FUCKING WOMEN!"

"Then," Bukowski said, "she jumped in her car and tried to run me over!"

I couldn't think of what to say. I would have thought he was kidding if he hadn't looked so shook up.

"She did this because I told her about you when she phoned on the day I bought the mattress."

He bent down, kissed me gently on the lips and said, "God, I'm so glad you weren't here!"

It was unsettling, but I didn't feel threatened. I never met Linda King, but had heard horror stories about how she had attacked other women Bukowski showed an interest in. Shortly after this incident, she moved to Arizona.

However, there are always two sides to every story. I now suspect Bukowski, for whatever reason, loved to provoke her. He knew she had a volatile temper and I believe he enjoyed igniting it. I also believe he called her, not the other way around, to taunt her about his latest, young conquest.

Though he was a man with many good qualities, he was also deeply flawed. I don't know why, but he seemed to derive perverse pleasure from instigating trouble, particularly between women. Maybe he found it amusing and good fodder for his writing, or maybe it made him feel loved and wanted. Of course, I wasn't aware of this at the time, so I gave him a big hug and told him not to worry anymore—Cupcakes is here and everything will be okay.

He grabbed a couple beers from the fridge and he seemed more relaxed. I then confronted him about the unflattering poem.

"Georgia called me earlier. She was excited about a poem you wrote about us in your column. I wasn't quite as happy about it as she was. Did you really think we were hookers?"

"Hey, Baby, I wrote that before I knew you. And besides, in this neighborhood you never know."

"Boy, that's the truth," I said.

"Another beer?" he asked.

"No thanks, I've got to work tonight. I better get going."

"When will I see you again?" he asked.

"Call me tomorrow afternoon," I said, as I gave him a quick goodbye kiss.

When I got home from work the next night, there was a note from Bukowski. In it, he told me to kick him in the ass if he ever mentioned Linda again. Under the note was a book of poems. It was a copy of *Mockingbird Wish Me Luck*, with the inscription: "For Pamela—Who makes me dance and rumble inside. Yes, yes, yes. Charles Bukowski." This was the same book he had dedicated to Linda King.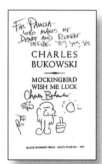

When I got up at noon the next day, there it was on the floor in the living room—an eviction notice that the landlord had pushed under the front door. It was about two weeks before Christmas. So much for Peace on Earth, Good Will Toward Men.

I decided to check up on Bukowski to make sure Linda hadn't come back to finish the job, and to fill him in on my news. When I got to his place, I could hear him at his kitchen table typing away.

He answered the door and stood in the doorway. He looked defeated.

"Why the long face, Mr. Ed?"

"Sorry, Red. I'm just a little frustrated. I had to buy a new typer and I'm trying to get used to it. I also had to pay to have the windows replaced."

"Why don't you get Linda to pay?" I asked.

"It's not worth the bother," he said. "I want her out of my life."

"Let's go out for a drink," I said. "I need to talk to you about something."

"I need to finish these letters and get this receipt off to John. He agreed to pay for the machine."

"Oh, good," I said. "Well, can I come in? I want to see your new writing machine."

He stepped aside so I could walk first through the door. He was mannerly, almost in a quaint way, when he was sober and sometimes even when he was drunk. I figured he'd been brought up learning old-world politeness and courtesy from his German mother.

We walked into the kitchen to view the new typewriter. It looked similar to the old one, but it was new to him and it didn't feel the same as his good old faithful Royal. We sat at the table drinking beer. He was still visibly shaken by the Linda ordeal. His hands trembled as he lit a cigarette. I felt guilty telling him about my eviction when he had his own problems.

"Shit, I loved that typer," he said. "I feel like I've lost a piece of my soul."

"Where is it now?" I asked.

"In the trash can," he said. "It seems wrong leaving it there. I feel like I should bury it and have a funeral service or something. It's been good to me—it deserves some grace."

"Yeah—maybe we can have a wake for it—with an open casket," I said. "Come on, cheer up, Hank. Maybe it's for the best. Maybe this one is magic and you'll write all kinds of amazing new stuff on it."

A smile crept onto his mouth, as if he'd forgotten how to be happy and was trying to learn all over again.

"You always cheer me up, little Red," he said.

For a while, that was the essence of our relationship. I'd kid around with him until his depression lifted, then we'd go out and have fun like a couple of carefree kids.

"How'd you like to come to my mom's place for Christmas Eve dinner?" I asked, and then added, "She wants to meet you."

"You told her about me?" he said, looking pleased.

"I told her you were a famous author. I told her you wrote children's books," I said. "She was impressed."

"Who's going to be there?"

"Stacey, my brother Larry, my sister Tracey, and my mom."

"Sounds too festive for me, Kid," he said.

"Come on," I said. "You'll have fun. We're going to cook a duck."

"I hope its Donald," he said.

"Now you're getting Daffy."

I wanted to bring up the subject of my eviction. I knew he could figure out something for me to do. But it just didn't seem like the right time to bring it up.

All of a sudden, he said, "What did you want to talk to me about?"

"I'm getting kicked out of my house."

"Why?" he said. "Because of what happened with the landlord?"

"That's probably part of it. But then again, I haven't paid the rent in a couple of months."

At this point, Bukowski and I had only known each other about a month, and we had only slept together once. That's why I was surprised when he told me that the place next to his was available. Why would he want me to move next door? Wouldn't he feel awkward having other women coming over if I was just a few feet away? I assumed he was already serious about me and had no plans to see other women. These were just vague thoughts running across my mind. I didn't think too deeply about his offer or its ramifications.

Instead, I was already acting as if the move had been settled. I asked him about the rent, whether the complex allowed children, and when the place was available. Though the rent payment was not much less than what I was already paying, and I did express some concern about being able to meet the monthly obligation, Bukowski said he had "connections" and that would never be a problem as long as he was around. He said he would even be able to get the last months rent, which was required to be paid in advance, waived for me. I was excited. _This is too good to be true_, I thought.

I had no reservations about living next door to Bukowski. He was solicitous and protective, something I badly needed in my life. He was wise and I felt he could help me figure things out—he'd not only be my boyfriend, but also my guide and mentor.

What could possibly go wrong?

NINE

Mom had a good time talking with Bukowski. She really liked him . . . She also told me that he had the saddest eyes she'd ever seen on a human being.

I don't know what Bukowski usually did for the Christmas holidays. His parents had been dead for years and he had no siblings. I didn't know if he spent the holidays with his daughter Marina and her mother Frances Smith. I didn't know if he spent time with friends. I didn't know if he just stayed home by himself. Like me, he had been raised Catholic, so he must have had some sentiments about the holidays. When I invited him to spend Christmas Eve at my mom's place, I never thought to ask if he had any other plans.

My mom, Rose, was fifty-one when I first met Bukowski, which meant she was four years younger than he was. I never viewed Bukowski as her contemporary. My mom seemed so much older.

Mom wasn't much of a cook and neither was I. My sister Tracey had come home from Albuquerque for the holidays. Tracey was twenty-one and had recently graduated from broadcasting school. She had just landed her first job as a newscaster at KOB radio in Albuquerque, New Mexico. Of the three of us, Tracey was the best cook. She suggested we roast a duck and even offered to go out and buy it. Mom and I were ecstatic that we didn't have to worry about the main course. It was enough for us to throw together a green salad, open a can of corn, and put chips and dip on the table.

Italian on both sides, my mom had grown up with the tradition of Christmas Eve, not Christmas, being the real holiday.

Mom had to work for a living and didn't have much time for cooking, baking, and entertaining. We were raised on Burger Chef and Swanson TV Dinners. But she did her best—and always had a big Christmas tree, with holly and garlands around her apartment. She also had a marvelous knack for decorating on a shoestring, and loved to scour thrift shops like the Goodwill for unique hidden treasures, like the black Santa that sang the Christmas Blues, and abstract papermâché ornaments that looked like Salvador Dali had designed them. She bought eggnog, candy canes, chocolate Santas and anything else that was quick and easy. My point is—she tried.

When the doorbell rang, I opened the door and my brother Larry came in. He was twenty-seven, on the short side, and had bright orange hair, which he wore in an Afro. He made up in brains what he lacked in looks. But despite his brilliance, Larry could never make a go of anything—school, work, or relationships. My mom pampered him and gave him money, but nothing she did seemed to make a difference. He was usually out of work and hard up for cash. Mom and Larry were codependent even before there was a word for it. Unlike me, he had a sense of entitlement. Though I wasn't much better—at least I tried, and always felt guilty about leaning too hard on her.

My mom was always happy to see him, though, and ran over to give him a hug. She walked into the living room just in time to see Georgia, her boyfriend Bill, and Georgia's two little daughters stream through the door.

"There's no fucking place to park on this block," Georgia said, handing my mom two bottles of wine and adding, "Merry Christmas, Rose."

Without saying a word, Mom turned and headed for the kitchen, where Tracey was basting the duck. She looked at me and nodded her head toward the kitchen. I followed her.

"What are they doing here?" Mom whispered.

"I don't know," I said, and I really didn't. "Maybe Larry invited them."

My mom's face relaxed. If Larry had invited Georgia and her crew, it was okay. If I'd invited them, it would not have been okay.

Larry came in the kitchen and grabbed a corkscrew and three wine glasses with one hand and took the two bottles of wine from my mom with his other hand. As he did this, he bent down and kissed her on the cheek.

Larry was nine when my parents got divorced, and he took it the hardest. My mom tried to do everything she could to, as she said, "Do right by Larry," but all of her spoiling didn't do him any good. If anything, her trying to make life easier for him had made his life harder in the long run. She felt tremendous guilt for depriving her only son of a father and over-compensated for it.

I glanced at the clock. It was almost time for Bukowski to arrive.

"Can I help you with that, Tracey?" I asked my sister.

She removed the meat thermometer from the duck and looked at it.

"The duck won't be ready for at least another hour," she said.

"Maybe you should just turn up the heat," I said. "It'll cook faster."

She laughed, thinking I was kidding. But I actually knew virtually nothing about cooking. I thought you could cook something faster by turning up the heat.

My sister, Tracey

I had spent most of the day with Tracey, so I was pretty much caught up on how things were going in Albuquerque. She'd given me my Christmas gift early—a stunning silver and turquoise necklace and bracelet that she'd bought at an Indian reservation. Tracey told me she liked her job and the people, and even liked Albuquerque. But she was lonely living so far away and couldn't wait until she got a job in Los Angeles. (Six years later she would be back in Los Angeles working with the famous radio team Loman and Barkley on KFI radio. In 1989, she would go on to become the first female to host her own show in Los Angeles on KFI called "TNT in the Morning—*The Tracey Miller and Terry Rae Elmer Morning Show.*)

The doorbell rang. When I stepped into the living room, I saw Bukowski surrounded by Larry, Bill, and Georgia—all of them big fans. They were all chattering at once. I don't think Bukowski was expecting this kind of reception. He looked lost and confused, as if he'd just gotten off the bus at the wrong stop.

Well, at least the kids were having a good time. Stacey and Georgia's girls, Maureen and Stephanie, were playing with Stacey's baby dolls next to the Christmas tree, where lots of presents were waiting. The kids weren't about to move from that spot until it was time to open the gifts.

By the time I reached Bukowski and kissed him on the cheek, Larry had already poured him a glass of wine and ushered him to the throne-like upholstered chair that faced the TV.

"Mommy, we're hungry," Stacey said.

I made my way back to the kitchen, where Tracey was peeling potatoes. She had already made a salad, which was in the refrigerator, and a green bean casserole.

Tracey did everything with good humor and without complaining. She was a gem, a delight, and the best sister anybody could ever have. She also inherited all the artistic gifts. She would learn early on what not to do in life by watching her sister and brother. Though we were complete opposites, physically and temperamentally, we were as close as two people could be. She was witty, kind, beautiful and unassuming—I adored her.

But right now I felt guilty about not helping more with the cooking.

"Go in and visit with your friends," she said. "Everything's under control."

"Where's Mom?" I asked.

"She went to visit one of her friends."

I figured Mom was mad because of Georgia. She couldn't stand Georgia—and thought she was a debauched, debased drug addict who was leading both Larry and me down the road to perdition. She warned both of us repeatedly not to have anything to do with her and was furious that we never listened to her advice.

"Is she coming back?"

"I hope so," Tracey said. "Who's going to eat all this duck?"

"That reminds me," I said. "The kids are hungry—how much longer before we eat?"

"Better give them some crackers or something," Tracey said. "It's going to be at least an hour before this goose is cooked."

I watched Tracey for a few seconds, and, when she wasn't looking, I turned up the oven setting from 325 to 400. The duck would cook a lot faster, I figured, and the kids wouldn't get filled up on potato chips and crackers.

Bukowski sent a "rescue me" look my way. He really didn't like his fans, and he hated it when people played up to him. Larry and Georgia were trying to outdo each other rattling off things they remembered from Bukowski's work. You'd think Georgia had just met the guy by the way she was fawning over him. I gave Bukowski an apologetic shrug, then went over and put my arm around his shoulder.

Tracey took a break and joined us in the living room. I introduced her to Bukowski and he stared at her for what seemed a minute before saying, "Pleased to meet you, Tracey." As I've mentioned before, when he was relatively sober, he was always very polite.

Tracey and I looked nothing alike and people never believed we were sisters. During the 1990s, they used to call us Thelma & Louise, due to her resemblance to Geena Davis and mine to Susan Sarandon.

But back in 1975, Tracey was a tall, dark, gorgeous, exotic-looking, young woman. Men were mad for her. Over the years, she'd get a dozen serious proposals of marriage. On this night, Bukowski was smitten with Tracey's beauty, charm, grace, and warmth.

Just then, something happened that made us all turn and look in the same direction. The kitchen was on fire. Flames were shooting out of the oven and the room was filling with smoke.

Bill and Larry ran into the kitchen, opened the oven and beat the burning duck with dishtowels and doused it with glasses of water.

"Jesus and the beads!" Georgia yelled.

Mom arrived back home just in time to witness the demise of our Christmas Eve dinner.

"Oh, Dear God, what the hell has happened? Someone pour me a glass of wine!" Mom said. She was a teetotaler, so I figured she must really need a drink.

I looked at Bukowski. He was grinning so wide that he looked like a cartoon. This was the kind of situation he loved—when everything went to hell and people just ended up saying, "Fuck it."

"We're hungry," the little girls said.

"Let's order a pizza," Bukowski said. "I'll pay."

"Everything's closed, man," Larry said.

"I'll make you some peanut butter and jelly sandwiches," I told the girls.

"While you're at it," Bukowski said to me, "check if you have anything more to drink."

There was plenty more to drink that day. The little girls fell asleep in Stacey's room, and after that we really started drinking—and even Mom didn't seem to mind. What else could you do when you had to cope with a disaster?

Mom had a good time talking with Bukowski. She really liked him and told me later that she felt he was a decent man and knew he would take good care of me. She also told me that he had the saddest eyes she'd ever seen on a human being.

Bukowski dressed for Christmas Eve dinner with the Millers
(photo courtesy of Pamela Miller Wood)

Years later I would read in Howard Sounes' excellent Bukowski biography *Locked in the Arms of a Crazy Life* that Bukowski stopped by the home of George DiCaprio after leaving our Christmas Eve celebration. George is the father of actor Leo DiCaprio, who was only a few months old at the time. George was a comic book distributor and he and Bukowski would often talk when they ran into each other at the local coffee stand on Western Avenue.

Though I never met the DiCaprios, they only lived a couple blocks from our Carlton Way bungalow, near Hollywood and Western. By all accounts, Bukowski was very drunk when he showed up at George's door and made quite a scene. That didn't surprise me at all, given the amount of liquor he consumed that day. He never mentioned it to me. That didn't surprise me, either.

 **TEN**

I needed guidance, and I felt that under Bukowski's wise tutelage, I might find it.

I came back to the guesthouse a few days later and found the landlady, Mrs. Walters, rifling through my things.

"What in the hell are you doing?" I said. "I told you I'd be out before the end of the month."

Mrs. Walters picked up a pile of stuff from the bed and began to walk out. There were books, records, scarves, perfume, and on top of the pile was the jewelry Tracey had given me for Christmas. I reached for the necklace, but Mrs. Walters ducked under my arm and rushed toward the back door.

"You owe me back rent," she said. "I have a right to take this."

When she left, I felt like crying. What if the jewelry had been a family heirloom? Well, that would have made it worse and I would have lost it anyway, I guessed.

I was so sick of being broke, so sick of having to worry about the rent, so sick of slaving away, so sick of feeling that I had no control over my own life.

This would all change, I hoped, when I moved next door to Bukowski. I would settle down, take great care of Stacey, and get my life together. I needed guidance, and I felt that under Bukowski's wise tutelage, I might find it.

Bukowski stopped by the Alpine Inn the following week. The end of the month was approaching and Roz was off that night, so I had the bar all to myself. I pulled a draft for Bukowski and set it in front of him.

"Thanks, Red," he said.

Then he asked whether Tracey had gone back to Albuquerque. The day after Christmas, the three of us had gone to a piano bar in Hollywood called the Sneak Inn, where Tracey had sung Patsy Cline tunes in a voice nearly as good as the original. We'd had a great time, and I could see that Bukowski adored Tracey almost as much as I did. Eight months later, before I left to visit Tracey in Albuquerque, Bukowski would inscribe a copy of *Scarlet* and ask me to give it to her. It read: "To Tracey—I'll always remember you that night Pam and you and me drank together awhile. That moment, that night, you were the most beautiful creature-woman I had ever seen. I still remember you that way. Love, Charles Bukowski."

Rita, the owner, slid behind the bar and whispered, "I need to talk to you" in my ear.

I glanced over at Bukowski, excused myself, and followed Rita into the kitchen. I knew what was coming.

"Pam, I'm sorry," she said, "but we're going to have to let you go."

I didn't ask for an explanation and she didn't offer one. Anyway, I didn't want to know. I could collect unemployment! Hooray! At eighty dollars a week, it was almost as much as I was making by working five stinking nights a week.

When I went back to the bar, I told Bukowski what had happened.

"Do you have to give back the outfit?" he asked, pointing to my dirndl.

"I suppose so," I said. "Though I don't have anything else to wear home tonight."

"Just a second," he said, then got up and walked out.

A minute later, he was back carrying a camera.

"I need a picture to remember this by," he said.

He waved for me to pose in front of a rustic-looking wall.

"Say 'freedom'," he said.

I smiled and felt as if I were truly beaming. I was ecstatic. No more jobs for a while!

Photo taken at the Alpine Inn by Charles Bukowski

When the picture developed, Bukowski showed it to me—a happy redhead in a dirndl.

After Bukowski died in 1994, one of his friends was invited to look through some of his effects—things that were designated as nonessential. During the search, the 1975 photo of me in my dirndl turned up. It was enough of a keepsake that Bukowski had held onto it for nearly twenty years.

A couple days after the New Year, Bukowski helped me move into my new apartment on Carlton Way. It was a spacious single with a pull-down Murphy bed. It was located on the second floor adjacent to his bungalow. There was a small balcony off the living room and I could look down through his window and see him typing at his kitchen table.

I would start the year in a new apartment, with a new man, and without a job. I figured everything was in place so I could get myself together and figure out what I wanted to do with my life.

Entrance into the Carlton Way apartment where Bukowski lived for several years. I would eventually take a separate apartment in the complex with my daughter, Stacey.

(courtesy of Thomas Schmitt)

11 ELEVEN

Georgia was spoiled rotten and never did any work or really had to struggle in any way. She just managed to get people to take care of her, baby her, coddle her, and chauffeur her around town.

The year 1976 would turn out to be one big party. America was celebrating two hundred years of independence, and I was celebrating my own liberation from the daily grind.

I told myself that after I settled in, even though it wasn't the greatest environment to raise a child, I'd keep Stacey with me full time. As it was, I was still taking her to my mom's after school, then picking her up in the morning. I felt I was doing the right thing by keeping her in a more stable atmosphere provided by her grandma. When I wasn't with Stacey, Bukowski and I would spend the rest of the day doing what two people do when they're getting to know each other.

During January 1976, Bukowski and I kicked off the year in style. We spent a lot of time together. We'd go out drinking, stay in drinking, have sex, go out to eat, attend boxing matches and go to the racetrack. Sometimes we stayed up all night talking. Other times, he stayed up all night writing and listening to the radio, and I'd watch TV in the bedroom.

January was a month of blissful compatibility. We made each other happy. We made each other laugh.

In the middle of the month, Bukowski had to fly to Chicago for a poetry reading. Even though I was out of work, I'd keep myself busy by decorating my new apartment, visiting Georgia or running errands.

At least once a week, Georgia called me to drive her someplace or other—usually to the welfare office or to a "friend's" house to pick up "something." She was collecting a couple hundred bucks a month in public assistance and most of the money went for drugs. Her live-in boyfriend,

67

67

Bill, was a steady worker and he made sure her rent and utilities were always up to date. He also appeared to take good care of her girls.

Georgia was really lucky to have Bill, though she either didn't realize it or she didn't let on. Bill was a good guy—nice, kindhearted, and good-looking—and he absolutely idolized Georgia. He was an enigma to me and I never fully understood his attraction to her. Sure she had a unique personality, but who could put up with all the baggage that came with it? Whatever they had, seemed to work. They would remain together for a few years.

When I pulled up in front of Georgia's place, she stuck her head out of the door and yelled, "Just another minute."

I figured I'd be lucky if she came out in ten minutes. I lit a cigarette and turned on the radio, changing the stations until I heard "Bungle in the Jungle" by Jethro Tull. I sang along, smoking and tapping on the steering wheel. After the song, I put out one cigarette and lit another. I took a pill out of my jeans pocket—one that I'd put there just in case I needed it. Now I really needed it. I popped it in my mouth and swallowed it dry. I switched the stations back and forth until I caught "One of these Nights" by the Eagles. The song was half over, but it was one of my favorites. While I was singing and smoking and drumming on the steering wheel, I was putting on mascara, looking at myself in the rearview mirror. The song was over so I turned the radio dial until I caught "Lady Marmalade" by Patti LaBelle. I was getting all set to sing along, the French parts, too, but just then Georgia hopped in the car.

"Gee-zue Christo," I said, "what took you so long?"

I took my first good look at her. She didn't look well. She was shaking, and her nose was running.

"Do you have the flu? If you're sick, let's go see a doctor," I said. "We can go to the welfare office tomorrow."

"I need to go there today or I'm not gonna get my fuckin' check this month," she said. "Come on, let's go."

Georgia didn't say anything as we drove down Hollywood Boulevard. She was clutching a book in her hand.

"Whatta ya' readin'?" I asked, breaking the silence.

"*Even Cowgirls Get the Blues.*"

"Is it any good?" I asked.

"Yeah, it's fuckin' great—just drive, please. You're a scintillating conversationalist, but I don't feel like talking, okay?"

That was Georgia. Even though you were going out of your way to do her a favor, she made it seem as if she were gracing you with her presence. I decided to drop the small talk and try to get this over with as quickly as possible.

When we got to the welfare office, I double-parked and waited for Georgia to get out of the car.

"Aren't you coming in?" she said.

"I'm going to run a couple of errands. By the time your turn rolls around, I'll be back."

"You should come in and see what number I get," she said. "Maybe they'll take me right away."

"You always have to wait."

"I don't want to be waiting around for you to pick me up," she said. "I want to go home and crash."

"I've got a doctor's appointment and besides, there's no place to park. You've got a book to read. I'll be right back—don't spaz out."

I was hoping to check out a doctor over on Santa Monica Boulevard, near Sunset. He had a walk-in clinic and I needed another prescription. I had gained two pounds since I quit work and I wanted to have it, just in case. It was like an insurance policy. I knew Georgia had lots of uppers, but I just couldn't take that bathtub garbage she was now buying. It made me feel sick and nervous.

"You better go in with me, Pam," Georgia said. "After all the favors I've done for you."

If anything, it was the other way around; I was always babysitting for her, chauffeuring her around, loaning her money, buying her food, and taking her out for drinks.

"What kind of favors are you talking about?" I asked.

"Last night, I gave Larry half my stash so he could get high," she said. "And now I'm strung out."

"And that's a favor you did for me?" I said.

I didn't want to let on that this was the first I'd heard that my brother was shooting heroin. And now I was certain she was too.

"He said you were going to pay me back," Georgia said. "You owe me twenty bucks."

I knew Larry and Georgia were close, but I didn't know they were this intimate.

I was beginning to realize that it may be time to break loose from Georgia. I wanted to start over in my new apartment with my new boyfriend and my newfound freedom from work. I was ready to sever my ties with Georgia and my brother.

"I don't have time to wait inside with you, Georgia," I said. "I guess you'll have to take the bus home."

"Bus?!" She screamed the word the way a woman would scream "Rape!"

Georgia was spoiled rotten and never did any work or really had to struggle in any way. She just managed to get people to take care of her, baby her, coddle her, and chauffeur her around town. I suppose I should have had more compassion for the underlying psychological issues that brought her to this place, but I had my own to deal with and was becoming weary of her. She was heading the way of most addicts—completely selfish and manipulative.

"I want my money," she said, throwing open the car door.

"Get it from Larry!" I said.

She got out of the car and slammed the door. Then she tried to kick the car as I was driving away. In my rearview mirror, I saw one of her platform shoes fly into the middle of Hollywood Boulevard. She had to limp into the street, darting around cars, to retrieve her shoe. It was a pathetic scene, but I couldn't help laughing.

I spent my last sixty dollars to get the pills—fifty dollars for the doctor visit and ten dollars to have the prescription filled. The prescription included those two dreaded words: No refills.

I'd asked for a Dexedrine prescription. At the time, these drugs had been reclassified as Schedule II drugs by Congress in 1971, which made them more difficult to come by, but not impossible. Doctors were hesitant to prescribe them unless absolutely necessary. But there were still some unscrupulous doctors, who, for a price, would write them—and we knew them all. Back then there were no computers, so you could get several prescriptions at once without fear of cross-referencing as long as you alternated pharmacies. I managed to fill the scrip and pick up Georgia in time to take her home.

When Bukowski got back a couple of days later, we were both happy to see each other. He wanted to go right to bed.

"How was Chicago?"

"It was like hell," he said. "Cold and snowy."

"I thought hell was hot and fiery."

"I used to think so, too," he said, "until I experienced January in Chicago."

It was about three in the afternoon, with only a couple hours of daylight left. I wanted to go out and do something. But, I figured, after his trip that was the last thing he'd want to do. I thought if I could make him feel sorry for me, maybe he'd go along with it. I stuck out my lip and pouted.

"What's wrong?" he said, slumping into his striped chair.

"I'm hungry," I told him, taking a seat on his lap. "Let's go out to eat."

"Make yourself some scrambled eggs," he told me.

"I've been eating eggs since you left," I said.

I jumped up and started to bob and dance around, flapping my arms like an idiot. I twirled around a couple of times and said, "Hank, watch me do the starving Funky Chicken."

I danced around like a maniac, singing and making up words to a song, "I'm a hungry, hungry, funky, funky chick-chick-chick-on."

He started to laugh from deep in his stomach. The laughter just rumbled out of him. I was acting so stupid, it was funny.

"You're crazy, Red."

"Let's go out to eat, please," I purred, sitting back on his lap.

"Okay," he said. "Let's go down the street."

"Where?"

"Pioneer Chicken."

"No! No! No!" I said. "I want to go to . . ."

Before I could say Musso's, Bukowski's head fell to his chest, and he began to snore. He was fast asleep, slumped over on his striped throne. I decided to let him sleep. I covered him with a blanket, then went into the kitchen and made myself some scrambled eggs.

He woke in his chair a couple hours later. I was in bed watching the news. He came in and lied down beside me. We had a short, but sweet session and he fell asleep again with his arm across my waist.

The next morning, I reached under the bed hoping to find my pack of cigarettes. My hand touched a pile of papers. I grabbed some pages and pulled them out. They were watercolors painted on flimsy 24" x 36" recycled packing paper. I found the simple, colorful paintings charming and wondered who had drawn them. At first glance I thought it may have been his daughter.

Just then, Bukowski came into the bedroom with a beer in one hand and a hardboiled, salt covered egg in the other.

"What are you doing?" he said.

"Look what I found under your bed."

"They're no good," he said, chomping into the egg.

"You painted these?"

Bukowski nodded, then shrugged.

"I've never seen you paint."

"Who would want to paint with you around?"

I found the paintings delightful. They were whimsical and childlike. One was a large blue face that looked like a mask; another was a man outlined in black with an angel flying next to him. Still another was a green face outlined in red, followed by a red face outlined in green. I spread the paintings all around me on the mattress, then reached under the bed and grabbed another stack.

"Leave them under there," Bukowski said.

"You can't leave your paintings under the bed."

"They're lousy. That's where they belong."

"You don't want them?"

"Not really."

"Well, if you don't want them," I said, "I guess they're mine."

I stacked all the paintings on top of my head, got up off the floor, and made my way to the door, barefooted.

Bukowski stuck the last bit of egg in his mouth and took a swig of beer. He watched me approach the door and laughed. I guess he thought I was just fooling around. When I opened the door, he must have realized I was really serious.

"Come back," he yelled in-between his laughter.

"Come get me," I said, as I ran out the door and then up the walk to my apartment.

I turned around and saw him standing on his porch still laughing. It was raining that day and I slipped on the stairs as I headed up to my door. I heard a loud cackle. He thought that was hilarious. I didn't return the paintings, and he never asked for them back.

 **TWELVE**

He seemed so delighted to be with me, and to have people see us together.

Bukowski hated to travel, hated to be anyplace other than L.A. When he got back from Chicago, we settled into a routine. The day usually started with Bukowski's hangover.

The first thing he did in the morning was vomit. After maybe ten minutes of this, he went into the kitchen, drank a beer, and tried to keep it down. He usually failed and was back in the bathroom retching. Then he went into the kitchen and drank another beer. If he was lucky, it would stay down, and the day would begin.

Even though his place was a dirty mess, his personal hygiene was quite good. In the morning, he would usually take a hot shower and come back to bed. Sometimes we would make love. Sometimes we would just lie in bed cuddling and talking.

Bukowski was a great storyteller and had a seemingly endless supply of tales. He rarely repeated himself, and usually remembered if he had already told you something. He would regale me with interesting stories like the one about a woman friend of his whose husband had died and she had him cremated. She wore a locket around her neck filled with her dead husband's ashes. At each meal, she would open the locket and take a pinch of his ashes and sprinkle them on her food like seasoning salt. This was her way of staying one with him. Bukowski never told me the back story on this woman, but years later I would come to find out that this female friend was Gypsy Lou Webb, co-founder of the Loujon Press in Louisiana. She and her husband Jon would publish two beautiful ornate books of poetry by Bukowski, *It Catches My Heart in its Hands* and *Crucifix in a Deathhand*. This would mark a pivotal moment in his career. Prior to meeting the Webbs he had been published in mostly obscure, small press publications. These two books showcased only Bukowski's work, which would garner more attention and give him additional credibility as a legitimate writer.

He also told me an interesting story about a lovely looking young woman who made her living as a prostitute. She was a regular in a bar that Bukowski frequented. Though she was strikingly beautiful, she was very unhappy. One day she took a seat near Bukowski at the bar. She ordered a drink, then took out a razor blade. Much to the horror of all the patrons, she began cutting up her face. A few days later he was told she had committed suicide. This was obviously the basis for the story he wrote titled, "The Most Beautiful Woman In Town." I assumed this was a true story, because he was clearly moved by it.

There were a few topics he would bring up more than once. His major repetitive topic was Jane, his first love and the inspiration for his screenplay, _Barfly_. She drank herself to death. Over and over, he would tell me how guilty he felt about abandoning Jane toward the end of her life. He had loved her dearly, and he had many great memories of their time together. But he just couldn't seem to forgive himself for how she had died. Jane loved him before he was "Charles Bukowski" and she would always have a special place in his heart.

Another subject he mentioned more than once was his divorce from Barbara Frye. He couldn't believe she'd divorced him on the grounds of "mental cruelty." He didn't seem to mind that she divorced him. It was the reason she gave for it that upset him. He kept the divorce papers in the top drawer of his dresser, and pulled them out—gazing at the documents and shaking his head in disbelief.

"Look at this document," he'd say, handing me the divorce papers. "You know me, I'm a gentle guy. How could she accuse me of something like this?" This truly bothered him.

Another repetitive subject was his father. Though he refused to discuss his mother, his father was a tremendous source of mental anguish, one he couldn't seem to resolve. He told me about all the irrational physical and mental abuse his father would subject him to from the time he was a young boy all the way through his adolescence. By all accounts, his father was a very vicious, sadistic, miserable human being. And, ironically, most likely the impetus for his exceptional talent, though I suspect Bukowski would have gladly forgone the fame in exchange for a happy childhood.

When I would ask about his mother, he would just sigh wistfully and offer, "I have nothing to say about her." My feeling was that she had loved and nurtured him. She was alone in a foreign country living with a monster for a husband, and he was her only child. Bukowski must have been the center of her universe. Though he had suffered extraordinary emotional and physical abuse, first from his father then later from a shallow, prejudicial society because of his unusual appearance, he still maintained a very healthy ego. I felt someone in his youth had given him positive reinforcement and a feeling of self-worth. I believe it was his mother. From what little I managed to glean about her, she appeared to be a gentle refined woman and most likely the one responsible for his appreciation of classical music. But he could never forgive her need for self-preservation by siding with his wicked father who would assault him mercilessly while she passively stood by. He tried to deem her irrelevant, but the pain and disappointment he still harbored over this perceived betrayal was evident.

He spoke of his daughter Marina with love and pride. He often told me how smart and beautiful she was and what a great kid she was. I'm not certain how often he saw Marina, but I had the impression they got together every few weeks. On occasion, he would talk about his visits with her when he returned and couldn't get over how amazing she was. Marina never came to Bukowski's place, at least not while I was there, and I never had the pleasure of meeting her. And though he didn't speak often about her mother, Frances, he always adopted a gentle, respectful tone when she was mentioned. His love and respect for both was unquestionable.

Bukowski did get to know my daughter Stacey. He was cordial to her, though not overly friendly. At times he would become impatient having a little one around when he was trying to court her mother. Sometimes he would remind me of W. C. Fields trying to cope with an annoying child: "Hey, Kid, you're cute, but you're in my way." But for the most part, he was very kind toward her. I was proud of Stacey, and even though, at times, I had a strange way of showing it, I loved her with all my heart. Despite her unconventional mother and lifestyle, she was a perfect child in every way— bright, beautiful, charming, sweet, obedient, and easygoing. She was even in the gifted program at school. I knew I was fortunate to have such a wonderful, seemingly well-adjusted child.

After we got out of bed, Bukowski usually had a couple of hardboiled eggs and a couple of beers for breakfast. Once in a while, we'd go out for Philly cheese and steak sandwiches around the corner on Hollywood Boulevard. Bukowski thought the greasy sandwiches cured his hangovers.

Bukowski rarely skipped a meal—one reason I believe he was able to function so well, despite his alcoholism. I was averse to cooking and so was Bukowski. For dinner, we'd often get takeout food, make sandwiches, or go to a restaurant. My favorite was Musso & Frank on Hollywood Boulevard. I believe I was the first person to introduce him to the restaurant. It would become one of his favorite places to dine and drink.

We were out one afternoon running errands on Hollywood Boulevard, which we did frequently (probably making a drugstore run). We were both

Seated: *Manny Felix*   Standing: *Craig Vallone*
I introduced Hank to Musso and Frank Grill. It would become one of his favorite restaurants. Above is the exact table where Hank and I would sit— last table on the left as you enter the front door. Manny Felix worked at Musso and Frank's since 1974 and has many great stories to share about Bukowski and his visits to the restaurant.
(© Taylor Brittenham)

hungry, so I suggested we have lunch at Musso and Frank Grill, which was right up the street. Bob, my former boyfriend, the screenplay writer, used to take me there often. It was a well-known hangout for writers because the Writers Guild was right around the corner on Cherokee Avenue. I was worried that Bukowski would feel uncomfortable because it was slightly on the fancy side. He was a very self-conscious man and hated going out to public places, especially where a standard of decorum or protocol was expected. Not certain how he would react, we walked into the restaurant and were seated immediately. We sat at the last table at the end of the first row of booths on the left side of the entrance. Bukowski looked around, and though it was an upscale restaurant with waiters wearing white dress shirts, black trousers and bow-ties, it had a warm, cozy atmosphere reminiscent of an old-fashioned gentlemen's club, with lots of dark wood and comfortable, red leather-tufted booths. I waited for his reaction, expecting him to say something negative. Much to my surprise he seemed to really like the place.

I went on to tell him about its history and that it was a favorite haunt of many great writers. This seemed to delight him—another reaction I did not expect. Then he really blew me away when the waiter came to take our order and he requested the Sand Dabs. Sand Dabs! I had never heard of them. It sounded like the type of dish an aristocrat would order. He displayed an air of sophistication I had never witnessed in him, nor could I have imagined up to that point in our relationship. He seemed uncharacteristically comfortable. I was pleased.

We ordered a couple of bottles of wine before the meal was over. I went on to tell him that I always fantasized that this restaurant was the west coast version of the Algonquin Club in New York. I would pretend we were members of the "Vicious Circle." I was Dorothy Parker and he was Raymond Chandler, or maybe Hemingway. "How 'bout Charles Bukowski?" he suggested.

If we weren't out running errands during the day, buying takeout food, filling a prescription, or taking his clothes and bedding to the Chinese laundry, we'd just hang around his apartment and drink. Both of us were fairly antisocial and didn't care much about the outside world. We were content just being alone together. Occasionally we'd venture out to a bar, like the Frolic Room, and drink and play pool (I was a much better player than him). Or we would go to the racetrack (where I always ended up getting lost) when the horses were running at Hollywood Park or Santa Anita.

One other form of entertainment Bukowski enjoyed, was watching boxing matches. I wasn't a huge fan, but did become somewhat interested in the sport in the 1960s when the charismatic Muhammad Ali, who was then known as Cassius Clay, came on the scene. I loved to watch him fight. He was also a great entertainer outside the ring.

The first time Bukowski took me to the Grand Olympic Auditorium, I had no idea what to expect. I imagined we were going to a gritty little gym somewhere on the east side. Instead, we went downtown, and pulled up in front of an enormous edifice that reminded me of a Greek temple. Bukowski told me that the place was called the Grand Olympic because it had been built to accommodate boxing events for the 1932 Summer Olympic Games.

When we entered the auditorium, I felt as if thousands of eyes were on me. Men hooted, hollered, whooped it up, whistled, stomped their feet, clapped, and beat on the seats. At first, I didn't know what was going on. I kept turning around to see if a celebrity such as Warren Beatty or Faye Dunaway was coming in behind me.

After I realized the men were putting on a show for me, my face turned a nice shade of red to match my hair. I felt like crawling under one of the seats. I didn't think my clothes were particularly sexy—just my usual jeans, high heels, crop-top, and preppy jacket. Bukowski seemed to be enjoying this madness, egging the men on, raising his arms like a conductor leading an orchestra. He grinned until his eyes crinkled shut. I later realized he liked to appear in public with an attractive woman on his arm—it bolstered his ego and reinforced his opinion of himself as a great lover. I had never viewed myself as a stunning beauty, but that day I felt like one.

As for the actual fights, I had never seen one in person. I don't like violence of any kind, and felt ill when each punch landed. I closed my eyes, but I could still hear the fighters punching and jabbing at each other. I understood why Bukowski enjoyed the sport. It was the purest form of survival of the fittest. It was the twentieth century version of the Roman gladiator, except (most of the time) no one ended up dead.

Later, he would tell me he loved how real and immediate the sport was. You put two men in a ring and wouldn't know what would happen until the bell rang. With each movement, each right or left, the game shifted. You had to pay attention. You had to watch. You could not let your mind drift. You had to be in the moment. Boxing seemed to be a form of Zen to Bukowski, an exercise in living in the now.

I think, too, he enjoyed the primal aspects of the sport. You are thrown in the ring, and you try to survive—dancing around, hanging on the ropes, throwing punches, but never quitting until you go down for the count. This was how Bukowski lived his life. It was a struggle, it was full of uncertainty and pain and suffering, and if you were lucky you had a few joyful moments, a few perfect rights or lefts that made it all worthwhile.

It was a bloody match, but an even one—each fighter giving the other everything he had. Between rounds, I watched the faces of the fighters. Both men looked dazed as if wondering how they got there, covered with spatters of blood on their faces and trunks.

I turned to Bukowski and said, "The looks on those poor guys' faces between rounds bothers me more than the violence. They look so lost and pathetic."

He squeezed my hand and said, "Sexy and sensitive . . . I hate that in a woman."

When we left that night, it was to more appreciation from the crowd—mostly working-class guys who looked as if they'd been through their share of fights. Bukowski held my arm as we walked out. He smiled and waved and nodded to the men in the crowd. He seemed so delighted to be with me and to have people see us together. I was glad he didn't appear threatened if other men showed their appreciation for me. I decided to just let myself enjoy the attention as if it were a fantasy come true—little Cupcakes surrounded by a thousand adoring men.

"Hey, maybe I can get a job as one of the girls that holds up the sign between rounds," I said.

"Yeah, maybe you could, Red."

THIRTEEN

When Bukowski was sober (meaning less than six beers), his manners were impeccable.

"*Quit* bothering me, asshole," Bukowski yelled into the phone, then slammed down the receiver.

In contrast to how Bukowski responded to female admirers, this was his usual reaction when fawning male fans called. The more they gushed about his writing, the more Bukowski seemed to despise them.

When I told him not to be so rude—after all, these guys were only guilty of loving his books—Bukowski would say, "They're losers. They think they're writers or poets and want me to help them get published. They're fucking cunts."

So it was with more than a little trepidation that I asked Bukowski if my brother Larry could stop by for a visit. Larry was a huge fan, which Bukowski had learned during their conversation on Christmas Eve.

"Shit, Baby, does he have to?" Bukowski groaned.

"He won't stay long, Hank," I said, with the hope this would turn out to be true.

"You're going to owe me," Bukowski said, pinching my fanny.

I draped my arms over his shoulders and said, "You won't be sorry. I've got something special in mind for you later." Then I gave him a big kiss to seal the deal.

When I called Larry and told him it was okay to come over, I said, "Could you bring a six-pack?"

There was a long silence on the other end of the phone.

"What's the matter?" I asked.

"I'm broke," Larry said.

He was always broke and was always borrowing money from my mom or one of his friends. I knew better than to give him any money—even though he hit me up for it, especially when he knew I'd just gotten an unemployment check. Not that I was much better with my finances, but for God's sake, he was four years older than I was—if anything, he should help me.

Rather than goad him into bringing some beer, I decided to let it drop. This was Larry's way—he felt entitled. Unlike the rest of us poor slobs, he didn't have to bring something to the party. He was exempt.

A few years before, Larry was asked to bring dessert for our Thanksgiving dinner. When the meal was over, I turned to him.

"So, Larry, what's for dessert?" I said.

Without skipping a beat, he reached into his pocket, pulled out a package of Dentyne, and said, "Gum, anyone?"

Larry could always disarm you with a quip like that. It was his major survival skill. But his wit wasn't enough these days. I didn't want to spend time with him, but felt guilty about pushing him away. I just wished he would find himself and quit waiting for somebody else to make things right in his life. I had too many responsibilities of my own that I couldn't handle—I didn't want to have to worry about him too.

My feelings toward Larry were ambivalent at best, the scales often tilting toward the negative. Growing up, he had bullied his two younger sisters, mainly me. After our parents were divorced, he took out his rage by frequently pummeling me with his fists.

Part of me figured he was a lost cause, but another part hoped he could do something with his life. I thought Bukowski might be able to give Larry some direction. Larry was a classic underachiever—a brilliant mind, but aimless and lazy—and really needed a father figure.

The evening of his visit, he was supposed to show up at eight o'clock. The doorbell rang at seven, when Bukowski and I were just about to dig into our favorite takeout feast from Pioneer Chicken. I was a big fan of the fried gizzards, and told Bukowski not to get me  anything else. When I was taking diet pills, I had to force myself to eat, which usually resulted in one meal a day. Rather than let food go to waste, he'd only ordered a few pieces of chicken, and some rolls, fries, and coleslaw for himself and my beloved gizzards.

"Who is it?" I asked, before peering out the Venetian blinds.

"It's the Vice Squad—open up."

When I opened the door, I could see that Larry had already had a few beers—and might be speeding too. He launched into his Jack Webb impersonation:

"This is the city. I work here. I carry a badge. Your neighbors are complaining that they see a lot of undesirables coming in and out of here. Hippies, nonconformist potheads, pinko-commies, you know, unclean dissenter types, ma'am."

"Larry, I said eight," I told him. "It's only seven."

He stepped through the door and said, "I thought we were supposed to turn back the clock tonight."

"It's February," I said.

"Do you want me to come back in the fall?" he asked.

I had to fight the urge to say, "Yes!"

I ushered him over to the couch across from where Bukowski was sitting in his striped chair. Larry nodded at him, but it came across as a bow.

"Good to see you, man," Larry said, taking a seat on the couch.

After meeting Bukowski at my mom's on Christmas Eve, Larry told me how much he "identified" with Bukowski. Though he had been a journalism major at UCLA and wanted to be a writer, I think this was more a physical kinship. Like Bukowski, Larry was an unattractive man whose looks were further marred by acne scars.

Right now, I could almost hear Larry's thoughts: *If this ugly son-of-a-bitch can make it, so the hell can I.*

Well, it's one thing to be unattractive and another thing to have a complex about it. Larry definitely had hang-ups about his looks. He realized he was unattractive at sixteen, when my mom told him she'd made appointments for him to get his nose fixed and skin resurfaced. But that wasn't enough. She also started to dye his hair brown because, she said, the orange color made him look less attractive. Who wouldn't have a complex?

Right now, looking at Bukowski and Larry, I could see this was a one-way kinship. Bukowski didn't care for Larry—he could see right through him. Bukowski had no sympathy for people who felt sorry for themselves and blamed other people for their problems. Because Larry was my brother, Bukowski made an extra effort not to be rude.

When Bukowski was sober (meaning less than six beers), as he was now, his manners were impeccable. He looked at the food on the table, really only enough for one—not counting my gizzards—and asked Larry, "Have you eaten?"

Larry said, "No, I came right from work."

Bukowski waved his hand toward the food and said, "Dig in."

I was hoping Larry would look at me. I wanted to shake my head to let him know it was not okay to eat Bukowski's chicken dinner. But he didn't glance up from the food on the table. I felt like ripping his bushy orange hair out by the roots.

"Thanks, man," he said, then picked up a drumstick and chomped into it.

Bukowski stood up and headed toward the kitchen. When he opened the refrigerator, he called into the living room, "Care for a beer?"

"Okay," Larry said, wiping his greasy fingers on a paper napkin.

"Better watch out, Lar, you're going to mess up your good clothes," I said, referring to the dress shirt and corduroy pants he was wearing.

"I'll have mom throw them in the wash," he said.

He wasn't trying to be funny or ironic. He didn't see anything wrong with a twenty-seven-year-old man asking his mother to do his laundry. Though I wasn't one to give advice, I'd told my mom over and over that she wasn't doing Larry any favors by coddling him, but she believed that with a little help he would get his act together. Besides, she still felt so much guilt where he was concerned that she was willing to pay her penance by washing his clothes, paying his bills, and giving him money.

I remembered the time Larry had a paper route and mom would set the alarm for him. But he let the clock ring and ring, and cursed at her if she tried to make him get up. So she did the next best thing—dragged me out of bed at four in the morning. She and I rolled up the papers, put rubber bands around them, then went out and made the deliveries.

As he sat eating Bukowski's chicken and drinking Bukowski's beer, I thought of how clueless he was. The world revolved around him. He had no responsibilities. We only existed to serve him.

Bukowski and I sat there smoking cigarettes and drinking beer while Larry scarfed down the food. Between bites, he talked about the assholes he worked with at Aaron Brothers Art Mart, where he was a sales clerk. I said a silent thank you to God that at least he had a job these days.

When I got tired of listening to him talk about the finer points of selling art supplies, I said, "Hank paints."

Larry seemed surprised. He moved his jaw from side to side—a nervous speed habit that always made me feel jumpy—and said, "Do you want me to get you a discount?"

"No thanks, I've got enough paints and paper to last for years," Bukowski said.

I checked the clock. It was only 7:30. I was starting to get pains in my stomach. I needed to eat something if I was going to keep drinking. And as long as Larry was around, I was going to keep drinking.

I went over to the coffee table to look for my gizzards, but they, too, had been devoured. Larry didn't seem to notice that I was looking for some food. He was always blissfully oblivious to others.

When he was done eating, I cleared away the paper plates, plastic utensils, greasy napkins, and paper bags. While I was in the kitchen getting rid of the trash, I grabbed some more beers.

I got back to the living room in time to see Larry lean back, let out a satisfied sigh, put his feet on the coffee table, and light a cigarette. When I handed him the beer, he didn't even say thanks.

Despite it all, I loved him somewhere deep down—even though most of the time this speck of feeling was hard to find. Emotionally, he was a case of arrested development. But intellectually, he was brilliant. He was also incredibly well read and well versed in a wide range of subjects. It was just such a waste of talent. I hoped that Bukowski could say or do something to shake him into some newfound sense of purpose in life.

Bukowski stared at me over the edge of his beer can. I knew he was suffering. I would really have to make it up to him later.

Larry stroked his heavy orange beard for a few seconds, as if trying to figure out exactly the right words to say. He took a deep breath. I think I knew what was coming—the "you're a great writer, and I want to be a writer, and can you help me" spiel.

Before Larry could say anything, I cut in and started to chatter rapid-fire.

"Hey, have you seen Georgia lately? Hank really likes Georgia, don't you, Hank? He thinks she's very amusing. I haven't seen her for a while. What's she been . . . "

Larry said, "Shut the fuck up, Pam. I want to talk to Hank."

Bukowski gave Larry his icy blue stare. "Hey—show some manners, man," he said.

Larry looked shocked. Bukowski was the rough talking, thumb-your-nose-at-convention kind of guy. Was the old man kidding? Larry wasn't sure, but I could tell he was trying to figure it out. He decided to backpedal.

"Pardon moi, Princess Pamela," Larry said, his voice dripping sarcasm. He slid a Pall Mall out of his pocket and lit it.

"So what writers do you like, man?" Larry said.

Bukowski sighed, then stood up and walked toward the kitchen. When he reached the doorway, he turned around and stared at Larry.

"Brother Larry, you can do better than that, can't you?"

"What do you mean, man?"

"All you guys have the same fucking question. Do you think reading the books I like will help you learn to write?"

Larry stroked his beard and ran his jaw from side to side. He stayed like that for a few moments, then looked at Bukowski and said, "It might give me some inspiration."

"For inspiration, stick your soft ass in a hard chair and sit in front of a typewriter for seven or eight hours each day."

Larry laughed, but Bukowski wasn't kidding. Larry put out his cigarette and lit another. He was trying to figure out his next question. Bukowski went into the kitchen to get a beer. He brought back one for each of us.

"Where do you get your ideas, man?" Larry asked.

It looked as if Bukowski were weighing his options—no answer, snide answer, or straightforward answer. He looked at me. I could see in his eyes that he was enduring this for my sake. I smiled to let him know I appreciated his restraint.

"Larry," Bukowski said, "just write about what you know—like what happens to you."

"But nothing happens to me, man," Larry said.

Now it was Bukowski's turn to laugh. He began to chuckle, his stomach rising and falling, and then he broke out into nearly hysterical laughter.

Larry looked at me, trying to figure out what was going on. Bukowski was now howling.

"Let me in on the joke, man," Larry said.

We waited for Bukowski to settle down. His laughter turned into long sighs that finally tapered off.

"That's your problem," Bukowski said, "you don't notice anything that's happening. You're too busy thinking about Larry."

"I don't get you, man," Larry said.

"Of course you don't," Bukowski said.

I was trying my best to stay out of it. It was now eight o'clock—the time Larry was supposed to arrive. It seemed a good enough time for him to leave.

I stood up and raised my arms and let out a big yawn.

"Boy, I'm really tired. Hey, Lar, I've got to get up early tomorrow morning and take Stacey to school," I said. "Maybe you ought to go now."

"I just got here," he replied.

"Would you mind? I really am exhausted," I told him.

"You're so fucking rude, Pam," Larry said, standing up. He turned to Bukowski and said, "Do you want me to go?"

"I want whatever the lady wants," Bukowski told him.

Larry's head turned from me to Bukowski, then from Bukowski to me. When he got up to leave, I walked him to the door. On his way out he turned to me and whispered, "Hey, you got any shit?"

"No, Larry—goodnight," I said, shutting the door.

As soon as Larry was gone, we hopped in the car and headed over to Pioneer Chicken. By 8:30, we were back at Carlton Way with our food in front of us, as if Larry's visit had never happened. We went to bed early and Bukowski held me to my promise.

FOURTEEN

"Bitch."

$O\!ther$ than copies of his own books, Bukowski's personal library was virtually nonexistent. I never noticed other writers' works in his house, nor did I ever see him read anything but the newspaper and the racing form. I suppose it's because he considered most books—prose and poetry—not worth reading. That's why I was curious when I discovered a book of poetry by Catullus, a controversial Roman poet who'd lived during the first century B.C.

When I asked Bukowski about the book, he told me he loved the translation by Carl Sesar. He thought it was funny and fiery—and that many of the poems sounded as modern as a stand-up routine. "This cat's got some glitter," he said.

It was a warm winter day, and I decided to sit outside and read, taking Catullus with me.

I made myself comfortable on the lumpy sofa on the porch. I flipped open the book to a poem and laughed as I read Catullus's reasons for not giving his friend a loan, then felt bad about his unrequited love for Lesbia. The writing reminded me of Bukowski's, with its references to piss, snot, ass, shit and "the gods." Though a little stilted, I found the poems fun to read and timeless. Finally, I had pinpointed one of Bukowski's literary influences.

Besides Henry Miller, he rarely spoke of other writers. He never even mentioned John Fante, who Bukowski would later claim had the most significant impact and influence on his life and writing style.

After about an hour of reading, I looked up to see Bukowski drinking a beer and staring at me from his striped chair.

I closed the book and walked inside into the living room. Bukowski continued staring for a few seconds more and then asked if I dyed my hair. I had the impression that he'd been studying it the entire hour.

My hair was a strange red—it was more of an auburn color made up of many shades, even purple. In the sun, it had an unnatural look, so I could see how Bukowski could make that assumption. He would often refer to it as "like lightning from heaven." I have brownish-hazel eyes and a complexion that tans in the sun, which is unusual for a natural redhead, so I understood why someone might ask that question.

But what I found funny was that my pubic hair was the exact color—not that I sat on the porch with it exposed to the sun. But anyone who'd seen my mound of Venus—which Bukowski had—would know that my hair color was natural. The carpet clearly matched the drapes.

"You don't pay attention, silly," I said.

Bukowski took a swig from his bottle of Michelob, then said, "How so?"

I pulled down my jeans just enough to expose the top of my fiery mound. Bukowski gazed at my curly-cues for a moment, then looked up at my head, then glanced back at my crotch. He took another gulp of his beer, and the liquid began to drip from the corners of his mouth because he was smiling.

He put down the bottle and said, "So, I guess you don't henna your hair."

I zipped up my jeans and climbed onto his lap. I noticed a bottle of whiskey sitting on the floor beside him.

"What is that whiskey bottle doing on the floor?" I asked. "Are you mixing whiskey and beer? You know what that does to you. You're going to get crazy, Hank."

"Ghurrr," he growled, making a motion with his right hand like a lion attacking.

"Stop it! You're scaring me!" I teased.

"Come here you, you, little vixen! Give your daddy a kiss!"

He grabbed me by the back of my hair and smashed his mouth against mine, giving me a hard, smothering kiss. Then he picked me up in his arms and carried me into the bedroom. He dropped me on the bed and began taking off his clothes.

He was down to his briefs and T-shirt when he started on me. He pulled off my T-shirt, then my bra. I knew that within the hour while I was outside reading, he had been drinking beer, chasing it with whiskey—and was on his way to the dark side. He was now working on my jeans.

Though I was laughing through most of it, I was beginning to get a little nervous.

"HANK—STOP IT!" I yelled, not sure if he was being playful or truly becoming maniacal.

Thankfully, there was a knock on the door. It was our neighbor, Brad Darby.

Brad was a young, good-looking, twenty-something guy who lived in the front unit with his equally attractive wife Tina. He was tall and slender with perfect, blow-dried hair. He wore tight, form-fitting "outfits" that always appeared immaculate. He managed an adult bookstore in the neighborhood, while Tina worked as an exotic dancer at a local strip club. He was also the designated manager of the apartment building.

I would refer to him and his wife as Ken and Barbie. He was attractive, but rather bland—not at all my type. I don't care for men who appear to spend more time in front of a mirror than I do.

Bukowski was fond of Brad and Tina and they spent many evenings drinking together before I came along. Brad was like the Howard K. Stern of the complex—he was rarely without his camera. On the days his wife was working, or out for a day of shopping, Brad would get lonely and stop by Bukowski's for a visit.

"Open up," Brad yelled.

"Motherfuck!" Bukowski growled. "What does he want?"

Bukowski answered the door in his T-shirt and briefs. Even though I wasn't particularly fond of Brad, I was glad he stopped by when he did.

I stayed in the bedroom half-naked. I found a baggy, striped cardigan on the floor and quickly threw it on. Suddenly, I heard Bukowski yell:

"Hey, Cups—Come on out here!"

"Oh crap," I muttered, "I hope this doesn't take long."

I got up and walked out wearing the sweater and my blue jeans—not realizing until it was too late that the cardigan had no buttons. I clutched it in the center, to cover up my breasts.

When I entered the living room, Brad was standing there holding his camera.

Bukowski said, "Brad wants us to pose for a few pictures."

"What kind of pictures?" I asked.

"Here, just hold this," Brad said.

He handed me a long black hose with what looked like a lemon attached at the end. I couldn't figure out what it was, but assumed it was some kind of sex gadget from the adult bookstore where Brad worked.

"What am I suppose to do with this?" I asked.

"Just hold it," Brad said. "Now say, 'Who cut the cheese?'" Then he snapped the picture.

I didn't look up when he took the shot. I was still trying to figure out what I was holding.

Then Brad asked us to pose anyway we wanted. I was getting annoyed and began walking back to the bedroom. I wanted to at least put my T-shirt back on.

"This is ridiculous," I said, heading toward the bedroom door. Bukowski grabbed my arm, twirled me around, and said, "Come on, Cups—be a sport."

"I just want to take a couple more and then I'll leave," Brad said. "Just give me a couple funny poses."

Next thing I knew, Bukowski was leaning over me, still in his underwear, with his face locked in a grimace, while he held a plastic fork over my head. I went along with the silliness by sticking out my tongue and grabbing his thigh near his crotch, with an equally crazy look on my face. Brad snapped away.

"Okay, guys, it's a wrap. Thanks a lot," he said on his way out.

These photos would surface thirty years later in a book of photographs, *Bukowski in Pictures* by Howard Sounes.

Though I was glad that Brad showed up when he did, I was just as glad when he left. While I found his wife Tina friendly and charming, I found him difficult to communicate with. He never looked me in the eye when he spoke and I always felt as though he was uncomfortable around me. The two of us never quite connected.

Once Brad was gone, I opened my sweater and flashed Bukowski. He had been in such a good mood during our foolish photo shoot I expected him to laugh. Instead, he just glared at me. He'd had about four more beers during Brad's visit—adding that on top of whiskey and numerous beers he'd consumed earlier, he was now sloppy drunk.

"Don't think I didn't see the way you looked at him," Bukowski said. "You've been fucking Brad behind my back—haven't you?!"

Of course, I thought he was kidding. We had been together virtually all day and night for weeks. And he knew I thought Brad was a drag. He had to be joking.

I laughed, which seemed to enrage him more. His eyes glazed over, and he went into a rabid trance. He said all kinds of vulgar things and made horrible accusations. It was like watching a dirty-mouthed child throw a tantrum.

"YOU WOMEN ARE ALL ALIKE!" he screamed. "YOU'RE ALL NOTHING BUT FUCKING, GODDAMN WHORES!"

When he was sober, Bukowski was a kind, gentle, almost courtly soul. When he passed a certain stage of drunkenness, he turned into a mad man. But despite all of his invective, his abuse had never turned physical. He struck only with verbal assaults.

I sat on the couch and smoked a cigarette while Bukowski raged. I should have gone back to my own apartment, but was strangely fascinated by this drunken meltdown. I almost felt as if I were watching a sick version of an educational film—the kind the hygiene teacher shows an eighth grade class to warn of the perils of alcohol abuse.

Finally exhausted, he plopped down on the striped chair, downed a beer in a couple of gulps, belched a few times, and then sat in silence. It was as if he'd had a finite number of words for this particular tirade and he had just spewed out the last one, which had been "bitch."

I stared at him for a minute or so, then said, "You all done now?"

Right then, I felt eons older than he was. Even though I was far from sober, I was still relatively sane and rational, and I was trying to coax him out of his crazed fit. He hung his head low to his chest, sulking.

I came to understand how much Bukowski disliked and distrusted attractive people—men and women. He thought good-looking people lacked character, had never suffered, had never experienced rejection, did not understand pain, had it easy in life, and got by on their looks.

Because he considered Brad an attractive man, and he considered me an attractive woman, he figured we had no qualms about jumping into bed together.

Tonight's jealous rage wasn't the first time he had accused me of being disloyal and it wouldn't be the last. Over time, Bukowski would accuse me of jumping into bed with virtually everybody he knew—despite all evidence to the contrary. I would soon discover that jealousy was one of his pathological insecurities.

FIFTEEN

He grabbed a breadstick and lobbed it at me. I dipped my napkin in his glass of water and threw it at him.

The first glimpse I had into Bukowski's jealous disorder took place a couple weeks prior to the Brad incident. Whenever I asked Bukowski for a favor, he usually came through. I often asked him to drive me someplace, pick me up someplace, or pick up something I needed. He seemed to enjoy taking care of me—and never complained.

I frequently asked him to drop me off at a pharmacy so I could get a prescription filled. Most of the time, he waited in the car, which is what I thought he'd do on this particular day.

As he pulled up in front of the drugstore, I opened the car door and said, "Be right out."

"I need to get something," he said, turning off the engine.

When we got out of the car, he asked, "Do you have any change for the parking meter?"

"We'll be right out," I said.

"I don't want to get a ticket," he told me.

"So do what I do," I said. "Don't pay it."

"But I would pay it," he said, "and I don't want to have to lay out that kind of money for no reason."

"You're a real stickler, Hank," I said.

"Do you have any change or not?"

I fumbled around in my purse and pulled out a dime, which Bukowski stuck in the meter.

"We've got fifteen minutes," he said.

I had to wait in a long line at the pharmacy counter. I didn't worry about making Bukowski hang around the drugstore. He was a very patient man and never complained about things like that. When I looked around and didn't see him, I figured he was outside smoking a cigarette.

Finally, the line moved up, and it was my turn. I handed my prescription to the pharmacist, and he held it as if it were a used tampon. From his high perch, he stared down at me and shook his head.

"You'd better take this someplace else," he said.

His voice was loud and bellowing. Everybody in the store turned and gaped at me. I knew they were all thinking the same thing: Look at the junkie. The funny thing was, this was Hollywood in the '70s—and most of the gapers were real junkies.

I felt like telling off the officious pharmacist, but didn't think that would help me get what I wanted—a bottle of pharmaceutical-grade Dexedrine.

"Please call my doctor," I said. "His number is right there. He'll verify the prescription."

"Oh, it's real, all right," the pharmacist said. "But I've already filled one of them for you this month."

I was usually careful about rotating my pharmacies and wondered how I managed to make this mistake.

"Oh . . . well, I accidentally dropped the last bottle down the toilet and flushed before I could retrieve it," I lied. "Please, just call the doctor, he'll vouch for it."

"All right," he said, "but this is the last time."

He filled the prescription while I waited. I was still seething, but very relieved. *Who did this pompous ass think he was,* I thought, *God?!*

I still didn't see Bukowski in the store. I headed for the exit and a good-looking black man in his early twenties held the door for me as I barged out of the drugstore.

"Thanks," I said, as I walked in front of him.

The young man began singing a song called "You Sexy Thing," made popular by a group named Hot Chocolate.

"I believe in miracles—where ya' from—
    you sexy thing?" he crooned.

I looked up at him and smiled and continued walking toward Bukowski's blue Volkswagen.

"Say, Miss Lady . . . what's the matter? You got something against the brothers?"

I smiled back at him and shook my head, while I continued walking toward the car. I saw Bukowski shoving another coin in the meter. He apparently saw the exchange between me and the man at the door. He jumped in his car without acknowledging me and started the motor.

I hopped in the car. On the seat was a bag full of toiletries, including a tube of Preparation H. I set it on the floor. Bukowski didn't say a word, but I could see he wasn't happy. He had also purchased a new pair of big, black-framed sunglasses, which he was now wearing. They made him look like a praying mantis.

I thought he was annoyed that I'd told him

(courtesy of Thomas Schmitt)   not to put money in the parking meter. He was such a strange mixture of bohemian and bourgeois. In his apartment, there were no rules—you could do what you wanted whenever you wanted. But when he was out in public, he made sure to follow all the rules and obey all Ten Commandments. He probably had the strictest morals of anyone I'd ever known.

"That s.o.b. pharmacist gave me a hard time about my prescription. He almost refused to fill it," I said. "Boy, that was close. I better be more careful in the future. You'll have to help me keep track of these things."

Bukowski didn't say anything. His expression was a cross between a scowl and a pout—a spout? He continued staring straight ahead through the windshield and remained silent.

As he pulled into the street, I pointed at the parking meter and said, "Hey, we still have twelve minutes left. Want to go back and neck in the back seat for ten minutes?"

I laughed, thinking this was very funny. But Bukowski just continued driving west on Hollywood Blvd. I lit a cigarette and turned on the radio, changing stations until I found a song I liked. I sang along until I felt like changing the station and singing something else. When we were traveling together in his car, he always deferred to me when it came to the radio—such patience.

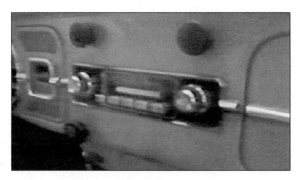

Radio in Buk's beloved Volkswagon
Regarding music, Buk has said he loves it all . . . "but some
music I can't stand" referring to most popular music. But he
always deferred to my sing-along taste when we drove,
allowing me to flip stations until I found a song I liked.
(courtesy of Thomas Schmitt)

When Bukowski pulled into a parking space about ten minutes later, I looked around, but couldn't figure out where he was headed. He got out of the car, slammed the door, walked to the parking meter and jammed some coins into it. I opened my car door and got out.

I watched Bukowski as he sauntered across the street and into the front door of Musso & Frank Grill. I followed behind.

We were seated at the same table in the back that we shared the first time I took him there. I slipped into the booth and stared at him. The waiter brought us menus. He ordered spaghetti and meat sauce and a glass of Chianti. I wasn't that hungry, but ordered a steak—very well done. Bukowski wouldn't look at me. He just sat there silently wearing his silly new sunglasses. Finally, the waiter brought the wine and poured it for us. Bukowski took a long sip, almost finishing the entire glass in one gulp. Then did the same with the second glass. Then he finally looked directly at me.

"I could break you in two," he said.

I figured he was just kidding around. I laughed.

"I could make you cry with a turn of a word."

I laughed again.

"I saw you talking to that guy," he snarled.

"What guy?"

"At the drugstore," he said. "He asked if he could give you a lift."

"No he didn't, and besides, that's not my fault."

"You were flirting with him," he said, "just like you come onto every guy that crosses your path."

"You're cracked, Hank. That's all in your mind."

"I could crush your skull with one hand," he said, still wearing those goofy looking sunglasses.

"What is with you?"

He continued to snarl at me with his lips curling like a rabid dog. I picked up a breadstick and threw it at him.

"Stop it, you're freaking me out! And please, take off those stupid sunglasses!" I said.

He grabbed a breadstick and lobbed it at me. I dipped my napkin in his glass of water and threw it at him. He did the same to me. I picked up the saltshaker and shook salt at him. He opened a packet of sugar and sprinkled it on me.

The maitre d' ran over to our table.

"Please, Sir," he said, "you're disturbing the other customers."

I began to open the ketchup bottle.

"If you don't stop," the maitre d' said, now looking at me, "you're going to have to leave."

Just then, our food arrived. The waiter placed it on the table. We ate without further incident.

SIXTEEN

The boozing, and the fights, and the jealousy were making me feel as if I were being buried alive.

Bukowski would write in the kitchen, often starting at around midnight and sometimes working until dawn. I was always amazed at how he was able to write for hours without ripping up anything he wrote to start over. I would never see him consult a dictionary or thesaurus. It was as though someone was channeling the words through him. He made it look so effortless.

Other times, he would write for a few hours and  then join me in the bedroom, where we would drink and talk the night away. He hated television, so when he came into the bedroom, I usually turned off the set. He just didn't understand how people could waste their time watching the idiot box. Sometimes I got the impression that he was jealous that I would find someone, or something, other than him, entertaining.

It's not as if he wanted to turn off the television so he could concentrate on a book. I rarely saw him read anything other than the *Los Angeles Herald-Examiner*. Even with the newspaper, it was just a cursory read. He didn't seem to care about politics, current events, or anything else in the news (with the possible exception of the sports page). He just wanted to have a working knowledge of what was going on in the world.

As for books, I assumed that he'd done most of his reading years before. He didn't seem to feel there were more than a few worthwhile books in the world, and he wasn't going to waste his time reading anything that was heavy-handed or boring. He just didn't see the value of most of the books that had been designated as literature.

Aside from the Catullus book, the only other author I recall him mentioning was Henry Miller. He said he liked "the old man's" earlier works, but felt he was too old and soft now, and may be slipping.

It was also around this time that he told me that he had received a letter from Miller's son. He praised Bukowski as a great writer—almost as good as his old man. I never saw the letter, but I would read his account of it in a book of his published letters, *Living on Luck*. In it there is correspondence to associates where he refers at least twice to this letter. Both times he tells the respective recipients that Miller's son "Larry" wrote the letter. What's odd about this is that my brother's name was Larry Miller, and my father was also a writer. Henry has only one son that I'm aware of and his name is Tony or Anthony. I now wonder if that letter he was so proud of was actually from my brother.

Since I never saw him read, I was surprised when he said, "Maybe you should try opening a book instead of watching so much of that mindless shit."

I felt hurt. I was already sensitive enough about my lack of education. I didn't need anybody else to make me self-conscious about it.

When I felt wounded in any way, I would never let anyone see it—I just couldn't stand to feel vulnerable and powerless. Instead, I would get defensive or angry—usually both. I would often kick back automatically. I was just more comfortable in this emotional zone—it made me feel more in control.

"I read all the time," I snapped at him.

My ex-boyfriend Bob had introduced me to a variety of eclectic authors, and I had read quite a few books while we were together. I knew that Bob was highly intelligent and well read, so I figured if he'd recommended the books, they must be good.

"What do you read?" he asked.

"All kinds of stuff. I like Richard Brautigan."

"He's a pussy."

"How about Hubert Selby, Jr.?"

"Overrated."

"How about . . . " I began.

". . . Charles Bukowski," he said, finishing my sentence.

I was wondering how long it would take before this subject came up. I had been dreading it. I hadn't read much of his work—just a couple of his poems and some sections of *Notes of a Dirty Old Man*. I still hadn't started *Post Office*.

"I've read your writing," I said.

"That's news to me," he said. "You never mention anything about it."

"Maybe I don't get it," I said.

"What don't you get?"

I didn't want to have this conversation. For a while now, I had been wondering what was so great about his writing. Many people seemed to adore it. But it didn't come across as extraordinary to me. His subject matter was often too raw and vulgar—full of bodily functions and dark references to death—and his writing style was almost childishly simple. I told myself that maybe I just wasn't advanced enough to appreciate it. The punk-rock scene was just beginning to emerge and I figured that was his core audience—the young, disaffected and angry.

To be honest, his writing wasn't that important to me. I was in the relationship because of the man, not because of the writer.

When I didn't answer his question, Bukowski left the room. I could hear him opening the refrigerator to get a beer. I turned on the television and hoped that would be the end of the conversation. I heard the typewriter clicking away for a few minutes, but then the sound stopped, and he was standing in the doorway.

"Why do you think people read my work?" he growled at me.

"Shock value," I said, without really thinking.

He turned off the television and stood in front of the set.

"That's the only reason?" he asked.

"Sure," I said. "Where else can they read about fucking, shitting, pissing, vomiting and death all in the same poem?"

"You have to look beyond the shit and the piss. Then you can see what gave rise to the shit and the piss," he said.

"And what will I see?"

"You know," he said, ignoring my question, "I went to the track the other day. I ran into a friend of mine. I told him about you. I also told him that you don't seem to show any interest in my writing. He told me I should smack you around first then dump you for that reason alone. He thinks I need someone who appreciates my work. And I'm beginning to wonder if he's right."

I jumped up and started to put on my clothes. I really, really didn't want to have this conversation. I needed to get away from him for a while. I decided to spend the night at my mom's apartment. Sometimes after spending several days or weeks with him I would begin to feel as though I was growing fungus. His place became like a mushroom cave and I would begin to feel depressed, and suffocated, as though my mind and body was screaming for fresh air and sunlight.

"I'll see you later," I said.

"Who are you going to meet?" he asked.

I could sense another one of his jealous rages coming on. I could have told him I was going to my mom's place, but he wouldn't have believed me. I decided to say nothing.

"Don't leave," he said, almost in a whisper.

"I feel like I can't breathe in here," I told him, slipping into my heels.

"Go ahead, go," he said. "I can write a lot better when you're not around."

"Great," I said, looking at him. "Maybe you can rhyme a few lines for a change or write about something other than ca-ca and pee-pee. Maybe you can give your poems some structure—and some yeast! So I can figure out what gave RISE to them!

He looked sad and shocked, as if I'd just kicked him in the stomach. Right away, I felt sorry for what I'd said, but I'd meant it. I was sick of bottling it up inside.

Besides, I never really thought he'd take my words to heart. I thought he'd laugh at me. After all, I was just a naive, uneducated kid who knew little about writing or literature.

I put on my jacket and picked up my purse.

"See ya later, Caligula," I said.

He put his hands on my shoulders, trying to make me turn around.

"Please, Cups," he said, his voice almost cracking. "Don't leave. Please stay. I'm sorry. I didn't mean to offend you. It's just that sometimes I don't think you really appreciate me. A man needs to feel appreciated by his woman—you know?"

I had to get out of there. The boozing, and the fights, and the jealousy were making me feel as if I were being buried alive. I don't know if any force in the world could have induced me to stay.

He followed me to the door, pleading with me not to leave. I thought it strange that the more difficult or distant I became, the more he seemed to want and need me.

"Hank, I do appreciate you, but right now I'd appreciate it if you'd get out of my way. I need to get out of here for a while," I said. "I have to get some air."

I pulled on the doorknob and he stepped aside. As I ran to my car, I heard him yell, "Go fuck Rod McKuen! And it's Catullus, not Caligula!"

I raced down to Franklin and headed east to my mom's apartment.

Within a few minutes, I saw a light flashing in my rearview mirror. A police car was behind me. I pulled over and put on my game face, fluffed up my hair, and got ready to use my redheaded survival skills. Even though I had been driving over the speed limit, even though I was buzzed on alcohol, even though I didn't have a driver's license or up-to-date license plates, I managed to talk myself out of a ticket. I was let go with a warning to stop speeding, sleep it off, get a driver's license, and renew my tags.

I tried not to think about Bukowski as I drove the rest of the way to my mom's. But I couldn't stop thinking about how heartbroken he had looked, and felt bad about some of the obtuse things I said about his writing, but I just had to get away for a while.

I stayed away for days. I didn't phone him. I didn't answer his calls to my mother's apartment. I realized that all of my high hopes about 1976— getting off the pills and getting myself together—were a joke. If anything, I was more strung out, less involved as a parent, and more confused than ever.

SEVENTEEN

. . . and he was always there for me.

After a few days with my mom and her nagging and nitpicking, I was overjoyed to fling myself headlong back to Bukowski's loose ship. With Bukowski, I could do what I wanted, when I wanted, and how I wanted. He tolerated just about anything and everything—loud music, outside noise, distractions, boozing, pill popping, singing, or dancing on the tables. There were no rules and no limits—and I liked it that way.

Whenever I returned to Bukowski after spending time with Mom, I felt as if I were in a safe harbor, where no one would judge me. At times like these, I wondered why I'd ever left. Most of the time, life was fun with Bukowski—a crazy, relaxed free-for-all.

Bukowski wasn't big on traditional romance—flowers, candlelit dinners, or boxes of chocolates—but he was sensitive and thoughtful. He often left affectionate notes—his brand of affection—outside my door, and he was always there for me.

He let me know how much he appreciated me—not just my body, but my mind and personality as well. He laughed at my jokes, listened to my stories, asked for my opinions, followed my advice—sometimes, anyway—and adored the way I looked. And, of course, the occasional striptease I'd treat him to didn't hurt either.

I think he cared for me so much that it drove him crazy. When he was drinking, he started to brood—and ended up wondering why I was with him. At times like these, he was convinced I was seeing other men—and he would sometimes erupt in a drunken rage.

But most of the time during the first few months of our relationship we did a lot of laughing and loving. On my birthday, March 31st, I turned twenty-four—and though by this time we had experienced some turbulence, Bukowski was even more affectionate than usual. He loved to kiss, hug, and cuddle, and we did lots of that—and more.

© Brad Darby

Bukowski also took me shopping at Frederick's of Hollywood, and had me try on spiked heels, asking me to strut back and forth in the store. He grinned at me as if I'd made him the happiest man in the world. After buying the sexy, red stilettos, we enjoyed a relaxing dinner at Musso & Frank. He was charming and well-behaved the entire evening, and, even though he had a lot to drink, remained sweet and loving.

Back at his apartment, Bukowski presented me with a package wrapped in brown paper that he'd painted with hearts and birds. I ripped open the box and squealed. It was just what I wanted. A Polaroid! A camera that gave you a photo instantly, in only a minute!

By now I had decided that maybe a career in show business in front of the camera wasn't so practical. This month I was onto a new fantasy of becoming a photographer.

A few weeks prior, I had discovered a book of photographs by Diane Arbus at my favorite bookstore, Chatterton's in Los Feliz. I told Bukowski at that time that I was inspired by her and had now decided to pursue a career in photography. That was the first and last I'd mentioned it to him, but he remembered. (This aspiration would die once I realized it takes more than just pointing and clicking to take a great photo.)

"Here," Bukowski said, "let me show you how to work that thing."

I put the camera above my head so he couldn't reach it. Then I jumped up and ran around the house, saying, "Try and catch me."

He chased me for a while until we both collapsed on the bed, laughing. Bukowski would have a lot of fun with this camera in the months to come. He often walked in on me while I was changing clothes and, like a menacing child, snapped photos of me in various states of undress.

A few days after my birthday, I stopped by Bukowski's place. He seemed to be receiving more guests than usual now. When I walked into the living room, I saw him sitting on the couch next to a slight, studious looking man. It was Jack Nitzsche, the award-winning music composer. I had never met him before and was delighted to make his acquaintance.

Jack was a well-known composer and arranger who had worked with many of the big names in the rock world—including The Rolling Stones, Phil Spector, and Neil Young. Tonight, Jack was well lubricated and looked quite depressed.

I wondered if Jack's mood had anything to do with his Oscar loss. He'd been nominated for best original score for *One Flew Over the Cuckoo's Nest* that year. I had watched the ceremony on television a couple of weeks prior and he lost the award to composer John Williams for the score of the movie *Jaws*.

After Jack and I exchanged greetings, Bukowski told Jack, "Forget about her, man. Get yourself a newer model with less maintenance."

He pulled me on his lap and gave me a big kiss.

"I'm in love with her," Jack said. He looked near tears.

"Don't ever get involved with an actress," Bukowski said. "They're too self-absorbed and insecure—they only care about themselves and how their hair looks."

"Oh, Hank," I said, "that's not true."

"She won't even talk to me," Jack said.

"Keep trying," I said. "She'll come around."

The actress Jack was in love with was Carrie Snodgress. He looked up and gave me a sad smile. He was a small man, almost frail looking. He was about forty, with long hair, wire-rimmed glasses, and a scraggly beard. I didn't find him attractive physically, but he had an intelligent goodness about him that made him appealing. He seemed hopelessly in love with Carrie.

After about an hour, Jack left, a little drunker and a lot sadder.

When Jack closed the door, I asked Bukowski, "What happened with Carrie?"

"Jack says she never has time for him," Bukowski said. "So they got into a brawl, and she kicked him out."

I couldn't imagine either Jack or Carrie raising their voices, let alone having a fight. They both seemed like such sweet, gentle people. I hadn't met Carrie in person yet, but had seen her in the film *Diary of a Mad House-*

wife—and thought she was wonderful in it. I had also seen her interviewed a few years earlier. She was a great actress—and seemed like a lovely person.

Bukowski told me that Jack had met Carrie when she was living with Neil Young in Northern California. Jack hadn't been the reason for their breakup, but had made his move as soon as Carrie was free. He told Bukowski that he'd fallen in love with her at first sight. Her child with Young had been born with cerebral palsy, and she spent most of her free time caring for the boy. I guess she just didn't have much room in her life for Jack.

Later that evening, when I was taking a shower, Bukowski burst in the bathroom and snapped a photo of me with the Polaroid. He did the same thing later when I walked into the bedroom—and the next morning when I was standing naked in my red stilettos.

For months afterwards, I never knew when he was going to sneak a photo of me when I was nude or partially dressed. He never got tired of this little game, and while I told him to stop, it just encouraged him. Sometimes he was like an impish, menacing child.

Bukowski shot photos of me until they were in piles all over the bedroom. I managed to retrieve most of them, but I've often wondered what happened to the rest of the pictures. Did he save them? Did he eventually destroy them? Are they, God forbid, filed away with his effects in a university library somewhere? I suppose I'm better off not knowing the answers to these questions.

EIGHTEEN

She looked up just in time to see Bukowski pull down his jeans and moon her—flashing his big, white, hairy butt.

My grade school friend Janet Marino left a message with my mom, asking me to call her. I hadn't heard from Janet for a couple of years, and though we had gone in different directions, we stayed in touch over the years.

On the phone, Janet told me she was still living at her parents' place in the San Fernando Valley. She said my mom told her I had an apartment in Hollywood. I don't know if my mom had made my life sound glamorous, but Janet seemed eager to come over for a visit. We made plans for her to stop by in the afternoon a few days later.

When I saw Janet pull into a spot across the street, I ran downstairs to meet her. As she got out of her 1970 convertible Opal GT, she gazed around with a dazed look as if someone had struck her on the head with a hammer. This wasn't the Hollywood she'd had in mind—bougainvillea, lemon trees, and Spanish tiles. This was the east side—vagrants, sex shops, hookers, and strip clubs.

Janet turned her eyes on me. There was an expression something like shock or maybe pity. I'm not very tall, but next to Janet, who was only 4'11", I felt like a giant. I looked down into her pitying eyes and smiled.

"Welcome to the neighborhood," I said, taking her by the elbow and leading her up to my apartment.

I'd met Janet in fifth grade, when I warned her that her former friend Cindy Sheehan was hatching a plot against her. Cindy told her clique, including me, that she wanted us to sing "Marino the Beano" to the tune of "My Momma Done Told Me" when Janet walked into the girls' bathroom at school. I assumed Cindy was jealous because Janet was a knockout—a cross between Rita Moreno and Sophia Loren in their heydays—and she was sick of Janet getting so much attention from the boys, more specifically her boyfriend.

After I warned her, Janet was so grateful that she asked me to be her best friend. We were an unlikely duo. When we reached middle-school, she was a Greaser and I was more of a Surfer, I guess—two types that rarely, if ever, hung out together. On top of that, my Italian mother wasn't sure about Janet's family. They were Sicilian, and Mom, who didn't normally have a prejudiced bone in her body, thought they were the type that gave the rest of the Italians a bad name. I think she was brought up with the stereotype that all Sicilians had mob ties. Despite all this, we became friends and remained in contact, even after I "moved" away in seventh grade.

Janet and I had chatted on the phone over the years, so we'd kept up with the major events in each other's lives. But this was the first time we'd been together in four or five years.

Janet's style hadn't changed much. Her dark hair was feathered and sprayed into a bouffant, Farah Fawcett style do. She wore tight, white pedal pushers with black, high-heeled slingbacks, and a sleeveless black silk blouse with a gold Italian cornucopia dangling from a thick chain around her neck. Her fingernails were long and painted bright pink and her wrists were loaded with jangly gold bracelets. She was in full make-up and wore bright pink lipstick that matched her nails.

I, on the other hand, had on a T-shirt, jeans, and was barefoot. My hair was loose and long, and I wasn't wearing any makeup, except a little mascara to darken my lashes.

Janet gave me the once-over, as if I were a poor soul who'd been ship-wrecked somewhere for years. I could see that she was trying to figure out what had happened to me. She seemed to be wondering how I could have sunk so low.

She gave my apartment the same stunned look. It was a mishmash of cast-off furniture, odds and ends, and hand-me-downs. Still, I'd tried to give the place some pizzazz and was especially proud of my white rattan fan chair, where Janet now sat like the Queen of the Valley.

After I poured her a glass of champagne, I handed her a framed photo of Stacey.

"This is my daughter Stacey," I said.

I waited for Janet to gush over Stacey, but she just glanced at the photo and put it on the beat-up coffee table.

"Cute," she finally said.

Cute? My daughter wasn't cute. She was gorgeous—a raving beauty who had just turned seven. She had Alice-in-Wonderland blonde hair down to her waist, beautiful green eyes, and was tall and slender, built like a ballerina.

"I can't believe you had a kid when you were only sixteen," Janet said.

"She's the best thing that ever happened to me," I told Janet.

Janet didn't ask any questions about Stacey, or even about me, for that matter. Instead she launched into a monologue about herself.

She was unhappy with her current boyfriend, her job, and having to live with her parents.

For a second, I thought she was going to ask if she could come and stay with me. But I doubted that she would allow herself to sink so low.

After we finished the champagne, I said, "How would you like to meet my boyfriend?"

Janet's eyes widened. She seemed surprised that I had a boyfriend, let alone one I wanted her to meet.

"I've gotta leave soon," she said.

"He lives right downstairs," I told her.

I grabbed her purse and helped her up from the rattan throne. In less than a minute, we were standing outside Bukowski's front door.

I opened the door and called out, "Haaannnk, you here?"

Bukowski shuffled out of the kitchen, wearing his usual outfit—plumber-style jeans and gut-hugging T-shirt. Classical music was playing on the radio. It was about three in the afternoon and his day was just getting started. He was probably on his third or fourth beer.

When Bukowski walked into the room, I glanced at Janet out of the corner of my eye. She looked as if she were going to faint and held onto my arm as if to steady herself.

When Bukowski was standing in front of us, I made the introductions.

Then I added, "Janet and I went to grade school together in the Valley."

Bukowski shifted his can of beer from his right hand to his left. He wiped his wet hand on his T-shirt, and then offered it to Janet. She barely made skin contact as she shook the ends of his fingertips.

"Have a seat," he said.

Janet looked around for a place to sit. The sofa was strewn with newspapers, Bukowski's socks, and a pair of underpants. A pair of my high heels was sitting on the striped chair. Dishes and full ashtrays were all over the place.

"That's okay," Janet said. "I gotta get going."

Bukowski sensed immediately how repulsed she was by him and his surroundings. Like a vulture spotting his prey, I knew she was about to get a royal dose of the Bukowski shock treatment.

"But you just got here," Bukowski said, knocking the high heels to the floor and plopping down into the chair. He then took a large swig of beer, allowing it to drip down the corner of his mouth and onto his shirt. He wiped his mouth with the back of his hand and belched.

"Get her a beer, Red," Bukowski said.

"No, really," Janet said. "I can only stay a minute."

"Don't worry, Kid," he said, "you'll get used to the filth and the dirt— it'll grow on you. Before you know it, you'll be craving it. You'll embrace it like a long lost lover."

She chuckled nervously as she pushed some newspapers out of the way and perched on the edge of the couch, her hands clasping her knees. Her eyes darted around as if expecting rats to jump out of the walls and bats to fly out of the closets.

"Hank's a writer, can't you tell?" I said, giving Bukowski the evil eye.

"Okay," Janet replied.

I waited for her to say something more or ask a question, but that was it.

"See those books over there?" I said, pointing to the makeshift book-case. "Hank wrote all of them."

"Uh huh," Janet said, then stood up quickly and began walking toward the door.

"Long drive back to the 'burbs'?" Bukowski asked.

"Yeah, don't want to get caught in rush hour traffic," she said.

"Well, you'd better get a move on," Bukowski said. "Don't want you to get stuck on the freeway."

"Right . . . okay," Janet said.

As she was walking to the door, she signaled for me to come close so she could talk to me privately. I leaned into her face. "Is this a fuckin' joke?" she whispered.

"What are you talking about?" I asked.

"Come on, Pam . . . this is a joke, right?" she said. Then she looked as though a light bulb turned on in her head.

"Am I on *Candid Camera*? Alan Funt . . . you can come out now," she yelled.

Certain that Bukowski heard her, I nudged her and laughed.

"Janet, don't be so rude!" I told her.

Once she realized it wasn't a joke, her skin took on a sickly green hue— apparent even through her bronzed makeup. She put a hand on her stomach, as if fighting back the urge to heave. The mere thought of living in a place like this with a man like this, was making her ill.

"I gotta go. Nice to see you, Pam," she said, looking at her shoes. She turned her head in Bukowski's direction and addressed the floor as she said, "Good to meet you."

Despite her disgust and scorn, I figured she couldn't wait to get back to the Valley, call up our old school friends and tell them all about it.

"Hey, Janet," Bukowski said, as she readied for her exit.

She looked up just in time to see Bukowski pull down his jeans and moon her—flashing his big, white, hairy butt.

Janet screamed as if a rat had just run up her leg.

"OH-MY-GOD! WHAT THE HELL IS GOING ON, PAM!?" she yelled.

I couldn't stop laughing. I doubled over and held my folded arms against my stomach. Bukowski flopped back into his chair and took a sip of beer.

Janet flung open the front door and raced in her high-heeled slingbacks down the courtyard to her car. As she ran, she screamed, "YOU'RE SICK! YOU'RE BOTH SICK!—YOU'RE CRAZY, PAM!"

Within seconds, she turned over the motor and was gunning it down the street.

After she left, I laughed nonstop for five minutes. When I finally settled down a little, I picked up a newspaper and smacked Bukowski with it. "Why did you do that?"

"I don't like her type," he said.

I waited for him to say something more, but he just downed his beer and went back to the kitchen to get another. We had a few more laughs over it and I almost felt sorry for my poor, little friend. I called Janet the next day and apologized, but it would be a few years before I heard from her again. I wish I had captured the look on her face with my new Polaroid.

Hank and me
(photo courtesy of Pamela Miller Wood)

NINETEEN

He rolled his stool closer to me. I could feel his hot breath on my bare arms.

Bukowski grabbed his car keys from the nightstand.

"See you later," he said.

It was about two o'clock on a weekday afternoon. Unless he was going to the racetrack, he rarely went anywhere this early. Usually he was on his second or third beer, and his day was just getting started.

"Got a hot date?" I teased, as I stood in front of the bathroom mirror trimming my hair.

Over the years, haircuts had been a source of intense trauma for me. My father and stepmother had pinned me down and cut off my waist-length hair to the scalp when I was thirteen—as punishment for being late for first period in the eighth grade. Then there were all the bad beauty shop experiences. I wouldn't even let Georgia touch my hair—and she was a trained beautician. Maybe it had something to do with her lack of sobriety when she was wielding scissors. For years now, I had cut my own hair.

Bukowski stood in the bathroom doorway gazing at me. My red hair was a totem of sorts for him. He seemed mesmerized by it and loved to watch me wash, comb, or brush it. I knew if he didn't have somewhere to go he'd probably stand there all day with his eyes on me.

"Don't chop off too much," he said.

"I've done this before, Hank," I said, snipping at my split ends.

The tiny hairs fell into the basin. Bukowski stepped over so he could see the red hair fall onto the white porcelain. This was the kind of thing he loved—these little details of the day.

"Don't you have someplace to go?" I said.

He snapped out of it and checked his wristwatch.

"Right," he said, "can't be late for the doctor."

I looked at my eyes in the mirror. They seemed to pop out as if I were a squeeze toy. *Did he say doctor?*

"Why didn't you tell me you were going to the doctor?" I said.

Bukowski's eyes softened, as if touched that I was concerned about him. I felt sort of guilty—because I was mainly interested in getting a new prescription for amphetamines.

I put the scissors in the medicine chest, and then rushed into the bedroom.

"I'm going with you," I said.

"Jeez, Kid, didn't know you cared so much. But I can't wait," he said. "If I don't get there on time, I'll miss my appointment."

"Why didn't you tell me you had an appointment?" I asked, as I threw off my robe, yanked on my jeans, and crammed my feet into red high heels.

I pulled on a black tank top, grabbed my purse, and raced for the door.

I was in the passenger seat layering on mascara by the time he reached the car.

"Why are you going to see the doctor?" I finally thought to ask.

"He lanced a boil on my ass and wants to check on it. I think he just likes looking at it."

Poor Bukowski seemed to have a lot of problems on that portion of his anatomy.

"Can't blame him," I said. "Look at the effect it had on my friend. You ought to have him cut off that red pointy tail while he's down there."

"We're only going a couple of blocks," he said, as he eased out of the parking space referring to my makeup job.

"When you stop the car, I'll be ready," I said, rolling on some lip gloss.

As he made a left from Western onto Sunset, I was adding another coat of mascara.

He made a right on Vermont, then drove down a couple of blocks and parked.

"Here we are," he said.

"And here I am," I said, turning to him.

"There you are," he agreed with a smile.

We went into a high-rise building and got into the elevator. As we were going up, it finally dawned on me to tell him the real reason why I wanted to tag along.

"Do you think your doctor can squeeze me in?" I said.

"What's wrong with you?" he asked.

"Come on, Hank," I said.

I knew that he knew what I wanted. I was down to my last couple of pills and needed a new prescription.

"I'll ask him," he said.

We walked up to a glass door with the name "Dr. Hedrick Gunther, General Practitioner" painted in black letters.

Before we opened the door, I said, "Is he any good?"

"He's German," Bukowski said, as if this were the highest possible praise.

We entered the small waiting room, where quite a crowd had gathered. I figured Dr. Gunther must be pretty good if so many people were waiting to see him.

I took a seat, and Bukowski ambled over to the receptionist and asked if the doctor could see me too.

"He's on his way back from lunch," said the receptionist, a woman in her fifties with tight gray curls. "He should be back shortly. Tell your friend to fill out this form."

She handed him a clipboard with a piece of paper attached to it. I was relieved she didn't refer to me as his daughter. He came back and gave it to me.

As I was filling out the form, Dr. Gunther strolled through the door. I looked up and saw an attractive man in his early forties wearing a crisp white doctor's coat over his clothes. Dr. Gunther looked around the waiting room, then spotted Bukowski and walked over to him.

"So, finally you are back," the doctor said, speaking with a pronounced German accent.

"She dragged me here," Bukowski said, turning to me.

Bukowski's chest seemed to puff up a little, and then he said, "This is my girlfriend, Pam."

The doctor's eyes flashed behind his wire-rimmed glasses. He looked to Bukowski, then back to me, then back to Bukowski. He shook his head and smiled.

"Think you can fit her in too?" Bukowski asked the good doctor.

"I think so," he answered.

The doctor then turned to the people in the waiting room and said, "Sorry to keep you waiting. I will be right back." All of his w's were pronounced like v's.

He headed out the door, and Bukowski got up and followed him.

After I gave the form to the receptionist, I browsed through the magazines, picked a couple, and sat back down. When the doctor breezed back into the room, I was reading an article in _Time_ magazine about Jimmy Carter's campaign to head the Democratic ticket. Unlike Bukowski, who was apolitical, I took an avid interest in politics—and prayed that a Democrat would be elected in November. The country was still suffering from a hangover caused by the previous corrupt Nixon administration and it was time for a change.

The door opened a few times and I thought Bukowski was coming back, but it was just another patient entering the waiting room—where there was now standing room only.

As I waited, I read about the guilty verdict for Patty Hearst, conflicts over desegregation in Boston, and the preparations for the Bicentennial celebration in Washington. I was about to start reading about the murder of Sal Mineo, when the receptionist called my name. I had been waiting over an hour.

She led me into an examining room, told me to sit on the table, and then closed the door.

After about five minutes, the doctor walked in. He nodded at me, and then sat on a stool with wheels on it, so his eyes were even with my knees.

"What can I do for you today?" he asked, his accent making him sound like Colonel Klink from the _Hogan's Heroes_ television program.

I'd hoped that Bukowski would tell the doctor what I wanted when they'd both left the waiting room. But I was on my own. I took a deep breath and launched into my appeal.

"I can't seem to get my weight under control," I said. "I need a prescription for diet pills."

The doctor squeezed my left knee and said, "Why do you want the diet pills? You are not fat."

He rolled his stool closer to me. I could feel his hot breath on my bare arms.

"Well," I said, "I'm not comfortable with my current weight. I feel better when I'm slimmer."

He didn't respond for a few seconds. He glanced at my high heels, then his eyes traveled up my legs, to my breasts, and finally to my face.

"Tell me," he said, "when was your last pelvic examination?"

I was stunned. Why would he ask that? I had seen many doctors while seeking amphetamines, but this would be the first time that one had asked to perform a pelvic examination. Either I'd been incredibly lucky in the past, or I was incredibly unlucky right now.

I didn't know how to handle the situation. I decided to ignore what he'd said.

"I've put on a few pounds recently," I said. "I really want to slim down."

"I need for you to answer my question," he said. "When was your last pelvic examination?"

I tried to reason with myself. Dr. Gunther was a general practitioner. A G.P. didn't perform pelvic exams. I figured he would just tell me to make an appointment with my gyno.

"It's probably been over a year," I said.

"Oh, that is far too long," he said. "You had better let me give you one right now."

I couldn't believe this. It was outright blackmail. He'd give me the prescription if I let him see my red snapper.

"Now?" I asked.

"Yes, now."

Giving him the benefit of the doubt, I wondered if there might be a correlation between diet pills and female problems. Did amphetamines cause yeast infections? Cervical tumors? Uterine congestion? Then my instincts kicked in. The word "pervert" kept firing in my brain.

I tried not to show what I was thinking—afraid that he'd withhold the prescription.

"Uh . . ." I stammered, "I have my period right now."

The doctor's expression shifted from lascivious expectation to scowling disappointment.

"Can I make an appointment for next week?"

His eyes brightened, but then his lids fell to half mast. He didn't really believe me, but what could he do?

He rolled over to his desk, wrote a prescription, then turned and handed it to me.

"You can make the appointment on your way out," he said, then stood up. Before I left the room, he said, "Now don't forget."

When I got back to the waiting room, Bukowski was there. He came up to the reception desk and paid for my visit.

I didn't say anything all the way down in the elevator or as we walked to the car. I wasn't sure how Bukowski would react if I told him about the doctor's aberrant request. I had what I wanted and didn't want to risk a scene. When we were driving down the street, I asked him to stop at Owl Drugs on Sunset so I could have the prescription filled.

Then I asked him, "Where did you go, anyway?"

"I went down the block to a strip club and had a few beers," he said.

I didn't respond. I figured he was trying to make me jealous, and it drove him crazy that it never seemed to work.

"So what did you think of my doctor?" Bukowski asked as he made a U-turn on Vermont.

"He gave me the prescription," I said.

"I guessed that," he said.

"And he wanted to give me a pelvic exam."

Bukowski let out a few chuckles—a reaction that made me feel angry and humiliated. Didn't he mind that his doctor had tried to take advantage of me? Didn't he think it was wrong? Didn't he care?

Then I took a deep breath and tried to calm down. After all, it wasn't Bukowski's fault—he was just trying to help me get what I needed. And it had worked. I had the prescription in my purse to prove it.

"What about you?" I asked. "I thought you needed to see him too."

"He looked at my ass when we were in the restroom," he said. "He told me it looks real pretty."

"I could have told you that."

TWENTY

"Let's see . . . I've got hemorrhoids, cockroaches and now you."

$\mathcal{H}ank$ and I got along much better when we were by ourselves. When other people were around, we always seemed to end up in an argument. While we preferred to spend time alone, it didn't always turn out that way. For a self-professed misanthrope, Bukowski seemed to have a lot of visitors. Friends, relatives, neighbors, and sometimes fans, were always popping in unexpectedly, frequently without calling first. Occasionally they'd phone to request a meeting or plead with him to come over. We just couldn't manage to fend off the intruders.

One evening, Bukowski and I were getting cozy on the couch when there was a loud banging on the door. Bukowski put a finger to his lips and I nodded. We figured we'd be extra quiet until whoever it was had gone away.

"Come on," an all-too-familiar voice said, "I know you're in there. Both of your cars are out front."

It was my brother Larry. I figured he'd run out of money and was looking for drugs, booze, cigarettes, and something to eat. I looked into Bukowski's world-weary eyes, let out a sigh, then got up and went to the door. When I opened it, Larry walked in, sauntered over to the couch and plunked himself down next to Bukowski.

"How's it goin', man? Do you mind?" Larry asked, as he helped himself to one of Bukowski's Pall Malls.

I noticed Larry wasn't speeding too badly, so I figured his visit wouldn't be a total train wreck.

I grabbed some beers and hoped he would leave after one round. But he started to jabber about how he'd just finished reading *Factotum* and seemed intent on dissecting every episode in the book with Bukowski.

Bukowski hated to discuss his work and I found it comical how many times he tried to change the subject. But Larry would not be deterred.

"Did your girlfriend really make a paper hat for your dick?" Larry asked.

His expression was earnest, with no hint of irony or humor, as if he were asking what kind of gas mileage Bukowski got with his Volks.

Just then, the phone rang. A "saved by the bell" look crossed Bukowski's face. He picked up the receiver.

"No, man, I don't think so," he said. He listened for a while, and then said, "We have company." He listened some more, then said, "Well, just for a few minutes."

When he hung up, Bukowski said that Brad wanted us to come over and say hello to a guy who used to live in the complex. He had lived in the same apartment I was now renting and Bukowski actually liked him. Brad also said he had some good shit and we should all stop by.

"I don't want to spend the afternoon with Brad," I said.

"I like Steve," Bukowski said. "He's an okay kid. I should at least say hello."

I was hoping that Larry would figure it was time for him to go home, but he stood up and followed Bukowski out the front door. This was not my idea of a good time. But rather than cause a scene, I decided to go along—hoping the visit with Brad and his buddy would be brief and that Larry would go home soon.

When we got to Brad's place, the front door was open and he yelled, "Come on in."

We filed into the living room, where Brad was sitting on the sectional with Steve and a woman I assumed to be Steve's girlfriend. Brad's wife Tina was working at the strip club and wouldn't be home until much later.

Bukowski walked over to Steve and said, "Hey, man, good ta see ya," as he shook his hand.

"You, too, man. It's been a long time. This is my fiancée, Mary. Mary, this is Charles Bukowski."

"I've heard so much about you from Steve. It's nice to finally meet The Great Bukowski," she beamed.

121

After Bukowski introduced Larry and me to Steve and Mary, we all settled down to some drinks. While I sipped my beer, I studied the lovely young couple.

They were in their early thirties. Both had dark hair—and his was longer than hers. They were dressed casually in jeans and T-shirts. They had an attractive, liberal, elitist look about them—style and class. Given Steve's good looks, I was surprised that Bukowski seemed so fond of him.

At first the conversation revolved around Steve and his career. He was a musician, which made me feel at ease—because I felt comfortable talking about music. Steve didn't belong to a well-known band, but he'd had some success. He told us that gigs had been few and far between, but he had some local upcoming play-dates and high hopes that things would pick up soon.

Then the conversation turned to literature, which made me feel uncomfortable—because I didn't know that much about the subject. I heard names fly past me—Hemingway, Fitzgerald, Faulkner, Mailer, Updike—and though familiar with the writers themselves, I had been limited in reading their work. I hoped the subject would change soon.

I began to feel insecure. I was out of my rock 'n' roll, counterculture element. I hadn't even read Bukowski's books, let alone the commercial greats. I began to shrink into myself. I just wanted to disappear. To combat my feelings of inadequacy, I began to drink more than usual.

Everyone was smoking cigarettes, except for Steve and Mary. Steve coughed a few times, then excused himself and went outside to get some fresh air. While the others were now discussing the works of Philip Roth, I decided to join Steve out front. Besides, I didn't know this Portnoy guy, and couldn't care less what he was complaining about.

I asked Steve questions about his music, and we discussed current bands, like The Eagles and Fleetwood Mac. I asked him what he thought about that new group, "Queen." He was a very smart, polite, nice guy, and I enjoyed talking to him.

After about fifteen minutes, we both went back inside. I was beginning to get woozy and feeling belligerent. The radio was on in the background. I heard the Captain and Tennille's "Love Will Keep Us Together."

"Hey, turn that up, Brad," I yelled. "I love this song!"

I began to sing along with the radio.

"Love, love will keep us together,
   think of me, babe, whenever,
   some sweet-talkin' girl comes along . . . "

Bukowski interrupted me, "Come on, Red, knock it off. We're right in the middle of a conversation."

"Yeah, settle down, Pam," Larry warned.

I stood up wobbling, and slurred in my most indignant tone, "Screw you both. I'm going upstairs. You two are boring me!"

I stumbled over the lovely couple on my way to the door. At that point, Steve stood up and announced that he and Mary had to leave too.

"Hey, you haven't finished your drink," Bukowski said.

"Sorry, Hank, got an audition tomorrow. Got to practice with the guys tonight," Steve said. "I'll come back another time. Good to see ya, man."

I was halfway down the court, heading for Bukowski's place to lift a couple beers before I went upstairs.

As I stumbled on the stairs, I called out to Steve and Mary, "Bye, nice to meet you both."

I grabbed the beers and ran up to my place. Then I pulled out my favorite Linda Ronstadt album and cranked up the volume on the record player. It was a hot day and all the windows were open.

At the top of my lungs, I sang,

"You and I travel to the beat of a different drum,
   ahh, can't you tell by the way I run,
   every time you make eyes at me,
   whoa-ooh."

Later that evening, I ran out of beer and felt like going another round. I was still buzzed from the afternoon session and decided to stop by Bukowski's to borrow a couple Michelobs. I knocked on his door and didn't hear anything for a couple minutes. Then I heard what sounded like his back door slamming. A minute later he opened his door.

"What do you want?" he asked.

"Got a couple beers I could borrow?"

"Get out of here, Red."

"What is your problem?"

"Let's see . . . I've got hemorrhoids, cockroaches and now you."

"Aren't you going to invite me in?"

"I'm busy right now. I'm not in any mood for your shit."

"Fine! I'm busy too!"

I headed back to my apartment. As I entered my front door, I heard his back door slam again. He must have company, I thought. Why else would he have been so rude? "Okay, two can play at this game," I mumbled to myself. I waited a few minutes, then walked over to my living room window. I turned to face the kitchen and yelled, "Could you bring me another glass of wine?" Then I ran into the kitchen. I dropped my voice as low as possible, and said, "Sure, Baby. Want ice in it?" Then I ran back to the living room window and said in a loud sexy voice, "Yes, that would be great!" Then I ran back to the kitchen and in my deepest man voice yelled, "Your wish is my command, Baby." I went on like this for about ten more minutes, laughing loudly in between the dialogue, then turned out the lights. I peeked out the window to see if Bukowski was in his kitchen. I hoped he heard my conversation with myself. I couldn't see anything, but after a few minutes I heard his back door slam again. I wondered why his date kept going in and out and wasn't using the front door. I ran to the window but still couldn't see anybody. I wondered who he was with, but too tired to make a scene. What was he so upset about? I only called him a bore. It had been a long day and I had too much to drink. *Oh well*, I thought, as I crawled into bed, to hell with him. I fell fast asleep.

I didn't leave my apartment until 2:30 the next afternoon. I had to pick up Stacey from school. On my way out I didn't stop at Bukowski's place because I wasn't sure what kind of reception I'd get, or who I'd find there with him.

He saw me walk by, then walked out on his porch and yelled, "Hey, where ya runnin' to, Kid?"

"To pick up Stacey," I said.

"You know, you acted like an ass yesterday. You shouldn't have followed Steve outside with his girlfriend there."

"I know," I said. "I'm sorry. I was just bored with the conversation. Besides, you know I'm never really comfortable around Brad. I don't think he likes me, either."

"Only boring people get bored," he said, and then repeated, "It didn't look good when you went outside with Steve. I think you upset Mary."

"All right already—I said I was sorry. She has nothing to be upset about. We were just talking!"

"But, you know . . ."

"Oh, cool it, Hank. I don't owe anybody an explanation. I didn't do anything wrong. Now buzz off!"

I knew he was exaggerating to make me feel bad. He was actually the one who felt insecure. Okay, so I was young and sometimes inconsiderate, but never disloyal to him. It would be several months before his prophecies would come true.

Stacey and I had dinner at my mom's that night. She was now in the habit of spending the night there during the week. After I put her to bed, I headed back to Carlton Way. As I approached my apartment, Bukowski heard me coming and poked his head out his door.

"Hey, Kid. I've got a bottle of your favorite champagne. Want to come in for a glass?"

"Sure, why not."

I parked myself on the sofa while he retrieved the champagne from the kitchen. After he uncorked the bottle and poured us both a glass, he sat across from me in his striped chair. We sat in silence for a couple minutes. We were each waiting for the other to make the first verbal move.

I finally said, "So . . . who came by last night?"

"What are you talking about?"

"It sounded like you had company last night. Like someone came in or out of your place a few times. I kept hearing your back door slam. What was going on? Were you trying to juggle two women at once?"

"Do you really care?"

"Of course I do. Why wouldn't I?"

"Sometimes I don't think you do."

"Well, you're wrong. I do care. You're just too damn sensitive and insecure, Hank."

"Maybe you're not sensitive enough."

"Okay, fine—maybe I'm not. Now tell me who was here."

"It's not important. No one you know. Who was at your place last night?"

"No one you know."

"Okay, Red. This conversation is boring me."

"You know what they say—only boring people get bored."

He chuckled and then raised his glass and said, "You win, Kid. You always win."

He hung his head and heaved a big sigh. His brow began to furrow. He was getting that sad, downcast, wistful look that always got to me. That same look he'd get when he talked about Jane.

I stood up from the sofa and walked over to him. I sat on his lap and put my arms around his neck.

"Don't look so sad, Hank. You know I love you."

He looked in my eyes and began to smile. Then he stood up holding me in his arms. He stumbled and fell back against the chair, almost falling over.

"Hey, that's not how it happens in the movies," he said, laughing.

He managed to catch himself before we both went tumbling to the floor. Considering the abuse he put his body through, he was exceptionally strong and well-conditioned. We both laughed as he headed for the bedroom carrying me in his arms.

After a great session of make-up sex, we relaxed in bed and lit our cigarettes. Then I asked him again.

"So tell me—who was here last night?"

"You tell me first. Who was with you last night?"

"Okay . . . promise not to laugh?"

"Promise," he said, propping his head up with his hand. He looked at me in great anticipation.

"No one was at my house. I thought since you had someone here, I'd make you think I was entertaining someone too."

"Come on, Red, you expect me to believe that? I heard a man up there," he said.

"That was me. Listen." I dropped my voice down low, and said, "Hey, Baby, how 'bout a kiss?"

He began laughing so hard the entire bed shook. He was howling toward the ceiling. Then he jumped out of bed and headed for the kitchen. He walked back to the bed with a bottle of beer in one hand and a glass of champagne in the other, with a big smile on his face. He handed the glass to me. He sat on the edge of the bed and raised his bottle toward me.

"You are some magnificent piece of work, little Red," he said. "Cheers, Baby."

We each took a sip, then I asked him again, "Ok, now it's your turn. Who was here with you last night?"

He began laughing again.

"Come on, Hank, what's so darn funny? Just tell me who was here last night?"

He continued laughing. My prodding seemed to make him laugh harder, as though I was tickling him. Tears began to form in his eyes. Then he finally caught his breath and said, "Oh, little one, we are a pair to draw from. There was no one here last night."

TWENTY-ONE

Scarlet was the highest compliment he could pay a woman.

April of 1976 marked our fifth month together. During that time, we'd come to accept each other as imperfect human beings, and realized that our relationship would never be predictable.

Bukowski was philosophical about my shortcomings, and I, with the exception of his irrational jealousy, accepted his limitations as a man. We'd had our share of turbulence and passionate quarrels, often bordering on the absurd, but it was clear we had now become dependent on each other, and had formed an irrevocable bond.

I was still walking through minefields in search of my niche—trying to attain some sense of personal satisfaction, which would continue to elude me as long as I kept my feet from touching the ground. I'd leave Bukowski without a word, spending time at my mother's house drying out. Sometimes I'd return to Carlton Way to find Bukowski gone. He always assured me it was "business," and I always believed him. But when I would leave for a few days, he would fall apart. It caused him extreme emotional whiplash. Like a manic-depressive, swinging from joy to despair with punishing regularity.

One day in April, after returning from a weeklong R&R session at Mom's, I stopped by to see Bukowski.

I opened the door and said, "Knock, knock, knock, anybody home?"

Bukowski came out of the kitchen with a beer in his hand. He set the bottle on the coffee table and scooped me up in his arms.

"Cups . . . Baby, where ya been?"

"I went to Mom's place for a few days. You should know by now that's where I usually am."

"I missed you, Kid."

Then he slapped himself on the forehead and said, "Oh, shit!"

He sat me down on the couch and said, "I've got a surprise for you, but, hold on, I have to call John first."

He sat next to me while he dialed the number of his publisher John Martin.

"Hi, it's me," he said into the phone. "I need you to do me a favor. Cupcakes is back, and I need you to take out those poems I told you to add the other day. Has the book gone to print yet?"

He paused, and then said, "Well, make sure you stop the presses, or you'll ruin my love life. And I know you don't want that to happen."

He squeezed my knee while he listened to what John was saying.

"Yes, I'm serious. She's back . . . we're back, and it's good, man. Come on, be a pal. It's for a worthy cause."

He let out a sigh, and then said, "You're okay, man. Thanks, I owe you one."

"What was that all about?" I asked as he hung up.

"Shit, that was close," he mumbled to himself. "Well, I told you I have a surprise for you, and I wanted to make sure you liked it. I wrote a book of poetry just for you, Baby."

"Really, Hank?" I said, putting my arms around his neck. "But, what did that call have to do with it?" I asked, backing away.

"Well, when you took off without telling me, I called John and told him to add a couple of nasty poems to the book. It was originally a tribute to you, but then I decided it might be more appropriate as an elegy. I felt better adding a little viciousness to it. I knew that would upset you, and I wanted to get back at you, Baby, but now I don't. And believe me, you would have been upset, especially with the one comparing you to a shark."

"A shark? That's not very nice, Hank. Why would you compare me to a shark?"

"Well, I told you, you hurt my feelings when you left, so I wanted to hurt yours. Don't worry, I caught it in time. Now give me a kiss."

"Aren't you afraid I'll bite your head off?"

"Give me those jaws, Baby."
We kissed and made up for lost time.

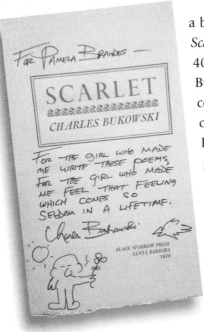

The book arrived a few weeks later. It was a beautifully bound hardcover book titled *Scarlet*. The book was limited to 180 copies, 40 of which include an original drawing by Bukowski. He inscribed a presentation copy with an original painting on the cover, which read: "For Pamela Brandes— For the girl who made me write these poems, for the girl who made me feel that feeling which comes so seldom in a lifetime." He signed it Charles Bukowski and added a drawing of his signature little man smiling, smoking a cigarette, holding a flower in his left hand, with the sun in the form of a heart above him on the right side, and a bird flying above on the left.

Before I sat down to read it, he took me to the Hollywood Ranch Market to pick up my favorite meal of chicken gizzards and coleslaw. He ordered the fried shrimp. We managed not to fight the entire evening.

Later, while Bukowski was typing away in the kitchen, I excitedly stretched out in bed to read *Scarlet*. It contained four poems. After reading the first poem, I sat up straight and read the other three. I was stunned and confused. The poems weren't what I'd expected. I thought—*you consider these love poems?* Like most of Bukowski's work, the poems were raw and real without pretense. They were also peppered with four-letter words and, yes, bodily functions.

I read the poems a few more times. I realized that coming from Bukowski—a man unskilled in the ways of romance—*Scarlet* was the highest compliment he could pay a woman. It was Bukowski's special way of expressing his love for me. But I was used to men expressing their love in more traditional ways, and didn't really know what to make of Bukowski's less-than-flowery display. I was expecting something more romantic along the lines of Yeats or Byron. I just wished that I could show it to my family and friends with pride, but knew that would never happen.

Even though I felt disappointed, I never let him know. I could be immature and self-absorbed—but not completely thoughtless. It would take some time before I truly appreciated the underlying beauty and poignancy of these profoundly meaningful poems. I read them now with a nostalgic smile. I realize that Bukowski had given me the ultimate gift.

(courtesy of Thomas Schmitt)

22 TWENTY-TWO

Sigh.

$\mathcal{B}$*ukowski* sighed a lot. To me, a sigh means something—I'm sad, I'm tired, I'm depressed, I'm weary. But Bukowski sighed on general principles. It was his response to being alive. *Sigh.*

When we first got together, I would ask him what was wrong after he let out a long sigh.

"Nothing," he'd say. "And everything—the whole goddamned world."

So I'd try to cheer him up.

"Come on," I'd say. "It can't be that bad. Let's go out and do something."

Sigh.

"Let's go for a walk."

Sigh.

"Let's go out to eat."

Sigh.

"Let's go for a drive."

Sigh.

"Let's drink some champagne."

Sigh.

"Let's go to the track."

"All right. Let's go."

It was April and the horses were running again at Hollywood Park, a racetrack in Inglewood, a few miles from Los Angeles airport.

Before we went to the track, Bukowski bought a *Daily Racing Form* and studied the horses. We left the apartment around eleven in the morning and got to the track before noon. This left about an hour before the first race—time that Bukowski spent studying the program and making notes on the horses and jockeys.

He usually waited until the last possible moment to place his bets. Bukowski based his selection on many factors—but primarily on how the odds changed after other people had made their wagers. When he saw how everybody else was betting, he usually bet on a different horse.

I found it funny that Bukowski was so dead serious at the track. I would watch him in awe as he analyzed the racing forms as though he was a mathematician trying to find the formula for a complicated algorithm. It looked like so much work. To me, it was a time to relax and have fun. Granted, Hollywood Park in the 1970s was nobody's idea of a classy spot. It could be viewed as a sad, dreary place populated mostly by desperate welfare recipients and deluded dreamers. Still, it was enjoyable to be outside on a spring day, drinking beer, and looking at the gorgeous horses and the jockeys in their bright silks.

While Bukowski and I had completely different betting styles—his was scientific, and though I did consider the odds and the jockey, mine was more instinctive, and we both got impatient waiting the thirty minutes between races. I usually wandered off to find a restroom or get a beer. I was born without an internal compass and would often get lost, resulting in Bukowski spending much of his time searching for me. Once causing him to miss placing his bet on a long shot—that won.

But even when he missed buying a ticket on a winning horse, he never complained or berated me for running off. While he was serious about playing the horses, he kept it all in perspective. If he won big on one horse, he didn't bet more on the next race.

Unlike many gamblers, he didn't deep down want to lose. He always wanted to win—and he was happy with accumulating small winnings throughout the day. In the end, it all added up. He usually won more than he lost. Bukowski was a fiercely competitive man by nature, and at the track his competition was the house.

Sometimes, during the lulls between races, when I wasn't running off and getting lost, Bukowski would mention Jane and how she'd first brought him to the track. The doctors had told him to stop drinking or he'd die. Bukowski asked Jane what he should do with his time. She told him, "Well, there's always the racetrack."

Bukowski didn't stop drinking, and he grew to love playing the ponies. It was his favorite diversion, and he seemed to approach it the way he approached his writing—with dedication, consistency, and discipline.

Of course, these were the qualities that I completely lacked—and ones that drew me to him. I always hoped that some of his steadiness would rub off on me. But I was too flighty, and usually running off somewhere.

Between races, I'd often turn to Bukowski and say, "Be right back."

Sigh.

TWENTY-THREE

I ran toward the front door, and he followed me.

After *Saturday Night Live* hit the air in October 1975, I tried to catch it whenever I could. When I was working the late shift at the Alpine Inn, I rarely saw the program. But since losing my job, I'd never missed it. I tried to get Bukowski to watch *SNL* with me, but he hated television. I sometimes thought he resented the program because I found something other than him so thoroughly entertaining.

I didn't watch a lot of television myself, but looked forward to *SNL*. For me, it was a major event—I absolutely loved the program and the entire cast.

On April 24, 1976, I was lying in bed drinking beer, smoking cigarettes, and laughing my head off. Raquel Welch and John Belushi, doing his Joe Cocker impersonation, were singing a duet of "Superstar," a great tune by Leon Russell. Belushi got funnier and funnier as the song went on—with his slurring words and spastic movements—until he finally collapsed onto the floor. I whooped it up so much that Bukowski yelled from the other room.

"Who's in there with you?"

"Come on in and find out," I yelled back.

But he kept typing away in the other room. It was around midnight, so Bukowski's writing session was just getting started. Fortunately, he could write in just about any circumstances and wasn't too bothered by noise or other distractions. In some ways, I think he felt good just knowing somebody was in the apartment with him.

I laughed through Dan Aykroyd's skit, where he played Joe Franklin from the U.S. Council of Standards and Measures. The bit was a tour de force, with Aykroyd/Franklin explaining, in a fast, clipped manner, how the alphabet would be reduced to just ten letters—the Decibet—to go along with the new metric system.

After a few more skits, Phoebe Snow sang "All Over." That may have been what got Bukowski into the bedroom. He loved the sound of women's voices—and Snow had a lovely, unique style that drew Bukowski like the Pied Piper. Though he was hopelessly out of touch with the pop culture scene, I did my best to bring him up to date.

He lit a cigarette and sat on the end of the bed as she sang. When the song was over, he turned to me and said, "Now that wasn't half bad."

He stood up and started to leave the room.

"Just watch one skit with me," I pleaded.

He reluctantly turned around and came back toward the bed.

"Just one," he said.

After the commercial, a title came on the screen that read, "The Claudine Longet Invitational."

About a month prior, a singer named Claudine Longet, the ex-wife of famous crooner Andy Williams, had shot and killed her live-in lover, a well-known skier named Spider Sabich. She contended that the gun went off by accident, and was out on bail awaiting trial. It was widely believed in the media and by the public that Longet had murdered her lover when he decided to leave her after a four-year relationship. Almost nobody bought her accident story.

In the skit, Chevy Chase and Jane Curtin stood near a ski lift. Chase announced that they were in Vale, Colorado, to host the Claudine Longet Invitational, a men's freestyle skiing competition. Chase and Curtin narrated as a skier named Helmut started down the slopes. A shot rang out and Helmut fell into the snow. Chevy Chase observed that Helmut had been accidentally shot by Claudine Longet. Next, a skier named Jean-Paul headed down the slopes. A shot rang out and Jean-Paul fell into the snow. Chevy Chase announced that Jean-Paul had been accidentally shot by Claudine Longet. Then Jean-Paul got up because he was only grazed. Another shot rang out. Jean-Paul fell back into the snow. He got up. A third shot rang out. He went down for good. Each time, he was accidentally shot by Claudine Longet. Next, there were highlights of the entire competition. Skiers fell one after the other. The reasons: Claudine dropped her gun and it went off; Claudine was showing the gun to a friend; Claudine was cleaning her gun. And again she was showing the gun to a friend. Finally, she put down the gun in the snow, and it went off by mistake.

I was shocked at the skit. I loved *SNL's* outrageous, sardonic humor, but this seemed in really bad taste. I was sorry that I'd asked Bukowski to watch it.

When the program cut to commercial, Bukowski laughed and then said, "Hey now that was all right." He then added, "But you must realize that parody is the lowest form of writing or humor."

"The skits are usually better than this one," I said.

"The whole premise of the show is uncreative and unoriginal," he said.

"Most of the stuff they do is very clever," I said. "You can't judge the show by one skit."

Bukowski shook his head and said, "It's easy to take something that already exists and use it in a piece of writing. It doesn't require any imagination."

"You're taking this too seriously," I said.

"I know something about writing," he said.

I was surprised when he said that. He was always so humble about his abilities as a writer and never tried to show off or act like the great scribe.

"So, what do you think is funny?" I asked, and then added, "Laurel and Hardy?"

"At least they were originals."

"Hank, it's 1976, not 1926."

"It doesn't matter," he said. "Humor should be timeless. This thing we just saw won't make any sense at all a few years from now."

He punched off the television and came back to bed. "You're looking good tonight, little Red," he said, changing the subject.

He moved closer to me and put his arm around my waist. He kissed my cheek, and then ran his fingers up and down my leg. He seemed to want and need me more each day, and I didn't know what to do with all that intensity. I was beginning to get that caged animal feeling again.

I slid out of bed, and pushed my feet into my shoes. I found my purse and my car keys and headed toward the door.

"You're kidding, right?" he said.

"Hank, I've got to get out of here for a while," I said.

He stood up and moved toward me. His neediness began to feel all-consuming. I needed some distance between us, so I used this little disagreement as an excuse. I needed to go someplace where I wouldn't feel smothered. These episodes of mine were becoming routine, and they felt similar to a panic attack.

I ran toward the front door, and he followed me. "Please don't go. I didn't mean to insult you. Here, I just turned the TV back on."

I could hear his voice cracking. I felt terrible, but not so terrible that I wanted to stay.

"I have to, Hank. I'm not feeling well. I just need to go out for a while," I said.

"Please don't go," he said. He was beginning to well up. I was petrified that if I stayed another moment, he'd begin to cry. I couldn't handle that.

Bukowski stood next to the front door. I walked to the back door, flung it open, and swiftly walked out. When I got to the sidewalk, I could see him standing next to my car.

"I need you to stay with me tonight, baby," he said. "Please."

"Please, Hank, don't do this to me. I told you, I don't feel well!" I pushed past him, opened the car door, and got in. He bent down and pressed his face against the windshield on the driver's side. I'm sure I saw tears in his eyes. I edged up the car, but he didn't stand back. I didn't want to run over him, but I couldn't stick around. I was having an anxiety attack. My breathing was coming in spurts. I felt if I didn't get away soon, I was going to pass out.

I rolled down my window and yelled, "I'll be back tomorrow, I promise." I hit the gas and got the hell out of there.

As I drove away, I didn't look in the rearview mirror. It seemed a long time ago when we'd had our first sweet evening together, and Bukowski had leaned through the car window and kissed me goodnight. That was only five months ago. I didn't know where I was going. I didn't know if I was going to my mom's, or to Georgia's, or to a bar. It was almost one a.m.

I tried not to think of Bukowski as I drove around Hollywood aimlessly. But I couldn't get his pitiful, grief-stricken face out of my mind. He looked so heartbroken; it was all so overwhelming to me. I didn't like feeling this way; it was too threatening. So I did what I always did when emotions came too close to the surface—thought about getting high. I had to fight the urge to stop for a drink or grab a pill.

Of all the turbulent days and nights we spent together, and all the ridiculous arguments we had, I feel the worst about this one. I feel ashamed of how I wasn't able to stay with him when he needed me the most. But I realize now, that's precisely why I fled. The intensity of his feelings for me was too much for me to cope with at that time. I wasn't capable of reciprocating with the depth of emotion and love that he expected and deserved. To this day, I sometimes see his face on that night, so full of love and pain, and it breaks my heart.

TWENTY-FOUR

"Get out of here, Larry," I said, starting to sob.

In less than a week, after my impulsive exit, I returned to my little hovel on Carlton Way. I was now refreshed with my batteries recharged and looking forward to seeing Bukowski, but he wasn't at home. A few days later I heard his Volks pull up in front. I had really missed him. To welcome him home, I put on my "Daisy-Mae" outfit that he loved—short cut-offs and a sleeveless, blue gingham, ruffled crop-top. I rushed over to his apartment in my bare feet.

When I ran in the door, he was slumped in his striped chair. I skipped over and slid into his lap.

"Where did you run off to?" I asked, giving him a big kiss. Before he could answer, I said, "You left all the doors and windows open when you left. Promise you won't get mad?"

"Promise."

"Georgia came by while you were gone and used your phone. I think she made several long-distance calls. I tried to stop her, but she was pretty high. Sorry, Hank."

He chuckled at my concern and said, "That's okay, Baby."

"Well . . . where were you?"

"I was in Texas," he said, sounding weary. "And I have to leave town again in a few days."

"Going back to Texas?" I asked.

After our argument last week something told me I didn't want to dig too deeply into where he'd been. I was just glad he was back.

"I have to do a reading in New York," he told me. "I'm leaving day after tomorrow."

"New York!" I said. "Oh, Hank, take me with you, please."

"If I did," he said, "it would cost me as much as I'd make doing the reading. I may as well stay home, which I'd prefer anyway. I hate New York."

"Oh, Haaank," I said, looking down.

I pouted and poked out my lower lip, trying for a comical effect. Bukowski laughed.

"Maybe John will pay for it," he said, referring to his publisher. "He thinks you're good for my writing—maybe he'll help me out."

I stayed on his lap while he made the call.

"Hello, John," Bukowski said into the phone.

I sat there with my fingers crossed, holding my breath. I kept my eyes shut tight as Bukowski explained why he was calling.

Finally, I heard him say, "You will? Thanks, man, I owe ya' again, Baby."

After a few more exchanges with John, Bukowski hung up.

"It's all settled," he said. "You're going."

I jumped off his lap and strutted my stuff in a victory dance.

"Yes, yes, yes!" I crowed, "I'm going to New York!"

"Come here, you redheaded rascal," he said, pulling me on his lap and giving me a big hug and kiss.

I spent the next day preparing for the trip. I had to find something to wear and do the laundry. But, most important, I had to get some pharmaceutical reinforcements—because I was petrified of flying.

The day before the trip, I stopped in to see Doctor Feelgood. I told him about my fear of flying and he wrote a prescription for a half dozen five-milligram Valium pills. Normally, I didn't like downers because they made me dopey—and I always preferred to feel hyper-alert. But in this case, dopey was just what I wanted.

After the doctor's visit, I went to my mom's place to do my laundry and make arrangements for her to watch Stacey while I was gone. But when I got there, she wasn't home.

As I started to load the washing machine, Larry walked in the door.

"Got any uppers?" he asked, not even bothering to say hello.

Normally, I didn't mind sharing. But this time I only had enough to hold me for the trip. I'd be jetlagged after losing three hours flying East, and I'd need a pick-me-up.

"No, I don't," I said.

"You don't have anything?"

"Just a scrip for Valium," I said, figuring Larry wouldn't be interested, since he'd asked for uppers.

"Valium! Give me the scrip!" Larry screamed.

"Sorry, Larry, I can't."

He looked at me for a few seconds. It was a cold, lidless look—the kind lizards use when stalking prey. He was going to try another approach.

"I'll have it filled if you give me some," he said in a soothing conman voice.

"He only wrote the scrip for a few pills," I said. "I need them for the plane ride. I'm going to New York with Hank tomorrow."

Larry

Larry was a textbook addict. He would do anything or try anything to get his fix. When his calm, cool approach didn't work, he quickly shifted to the opposite. He became a rabid wolf.

"Give me the scrip, Pam. Where is it?" he demanded, his voice bellowing through the house.

I took a step backwards. He looked as if he'd lost his mind. His eyes were wild and shifty. His red hair seemed to grow frizzier, as if he'd touched a live wire. I knew I needed to get away from him.

Larry saw my eyes drift toward the utility shelf, where I'd stashed my purse. He ran over to the shelf and scooped up the purse. I pushed him aside and tried to yank it out of his hands. While we were struggling over the purse, I reached inside and pulled out the prescription. As Larry lunged at me, I crammed the piece of paper into my mouth and pretended to swallow it. He jumped on top of me and we began to wrestle. He squeezed my face, and then put his hands around my neck, strangling me.

"Spit it out! Spit it out!" he yelled, banging my head against the floor.

I thought he was going to kill me, but I was too proud and stubborn to give him what he wanted. I would rather die.

"I swallowed it!" I lied.

He lightened up his grip, looking at me to determine if I was telling the truth. My adrenaline kicked in, and I managed to push him off of me. I ran to my mom's bedroom and locked the door.

"Get out of here, Larry," I said, starting to sob. "I'm calling the cops right now!"

I picked up the Princess phone on the nightstand and called Bukowski. I still had the prescription lodged between my cheek and gum. I told him that Larry was trying to kill me for my Valium prescription. He didn't ask any questions, but said he'd be right over. I heard the door slam in the other room.

I stayed in my mom's locked bedroom until I heard Bukowski's Volks pull up. I opened the door and tiptoed through the house, looking for Larry. But he was gone. When I met Bukowski at the door, I jumped in his arms, crying.

"Do you want me to kick the shit out of him?" he asked.

"No, just follow me home."

I grabbed my dirty clothes out of the washer, and we took off. On the drive to Carlton Way, I looked at the prescription. It was wrinkled, wet, and some of the ink had smeared. I doubted that I'd be able to get it filled.

When we arrived home, I called Georgia. I told her I was flying to New York and asked if she had any tranquilizers for my plane ride. She offered to give me a couple of Quaaludes.

When I arrived at her place, she was really stoned—nodding off and on, with a lit cigarette hanging from her mouth. She sat up in bed with an overflowing ashtray perched on one side and a half-eaten, two-day-old hamburger on the other. It was stifling hot in her place, and she was dressed only in a red lace teddy that was falling off her bony shoulders.

"Sooo, the Hollywood femme fatale is going to the Big Apple. Mothers lock up your sons," she slurred, while scratching her face and arms.

I grabbed her cigarette and crushed it out, taking the ashtray off the bed and putting it on the nightstand.

"Where are the pills, Georgia? Sorry, but I've gotta go. I have to pick up Stacey from school in a few minutes."

"No problem, Miss Vanderbilt. Give me my purse," she said, pointing to the foot of the bed. Like most female addicts, Georgia never let her purse out of her sight.

I handed her the huge, brown suede tote bag. She jammed her arm into the bottomless pit and in between nod-outs she swished around the bottom, moving in slow motion as she pulled out several vials until she finally found the right one.

"Come on, girl, I'm running late," I coaxed.

"Oh, Jesus, Mary, and Fred, settle the fuck down! Here," she said, as she handed me two Quaaludes.

"Thanks," I said, running for the door.

"Yeah, yeah," she said, as she attempted to find the filtered end of another cigarette.

The next day, around two in the afternoon, Bukowski came upstairs to help me with my bags, literally. I didn't own any luggage so I'd packed everything in brown paper grocery bags. There were about a half-dozen of them crammed full of dresses, blouses, blue jeans, shoes.

After several trips to the Volks, we were finally ready to move. Stacey and I hopped in the car, and we headed to my mom's.

As we were pulling away, I said, "Wait, I forgot something."

I ran over to my Camaro and dug through the layers of trash until I found the Polaroid camera that Bukowski had given me for my birthday. Camera in hand, I sprinted back to the Volks.

"I'm hungry," Stacey moaned. "I want a cheeseburger."

"Gramma will give you lunch," I said.

She burst into tears.

"I'm hungry now, Mommy," she yowled.

When we were a few blocks from Carlton Way, I yelled, "Wait. Turn around, I forgot my toothbrush!"

"You can use mine," he said. "We're not stopping for anything. We'll be lucky if we make it at all."

"Our plane doesn't leave for an hour," I said.

"Yeah, and we're an hour and fifteen minutes away, thanks to you."

Deep down, I knew I was probably trying to sabotage the trip because I was terrified about getting on the plane. I was feeling sick to my stomach.

When we got to my mom's house, she wasn't home.

Bukowski yelled from the car, "Dammit, Red, let's go!"

I didn't know where my mom was or how to get in touch with her. She was supposed to be home. Then again, maybe I'd forgotten to tell her what time we were going to show up.

"I want something to eat," Stacey said between sobs.

I found a bag of cookies in the pantry and poured her a glass of milk.

"Here, let's turn on the TV and you can eat your cookies," I said, stroking her hair. "Gram will make you lunch as soon as she gets home. She'll be here soon, very soon."

But Stacey wasn't buying it.

"No! No! No! Don't go, Mom!" she said, clinging to me.

Bukowski honked the horn over and over.

"Get the hell out here, Red," he yelled.

I hugged Stacey tight, kissed her goodbye, then stood up and walked toward the door. I turned and looked at her. The last thing I saw was Stacey's face, red and wet with tears.

I felt sick and sad as I walked through the door and locked it behind me.

"I love you, Baby," I shouted as I shut the door. I could still hear her crying.

"I'll be back soon. Be good for Gramma," I shouted through the door.

I ran down to the car and jumped inside.

Bukowski peeled out like a madman. He drove like a maniac—grinding the gears as he shifted from one to five in ten seconds.

I felt so bad about leaving Stacey that I took one of the Quaaludes on the way to the airport. I was unusually quiet for most of the drive there. By the time we arrived at LAX, I felt pleasantly high.

Bukowski pulled me through the terminal like a rag doll. Just as we were ready to board the plane, I noticed an insurance machine. I stopped and yanked my arm from him.

"Give me two quarters, Hank. I want to buy some insurance. I want to make sure Stacey is taken care of in case something happens to me."

"Oh my God, pleeease, Cups, don't do this to me. The plane is taking off in two minutes."

I stamped my feet and dug them in the floor.

"I'm not going until you give me some quarters," I yelled, pounding my fists against his arm like a kid throwing a tantrum.

Bukowski's face was redder than my hair. I thought he was going to hit me or have a heart attack. He took a deep breath and handed me two quarters.

After I filled out the short application, I tried to fit the paper into the slot. I was woozy, so it took me a couple of tries. When I finally accomplished my mission, I skipped off toward the boarding gate.

From his breathing, which came out in bull-like puffs and snorts, I could tell Bukowski was seething—but he didn't say a word.

We were the last ones to board, and the plane began to taxi as soon as our feet were inside. Bukowski stuffed my paper bags into the overhead compartment, and we plopped down in our seats. Bukowski let out a huge sigh.

After we settled into our seats, the stewardess asked if we'd like something to drink.

"We'll have four Vodka Tonics," he said.

The stewardess stared at him, as if trying to figure out if she'd heard him correctly.

He looked back at her and said, "We're expecting company."

She flashed a forced smile and left to get our order. We pulled down our trays, and soon we each had two drinks in front of us. I downed mine in record time and took my makeup bag and mirror from my purse. I began to apply mascara. As was my habit, my mouth hung open while I brushed on the mascara.

Bukowski loved to watch me put on makeup. It excited him. Often, he would walk into the bathroom and just gaze at me. I'd usually get self-conscious and push him out of the room. But this time, I was flying in more ways than one. I didn't care who was looking at me.

Between the pills and the booze, I was beginning to feel sleepy. I stashed my makeup under the seat and nestled against Bukowski. He leaned into me as I put my head on his shoulder and nuzzled him like a pillow.

He touched my face and whispered in my ear, "I love you, Kid."

"Umm, umm," I muttered.

The next thing I knew, a crowd was circled around me. A pretty stewardess was kneeling in front of me holding my face.

"Are you okay?" she asked.

"Where am I? What's going on?"

Then I focused on Bukowski.

He pulled me up into his arms and said, "Hey, little Reds, you gave me a scare. We made it. We're here, in the rotten apple. Can you get up and walk?"

"Yeah, sure, I'm fine. What's the big deal?"

"We thought you were dead, Cups. You scared the shit out of me."

TWENTY-FIVE

Bukowski held my hand as we strolled into the church. The crowd cheered and whistled as we edged our way through the mass of people, where it was standing room only.

$\mathcal{I}$ was still pretty groggy, but managed to get off the plane. I clutched a couple of my grocery bags in each hand while Bukowski held me around the waist, carrying the rest.

At the JFK terminal, a heavyset guy with a big smile greeted us. He grabbed a couple of our bags, then clutched Bukowski's hands and shook mine.

"Hi," he said. "I'm Harold. I'm going to take you to the hotel."

"Thanks, Harold," Bukowski said.

"My God," I said. "I feel like I'm in a steam cooker."

"Welcome to New York in June," Harold said. "It's not like the Irving Berlin song."

I couldn't believe how hot and muggy it was. Growing up in California, I had never experienced such humidity. I felt like I was in a sauna—it was suffocating. I was glad I'd worn a long white cotton dress. But poor Bukowski had on heavy jeans and a long-sleeved polyester shirt. Within a few minutes, we were both drenched in sweat.

It was nearly midnight when we made the drive from Queens to Manhattan. On the way, we stopped and picked up a young hipster named Brian. He gushed over Bukowski and was polite to me, but I noticed that he and Harold didn't exchange even one word. I figured they were rival poets in the New York scene.

As the lights of Manhattan rose in the distance, I was amazed at the height of the buildings. Just looking at them gave me vertigo. I couldn't believe people lived in these monster high-rises, and all so close together.

After we arrived at the hotel, Harold let us out of the car, gave us our stuff, and took off. As we stood on the sidewalk, Brian told us that the Chelsea was a legendary place where many famous artists stayed.

"You have Room 1010," Brian said. "That's where Janis Joplin always stayed when she was in town."

If only Georgia could see me now, I thought.

After hearing Brian brag about the Chelsea, I got excited. I was looking forward to staying in a really posh place and living it up. But when I stepped through the door, my fantasies evaporated. While the place did have some beautiful features—high ceilings, a wrought-iron spiral staircase, and fabulous artwork on the walls—it had a cold, sterile feel about it. It was dark and musty, even creepy.

After we checked in, Brian bid us goodnight, and we took the elevator to the tenth floor. Next to flying, the thing I hate most is riding in elevators—and this one was especially scary. The wrought-iron enclosure looked as if it had been built in the 1800s. The elevator creaked and jerked its way up, and seemed to take forever. During the nerve-wracking ride, I clutched tight to Bukowski. He laughed all the way up.

When we finally got to our room, I was even less impressed. It was bland and dreary—like being back home on Carlton Way, only hotter than hell. There was no air conditioning, or it wasn't working. I started to fan myself with one of my paper bags.

"Sit tight, Red," Bukowski said. "I'll be right back."

He left the room, and I sat like a statue on the edge of the bed. I was afraid to move, thinking a rat or a bug or a maniac would jump out at me.

About fifteen minutes later, Bukowski came back. He was dripping in sweat and carrying two frosty six-packs.

I couldn't remember when I'd enjoyed a cold beverage as much.

The next morning, we took a cab to St. Mark's, a nearly two-hundred-year-old church in the Bowery that was hosting the reading. As I stepped in front of the building, I was awed by the majesty of the place. It was surrounded by a black wrought-iron fence and had a high white steeple with a clock in the center. I could see tall white marble statues through the fence. The beautiful church was a welcome contrast to the austere Chelsea.

Brian, looking hip as ever, met us out front. I thought it funny how Bukowski did not look the part of the poet, while Brian did. But Bukowski was the one people were paying to see.

I could tell that Bukowski was tense. He had beads of sweat on his forehead and his skin looked pale and drawn. He hated to give readings. They made him nervous to the point of nausea. I only hoped he wouldn't get sick and throw up on the hallowed grounds of St. Mark's.

"Hey," Brian said, "before we go in, let me show you something really cool."

He led us around the back, where there was a cemetery. Brian pointed out all the famous people buried there. I could see that Bukowski was trying to keep from retching, but he just couldn't hold it back. He vomited all over a famous dead New Yorker.

"Are you okay, Hank?" I asked.

"I'm fine, Red," he said. "I'm okay, really."

We walked around to the front and peeked inside the church. The place was packed. People were standing in the doorways. The crowd was loud and getting restless.

"This way," Brian said, leading us to the back entrance.

We stepped into a room that looked like a partially renovated basement. All of a sudden, I felt queasy and self-conscious just thinking about the crowd in the other room. Like a mother, whose son was pitching at a little league baseball game, I was especially nervous for Bukowski. I checked my makeup, then took out my brush and began to run it through my hair, as if I was also performing on stage. I looked at Bukowski. He was leaning against the wall, bent over and holding his stomach.

"Come on, Hank, its show time," Brian said.

Bukowski straightened himself up, and then checked his face in the mirror for remnants of vomit.

"Is the beer out there?" he asked Brian.

"It's all set," Brian said. "Now, let's go."

Bukowski held my hand as we strolled into the church. The crowd cheered and whistled as we edged our way through the mass of people, where it was standing room only. As he approached the stage, Bukowski let go of my hand, and Brian led me to a chair in the front row.

At the hotel, we had finished most of the beer—so I was now feeling giddy, caught up in the excitement. As I watched Bukowski read, I grinned like the proud girlfriend that I was—especially when he read some of the love poems he'd written for me. My favorites were "Huge Ear Rings" and "The Promise." People looked at me as he read them, and I felt somewhat embarrassed, but excited by the attention.

(courtesy of Thomas Schmitt)

When Bukowski read his last poem of the evening, the audience went wild. The performance had lasted about an hour and a half. Afterwards, we ducked out the back and went straight to the hotel.

In the cab, I squeezed his hand and told him, "You did great, Hank. I'm proud of you, Baby."

He smiled and said, "It wasn't bad." I could tell he was pleased with his performance.

Back in our room, we toasted the successful reading with warm beer. We were in a happy mood. We fell back on the bed, giggling like little kids.

Then somebody banged on the door. The sound startled us out of our gleeful mood. Bukowski shook his head and his shoulders sagged.

"Who the hell can that be?" he whispered.

Then there were two more sharp raps on the door.

"Shit! Who is it?" Bukowski yelled out.

A man's voice said, "It's us, Dick Williams and Jane Miller."

Bukowski dragged himself toward the door and opened it.

In waltzed an attractive, Ivy League couple.

"What do you want?" Bukowski growled.

"To see you, of course," Dick said and laughed.

Bukowski wasn't amused.

Dick plopped onto the bed and Jane sat herself in a chair. Dick then began to tell us about his poetry and how Jane was supporting him while he wrote his magnum opus. He talked about books I'd never read and authors I'd never heard of. He was an arrogant, academic intellectual that you just felt like kicking in the ass.

After about ten minutes, Bukowski said, "Okay, you saw me. Now you can go."

He opened the door and waved for them to leave. For once, I was glad that he was rude.

After they left, we shed our clothes and went to bed. We both slept like stones. The next morning, we woke up refreshed. I hadn't eaten in a day, but didn't feel I could keep down any food. I popped a diet pill and washed it down with a hot bottle of beer. While I got dressed, Bukowski went out and grabbed something to eat. He came back about a half an hour later with more beer and a bottle of Smirnoff Vodka.

I was raring to go out and see the sights.

"Hey, let's go to the Empire State Building," I said.

"No, I don't feel like going to the Empire State Building."

"How 'bout Coney Island, are we near there?"

"No, I don't want to go to Coney Island."

"How about the Statue of Liberty?" I said.

"No, I don't want to see the Statue of Liberty."

"How about . . ."

"I'm tired, Baby," he said. "Those readings take it out of me. Come on, Kid, let's just relax."

"You're no fun," I said. "Here we are in New York and I can't see any of the famous places. Can we at least get out of this sauna and take a walk?"

"Okay, Red, we can take a walk," he said, sounding tired, bored, and annoyed all at the same time. "Let's go."

"Oh," I said. "Just one second."

I picked up the phone and dialed information. I asked the operator to give me the number for Eyton Ribner. I'd met Eyton when I'd modeled for him during his days as a student photographer at the Art Center College of Design in Pasadena, California. I had heard he'd recently moved to New York to pursue work as a fashion photographer.

"What borough?" the operator asked in a clipped, nasal voice.

"I think he lives in Queens," I said.

The operator yelled, "Call back when you're sure!" Then she hung up.

"Whoa, this town is really rude," I said to Bukowski, who was standing like a weary sentry by the door.

I grabbed my Polaroid, and we left the hotel. Outside, it was still hot and humid. I had on my coolest outfit—a blue tank top, jean peddle-pushers, and flip-flops—but was still sweating. Bukowski was sweating along with me in his baggy jeans and white T-shirt.

We moseyed down Twenty-Third Street for about a block. I spotted a newsstand, walked up to the display of publications, and began to scan the covers. I was looking for a *Village Voice*—thinking there might be a review of Bukowski's reading.

While I was browsing, the old man behind the counter yelled, "Hey, Sister, either buy somethin' or move on!"

I jumped back, shocked. Rudeness was the New York way, and I was getting an adult dose.

I looked at Bukowski, but he just shrugged, as if to say, "What did you expect?"

As we walked along, I felt like a heavy weight was crushing me. Everybody seemed anxious and fearful. Even the air seemed dirty and angry.

"Come on, Red, let's go back to the room."

"Hank," I coaxed, "can't you do just a little sightseeing for me?"

So we walked around for a while. We snapped a few photos. I took one of him in front of a sign that said, "Jesus Loves You." He took one of me standing under a sign that said, "Half-Price Sale."

"I'm serious, Red. I've got to go back to the room. It's too damn hot."

Up the street, I saw a furniture store, where beautiful leather chairs and roll-top desks were on display in the window. For as long as I could remember, my idea of success had been a cherry wood desk and an over-stuffed leather chair.

I ran over to the store and began to admire the leather chair. Out of the corner of my eye, I saw Bukowski turn around and walk the other way. It never occurred to me that he would leave me there, but he did. When I looked up, he was gone.

I walked back alone among the fearful New Yorkers. In L.A., men would have approached me, but the redheaded magic had no effect on this group. They were like the walking dead. They almost seemed afraid of me.

I thought about having to fly back to L.A. the following day and started to feel anxious. Then I remembered my prescription for Valium. I opened my purse and found the wadded piece of paper.

I walked for a few more blocks and saw a little hole-in-the-wall pharmacy on 8th Avenue.

Everything in the store seemed ancient. Murky light came through the smeary windows, giving everything a sickly yellow glaze. I walked to the back of the store and found an elderly man dressed in a white coat. I handed him my prescription. I didn't hold out much hope. I also didn't expect him to be polite, seeing as how everyone I'd encountered so far had been crude and rude.

"What is this?" he said, smoothing out the wrinkled prescription.

I was surprised at how pleasant he sounded. He was the first stranger I'd encountered all day who wasn't mean to me.

"I'm flying home to L.A. tomorrow," I said. "And I need to take a Valium when I get on the plane. I'm afraid of flying."

"I'm very sorry, Miss," he said, "but you should've had it filled in L.A."

"I didn't have time," I said.

"I'd like to help you," he said, "but I can't fill your prescription."

"And why is that?"

"It's from out of state," he said.

"But you can call my doctor," I said.

"Sorry," he said, "but we can't fill an out-of-state prescription. Besides, it's practically illegible."

"If you could fill it," I said, "how much would it cost?"

"Twelve dollars," he said. "But I can't fill this prescription. I'm sorry, dear. Have a few drinks on the plane instead."

I took the piece of paper out of his hand and left the place.

When I got back to the room, Bukowski was drinking vodka. I opened a beer and told him what had happened at the pharmacy.

"He just kept saying, 'I can't fill this prescription—I can't fill this prescription.' As though Thrifty's could? But if he could, it would cost twelve bucks. Twelve bucks! It only costs six back in L.A. How do people survive in this ungodly city?"

Bukowski listened, but didn't say anything. He looked totally wrung out from heat and exhaustion.

It was still like a sauna in the room. I walked over and straddled the windowsill. There was no screen on the window, and I propped my right leg on the sill and hung my left leg outside and began swinging it back and forth.

"Hey, Kid, you'd better get down from there," he said.

"I'm fine," I said. "It's much cooler over here. You should give it a try."

"Seriously," he said, "get the hell off that window sill. We're ten stories up."

I looked down over the city and began to feel dizzy. I lost my balance and fell sideways toward the outside of the window. I was teetering back and forth, then managed to grab the inside of the window with both hands and pull myself up and inside using my right leg as leverage. Bukowski jumped up to help me. I had given myself such a scare that I ran over to the bed holding my chest.

"Jesus, Kid," Bukowski said, "that was a close call. I've lost women before, but never like that. How would I explain that to your mother? You're crazy, Red."

Despite the adrenaline rush from nearly dying, all of a sudden the heat, the bennie, and the booze got to me. When Bukowski rolled over to hug me, I fell off the side of the bed. I fell fast asleep on the floor.

The next morning, we left for home. I couldn't wait to get back to civilized Hollywood. Like Bukowski, I hated New York.

26
TWENTY-SIX

"You're a fucking madman. I never want to see you again! You're cracked, Bukowski!"

$Shortly$ after we got back from New York, Bukowski told me he had another poetry reading.

"Where's this one?" I asked.

"The Golden Bear," he said, as if the name meant nothing to him.

As a music fanatic, I knew that the Golden Bear was a prestigious nightclub in Huntington Beach where many of the biggest names—including Bob Dylan, Jimi Hendrix, the Doors, and Janis Joplin—had played on their way up.

"Wow, you're getting popular, Big Daddy. That's great!"

"No, it's not great. I hate readings, but they pay the rent."

"How can you hate them? The audience loves you . . . at least they did in New York."

"The audience doesn't love me, and I don't love the audience. The people look at me like I'm a carnival freak with three eyes. They treat me like an ape that performs human tricks. 'Step right up, ladies and gentlemen. See the amazing Bukowski. He's half man, half ape. His mother was raped by King Kong.' Shee-iit, I hate the motherfucks."

I felt a pang of sorrow for him because I knew there was some truth to what he was saying. Even though the New York crowd had been huge and enthusiastic, there had been an element of ridicule. I could see why Bukowski wasn't looking forward to his reading at the Golden Bear.

"Would you go with me?" Bukowski asked.

"When's the reading?"

"This Friday," he said.

Stacey was going to stay with her grandma on Friday, so I told Bukowski I'd go with him. He pulled me onto his lap and gave me a big kiss.

"You're okay, Kid," he said, squeezing me tight.

We arrived at the Golden Bear about an hour early. Bukowski introduced me to the man in charge, who struck me as kind of a street-wise guy. He was a little unsavory looking, and I had an immediate negative reaction to him. Though he was very considerate of both of us, I didn't trust him.

Since we had time to kill, Bukowski and I went next door to a bar and had a few drinks.

"Try and go a little slower with the drinks this time, Hank. Last time you got pretty sloshed and started slurring your words a little toward the end," I said.

After about three rounds, we went back to the nightclub. Bukowski was beginning to get sick and paced backstage like a caged animal.

"Take care of my girl for me," he said to the guy in charge.

"Don't worry, Baby. We'll give her the royal treatment. I'll put her on my tab. What would ya like to drink, Sweetie?"

Just then, they announced Bukowski's name and he took a deep breath and walked onto the stage. The crowd clapped and howled at him.

"Settle down, ya pussies. I can take you all at once," Bukowski taunted.

That excited the crowd even more. People hooted and hollered obscenities. They were out of control. Finally, everyone began to quiet down as Bukowski began to read. In the meantime, the waitress was checking on me every ten minutes. It was like I had my own private servant. The drinks kept coming, and I kept draining them.

By the time Bukowski was finished with the reading, I was pretty wrecked. I found my way backstage, where Mr. Golden Bear was settling up with Bukowski.

"You were great, Baby," I gushed to Bukowski. "That was better than New York!"

"Yeah, yeah, thanks, Cups," Bukowski said, trying to make me stop. He hated compliments.

"Okay, now where were we?" Mr. Bear asked. "What did I say I'd pay you? Two hundred bucks, right?"

"Two hundred bucks!" I yelled. "You promised him five hundred. You better not try to screw him, man! I knew there was something about you that couldn't be trusted. I could tell just by looking at you! You've got mean eyes!"

"Hey, Red, cool it," Bukowski told me. "He was only joking."

Bukowski collected his pay and ushered me out the back door. I blabbered away all the way home.

When we got to Western and Carlton Way, Bukowski decided he was going to shut me up and sober me up. Instead of slowing down to make the turn onto Carlton, he sped up. He made a wide swing around the corner going at least fifty miles per hour barely missing the sidewalk.

"What are you doing, Hank? Stop it, you're scaring me!"

He began to laugh like a lunatic and continued to drive the same way. Instead of pulling up to the curb and parking in front of our building, he began to make donuts in the middle of the street at a fast pace. We spun around several times. Then he pulled into the parking lot across the street at Pizza Pete's and continued to spin and spin. I felt like I was going to vomit. All the while, I was screaming, "Stop it, Hank! You're going to kill us!"

I slumped down in my seat and braced my left foot on the dashboard with my other foot pressed against the windshield.

"You crazy son of a bitch! Stop this car now!"

Then I began to cry. He came to an abrupt stop—forcing the heel of my right shoe through the windshield of the Volks. I was glad I'd worn spiked heels. They probably saved my ankle from getting severed.

Cracked windshield on Bukowski's Volkswagon
(courtesy of Thomas Schmitt)

When the car stopped shaking, Bukowski said, "Oh come on, don't cry. That was fun. Didn't you think that was fun?"

159

I leaped out of the car and yelled, "You're a fucking madman. I never want to see you again! You're cracked, Bukowski!"

I ran across the street to the courtyard and sprinted in my stilettos up to my apartment. It took me a while to fall asleep. I couldn't stop trembling from the maniacal stunt driving exhibition.

The next day, Bukowski came up to my place acting contrite and apologetic. I could never stay mad at him for long, and he was patient with my antics too. I forgave him and life went on as usual.

That summer seemed hotter than normal in L.A., or maybe it was because neither one of us had air conditioning. We would often go for walks in the evening to get some fresh air. One night, we were walking down Carlton Way toward Western Avenue when I spotted a sign in front of a shabby little house that read "Psychic Readings, $5."

"Hey, Hank—look, a fortune teller. Let's get our palms read."

"I already know what the future holds, and it's not good."

"Oh, come on. It'll be fun. *Please.*"

"They're all frauds, Baby. Don't be a chump."

"*Pleease,*" I begged.

"Oh, shit, all right."

We knocked at the door and a chubby, teenage girl answered.

"We're here for a psychic reading," I said, while Bukowski stood in the background like a man out shopping with his wife.

"Oh, okay, hold on," she told us. Then she yelled into another room, "Ma, there's some people here who wanna reading." She turned to us and said, "Hold on," then headed for the other room.

A couple of minutes later, a middle-aged, haggard-looking woman shuffled out in flip-flops. She was wearing an old robe and looked like she just got out of bed.

"Would you prefer that we come back another time?" I asked.

"Nah, sit down here," she said, directing us to an old kitchen table that looked a lot like Bukowski's.

She brushed aside some magazines, then, in a thick Bronx accent, asked, "Okay, who wants ta go first?"

"You go first, Hank," I said.

"Give me ya palm."

He extended his right hand and she began to study it.

"Humm," she grunted. "I see you are a man who likes ta drink too much. That's not too good," she warned.

"Hey, lady, you're supposed to read my hand, not my face."

We both laughed, but the psychic remained serious.

"I see ya also have an eye for the young girls. This is not good, either. It will lead ta nothin' but heartbreak."

At this point, we both realized the woman couldn't even fake being a fraud.

Hank pulled his hand away, and said, "Okay, that's enough, lady. Let's get out of here, Cups."

He grabbed my arm and headed toward the door.

"Hey! That'll be five bucks, Mista."

Bukowski reached into his pants and pulled out a bill and disgustedly laid it on a table by the front door.

"Jeezus, Red," he said, when we reached the sidewalk. "I told you that would be a waste of money."

We headed back to our complex, turned on the fan, grabbed some cold beers, and did our best to beat the heat without a thought about what tomorrow would bring.

Que sera, sera.

TWENTY-SEVEN

I saw my "Mother of the Year" award going up in flames.

$\mathcal{S}tacey$ was out of school for summer vacation, so I was spending less time carousing with Bukowski. I guess that's why he and I were getting along better than usual.

One hot July day, Stacey and I stopped by to see how he was doing. He was in an unusually good mood and greeted us with a hug and an impish grin. He asked if I'd a like a beer and even brought Stacey a glass of 7-Up.

He was always pleasant to Stacey, but, for obvious reasons, preferred to be alone with me. At times, he could get impatient with her around. But this day he was upbeat and even had a bounce in his step as he walked to the kitchen to retrieve our drink order.

"Hey, what's got into you?" I said. "You seem almost happy for a change."

"I'm just glad to see you," he said.

After a few minutes, he told me about a call from a filmmaker by the name of Thomas Schmitt. Schmitt was with a film company based in Germany that wanted to make a documentary about Bukowski's day-to-day life. Bukowski asked if I'd like to take part in it. I was surprised that he was so enthusiastic about the film. He was always understated and somewhat dismissive about anything that involved the media. Half the time, I didn't know about interviews and photo shoots until they were over. He usually considered them a chore, but not this time. I told him that the project sounded like fun.

"They're going to be with us every day for maybe a week. Don't commit to this, Red, and then disappear on me."

I promised I'd be good and stick around for it. He seemed almost delighted.

About a week later, around noon, Bukowski came upstairs to retrieve me.

"Hey, Red, the Germans are here, the Germans are here," he said. "Get that cute little ass of yours downstairs and show them what you got."

When I arrived at Bukowski's place, I met Thomas and Alexandria Schmitt, an attractive couple in their early thirties. He was tall and slender with long black hair—and dressed like a local in jeans, T-shirt, and sandals. She, too, was tall and slender with beautiful, long, straight, blonde hair worn loose. She was wearing a fresh summer dress and looked like a model. They reminded me of the two best-looking members of the singing group ABBA. They shook my hand and were soft-spoken and polite. We sat in Bukowski's living room making small talk before they turned on the cameras. Though they both spoke with German accents, their English was very good.

Thomas told us they were staying at a Super 8 Motel on Western Avenue, a couple blocks from Carlton Way. It was a terrible place in a terrible neighborhood—and a vice magnet. They told us about hearing screams around three in the morning. A pimp was attempting to drown his prostitute because she'd withheld money from him. They heard the pimp yell, "Give me the money, bitch, or I'll kill you," and when they looked out their window, saw the man with his hands around the woman's neck, dunking her head in the swimming pool.

"Welcome to East Hollywood, my friends," Bukowski said with a chuckle. "This is where it's at—the pimps, the whores, the homeless, and the mindless. Life at its finest, Baby. We hear that melody every other night. If we don't, we figure something is wrong."

If the Schmitts had any doubts about Bukowski's reputation as the "poet of skid row," they were now convinced he was the real thing.

We had a couple of beers before they turned on the cameras. By the time we got started, I was beginning to feel very comfortable. In fact, I was getting sloshed.

Bukowski and I sat close together on his couch. For most of the interview, he had his arm around me. During the past few weeks, things had been going well between us. Our relationship was in an up cycle, and I felt our interplay on camera would be pleasant.

The Schmitts asked Bukowski several questions—mostly about his childhood and his days living in flophouses, when he'd existed on one candy bar a day. Bukowski regaled us with funny anecdotes. He was in such a good mood that he even sang his signature song to me. "Mean to me . . . why must you be so mean to me?"

That day, I was able to get my brother to keep Stacey for a couple of hours. Unfortunately, he had to drop her off on his way to work. She walked into the den of iniquity while we were still filming. The round coffee table in the middle of the living room was wall-to-wall beer bottles and overflowing ashtrays. It looked like the worst dive bar in Hollywood—an

With Buk and Stacey

unwholesome environment for a seventy-year-old, let alone a seven-year-old child. I saw my "Mother of the Year" award going up in flames.

Stacey was such a good little girl—despite her wayward mother. But she didn't seem daunted, and actually appeared to enjoy the high-energy atmosphere and all the attention. Years later, in 2004, she would see these clips in the documentary *Born into This*—and would be mortified.

When our neighbor Sam walked by, we yelled for him to come in and sit with us. Sam lived on the first floor—adjacent to my apartment and cattycorner to Bukowski's—and worked as a security guard at an adult bookstore down the street. He was tall, barrel-chested, around forty years old, and gentle, despite his imposing appearance. A New York transplant,

he kept watch over the court—and was the self-appointed doer of justice for Carlton Way. It wasn't unusual to see him stick his head outside his door or stop by Bukowski's place with a rifle clutched in his hands, asking if we'd "heard that," or if we'd "seen

Sam

someone suspicious." Bukowski and I appreciated his vigilance and were extremely fond of him.

The Schmitts asked Sam about his relationship with Bukowski. After answering a few questions, he took off. Before the Schmitts left, Stacey and I went upstairs to our place. I was beginning to see double and needed to lie down for a while. About an hour later, Alexandria came up to see us. She asked if she could shoot some footage of Stacey and me. We were glad to comply and hammed it up for the camera. The filmmakers left later that evening and promised to return around noon the following day.

The next day, the Schmitts showed up on schedule, and Bukowski came by to ask me if I wanted to join them. He planned to take them on a tour of his haunts, past and present, and run a few errands. I was feeling hungover and begged off.

When Bukowski came home later that afternoon, sans the Schmitts, I asked him where they'd been all day. He said they'd stopped to get some lunch at his favorite deli on Sunset—where they'd all enjoyed the greasy pastrami sandwiches that cured hangovers. Afterward, they'd dropped off his clothes at the Chinese laundry, and then went to the Post Office Terminal Annex in downtown Los Angeles where he'd worked for twelve years. As he told me about the day, I could see he felt tired and a little depressed. I wondered if the trip down memory lane had made him feel bad.

I walked across the street to Pizza Pete's and brought back a pepperoni pizza and large Pepsis for the three of us. We had a quiet dinner at his place, then Stacey and I left to go to bed early for a change.

The next day, the Schmitts showed up again around noon. This time, I'd made arrangements for Stacey to spend the day with her girlfriend Nina. I figured she'd seen enough debauchery for a while.

Though at first I enjoyed the attention, I began to feel uncomfortable— I felt as if I were under a microscope. I can understand why so many celebrities end up in rehab or dead from substance abuse. It's tough being under constant scrutiny—especially when you have a limited wardrobe. It was day three and though the focus was on Bukowski, I still felt under pressure to perform. It was beginning to wear on both of us.

I met the three of them at Bukowski's place. As usual, we all began drinking. Bukowski was sitting in his favorite striped chair, and I was on the floor beside him in front of the coffee table. This time, they focused on our relationship.

Bukowski was in a good mood, and we were both very playful with each other. The subject then turned to marriage. They asked if we had any plans to tie the knot—and we joked about going to a tacky wedding chapel in Vegas some day. We continued drinking, smoking, and laughing until they finally left in the early evening.

As soon as they walked out the door, Bukowski erupted.

28 TWENTY-EIGHT

"You're nothin' but a slut," he slurred.

"*You* whore!" he screamed. "I saw the way you were looking at him! Have you no decency? The man is with his woman and you're flirting with him! You thought I didn't notice, didn't you? You fucking, no good, fucking whore!"

His eyes were lifeless and his face was contorted. His mouth looked twisted and his lips trembled as he growled out the words. I had heard this song before, but not with such conviction and aggression. It scared the hell out of me. I thought, *Oh God, this is it—he's really lost it this time.*

In the past, when he went off on this tangent, I would just laugh, or say, "Knock it off, you're nuts, Bukowski." Or I would leave until he simmered down.

But this time was different. He got up from his chair and headed toward me. I was still on the floor in front of the coffee table when he lunged at me. I put my hands over my head to defend myself, and then managed to spring to my feet. I somehow made my way to the front door while he continued his vile tirade.

"You're nothin' but a slut," he slurred. "You're all the same! You better run, you fucking strumpet!"

When I knew I could safely leave his apartment, I stood at the door and went on the offensive. My instinct told me the best approach would be to act crazier than him. I began to yell like a raving lunatic.

"YOU SON OF A BITCH! DON'T YOU EVER TALK TO ME, OR THREATEN ME LIKE THAT AGAIN! I'VE HAD IT WITH YOU AND YOUR SICK, FUCKING DELUSIONS! WHAT IS YOUR FUCKING PROBLEM,

YOU INSANE BASTARD?! YOU'VE GOT AN ILLNESS, A DISEASE, AND YOU BETTER CURE IT FAST OR YOU'LL NEVER SEE ME AGAIN. I'M TIRED OF YOUR PARANOID RANTS, INSULTS AND ACCUSATIONS— FUCK YOU!"

He just stood there staring and panting like a rabid dog, and seemed stuck to the floor. He had never seen me this way and wasn't quite sure how to react. Even if I had been drinking, I rarely said the word "fuck." He knew this was serious.

I ran up to my apartment. I locked the door behind me and watched him from my balcony window. He turned out the lights, and I couldn't see what he was doing. I was still shaken by his unpredictable behavior and worried that he may try and break in. I had never seen such an extreme about-face from him. Nor had I ever seen him that physically threatening. Sure, I had been subjected to his jealous rages in the past, but this one caught me completely off guard. This had come out of nowhere and fast. It was truly frightening.

Though we'd had a lot to drink during the day, the adrenaline rush from the fear had made me completely sober. I turned out the lights and pulled my large wicker chair in front of the window to watch for any sign of him leaving his bungalow. I didn't see or hear anything, not even the clicking of his typewriter. I assumed he was sitting in the dark drinking the hard stuff and feeling sorry for himself.

Around six a.m. I woke up in the chair. I dragged myself into the bedroom to lie down for a couple more hours. Around eleven a.m., I was awakened by a knock on my door. I froze, knowing it was probably him, since Stacey was still with her girlfriend.

The pounding got louder, and then I heard him speak.

"Hey, little Reds, it's me, the madman downstairs," he said. "Open up. Hey, I'm sorry about last night. I wanna talk to you."

I remained silent and didn't move.

"Come on, Baby," he said. "Look, I said I'm sorry. Please come to the door. I'll buy you a new hat and high heels to match."

I didn't answer.

"Okay," he said. "I'm leaving, but I want you to know I am sorry."

Still no answer from me.

I didn't have a phone, so we did most of our communicating in person or with notes. I heard his footsteps going down the stairs. I waited a minute and then went to my window to make sure he was gone. I stood against the wall so he couldn't see me. I saw him walking into his house through his back door.

I threw on my jeans and a T-shirt. I didn't even bother with a bra or underpants. I brushed my teeth and ran a washcloth over my face. I had to pick up Stacey and wanted to get out of there before the filmmakers arrived. While I was brushing my hair, I heard something scampering outside my door. Again, I waited a minute, then looked out my window and saw him running back into his apartment like a menacing kid. I finished washing up and decided to go barefoot—my heels were too noisy.

I grabbed my purse, and just as I was getting ready to leave, the film-makers arrived. I looked out my window and saw Alexandria heading for my place. Shit—too late! I opened the door just as she was approaching the top stair. There was an envelope on the ground. I picked it up and stuffed it in my purse.

"Hello, Pamela," she said. "How are you? Hank tells me you are not feeling well."

"No, I'm not. I think I have the flu, so I won't be filming with you today."

I noticed she had a camera with her. I looked like death-warmed-over and asked her not to shoot any pictures of me.

"I'm so sorry you are not well. I hope you feel better soon. We are leaving today and I want to tell you how much I have enjoyed meeting you."

I told her the feeling was mutual and wanted to give her a big hug, but didn't want to expose her to my flu germs—real or imagined.

"Take good care of yourself, Pamela."

"Thank you, Alexandria. And please say goodbye to Thomas for me. Have a safe trip home," I said, as she descended the stairway back to Bukowski's place.

I waited a few minutes, grabbed my purse, and stood by the front door. I pulled the envelope from my purse and opened it. Though I was relieved that Bukowski seemed to have come to his senses, I was still shook up from the entire episode.

The note said that he was no good and asked for my forgiveness. He signed it "Horrible Hank" and drew his signature little man holding a bouquet of flowers. I stuffed it back in my purse and headed for my car.

There was only one exit to the street and that was the walkway in front of his apartment. I dashed by his front window as fast as I could, hoping they wouldn't see me. I made it to my car and peeled off toward Western Avenue.

I picked up Stacey at Nina's house. The girls were just finishing lunch. I thanked Nina's mom, Anna, and took off. I wasn't sure where to go next. I was still preoccupied with the night before.

We stopped at a liquor store to buy our usual assortment of junk food—a couple Yoo-hoos, Slim Jims for me, assorted candy bars and chips for Stacey. I decided to head for our favorite place, Echo Park Lake. Stacey and I went there a lot. It had a man-made lake and you could rent paddleboats for two dollars an hour. The park was quiet and peaceful—just what I needed.

Echo Park became a place where Stacey and I would go to reconnect. It was our refuge from our complicated life.
(© Taylor Brittenham)

We rented a boat and ate our nutritious snacks. I was still in a daze over the nightmare episode.

"Are you okay, Mom?" Stacey asked.

Snapping out of my funk, I said, "I'm fine, Honey." Then I smiled at her and asked, "How was your night?"

After about an hour of paddling up and down the lake, we went to my mom's house. We stayed for dinner and watched TV together. It was now the weekend and I asked my mom if she would mind if Stacey spent the night with her.

I wasn't going to take her back to Carlton Way, at least not for a while. I realized my lifestyle was unconventional and not the ideal surroundings for raising a child. But until I was ready to change, I always made sure Stacey was in a safe environment, shielded from most of the chaos and madness that was my life. Though there is no substitute for the security of a loving mother, it was the best I could do for her given my appetite for self-destruction.

I gave Stacey a hug and a kiss and told her I'd see her the next day.

Mom gave me the "I'm so disappointed in you" look as I walked out the door.

It was probably around nine p.m. when I arrived back at Carlton Way. As I pulled up, I saw Bukowski's blue Volkswagen, so I knew he was home. I hurried past his place toward my apartment.

His lights were on and I could hear classical music coming from his kitchen. I heard the rapid-fire clicking of the typewriter keys. Apparently, the wicked redhead had inspired him again. I managed to get upstairs and into my place without him noticing. I was exhausted from all the fighting and just wanted to turn in early.

I took off my jeans and crawled into bed with my journal. After fifteen minutes of writing, I heard a knock at the door. This time I answered. He stood there looking weary and dejected.

"Well, who do we have here?" I asked. "Dr. Jekyll or Mr. Hyde?"

"Can I come in? I won't stay long," he asked, looking at the floor.

"Sit down," I said, pointing to the Murphy bed in the middle of the living room. I sat across from him in the wicker chair.

"We missed you today," he said.

I didn't respond. I just sat there staring at him.

We were both silent for a minute. Finally, he spoke again.

"Look, Cups, I don't know what got into me. You have a way of . . . "

"Hey, don't blame this on me," I snapped.

"Okay, you're right," he said. "It's not your fault. It's me. I have this evil within me," he said touching his heart with his two fingers. "It's my father.

He was a very bad man, and I have some of his genes. I'll never be a whole person because of it. I'm damaged, Baby, don't you understand? I can't help it, I'm just wired wrong."

I continued staring at him. He seemed genuinely devastated by his bad behavior and DNA. I was beginning to soften up. That battered face of his was brutally expressive and pathetic. It looked like he was in so much pain. It always managed to get to me, but I remained silent.

"Okay . . . that's all," he said, heaving a heavy sigh.

He stood up and headed for the door. I stayed seated, staring in silence.

As he opened the door, he said, "I've got some champagne at my house if you get thirsty later."

"Cordon Rouge?" I asked.

"Of course," he said.

"Let me put on my pants.

As we walked out together, I turned to him and asked, "By the way—what's a strumpet?"

The documentary premiered in Germany, 1976, under the title:
Charles Bukowski
A Visit to the Underground Poet in Hollywood

TWENTY-NINE

He [Buk] wasn't a hypocrite and wouldn't preach about things he couldn't control himself.

A couple days after the German filmmakers left—(or so I thought)—Bukowski was booked for a reading at the Troubadour in West Hollywood. The Troub, as we called it, was a hot spot and considered one of the best venues for entertainment in Los Angeles. Though I didn't know it at the time, the Schmitts would also be there filming Bukowski's performance to complete their documentary.

(courtesy of Thomas Schmitt)

On July 11th, Bukowski was on the bill—opening for Steve Martin, who, at age thirty, was on the cusp of his eventual rock star-caliber fame. During the past several years, Steve had switched from writing to performing stand-up comedy—and had become a familiar face on programs hosted by Sonny & Cher, the Smothers Brothers, and Johnny Carson. With his crazy antics, funny stories, and banjo playing, Steve was a hit wherever he appeared. To be on the same bill with him was quite a coup for Bukowski.

In contrast, Bukowski hated to perform. I can't imagine a greater contrast to the bubbly, outgoing, audience-loving Steve Martin, than the dour, introverted, fan-hating Charles Bukowski.

As usual, we arrived early—Bukowski was a stickler for punctuality—then headed for the bar to enjoy a few drinks before announcing our presence to the Troubadour staff. I suggested that Bukowski stick with beer so he didn't get drunk too soon. I promised him I would watch it too.

Bukowski waved to someone in the crowd and steered me to the other side of the room. He was usually fairly antisocial at these events, so I wondered who could have made him not only wave but also smile. It was the poetess Joan Jobe Smith, accompanied by her new boyfriend.

I admired Joan's delightfully upbeat, outgoing personality. She exuded warmth and wit, and made both of us laugh. I liked her immediately. The four of us had a couple more drinks together, and then Bukowski and I excused ourselves to check in with Peter, the staffer in charge of entertainment.

By this time, the club was filling up—and Bukowski was starting to get nervous. He ran to the men's room, and I stood outside listening to him retch. Even though he sounded as if he were going to vomit out his guts, I wasn't worried. I'd been through this with him too many times before.

I was starting to feel giddy—caught up in the crowd's excitement, the venue's fame, the headliner's reputation, and the alcohol's effect.

When Bukowski came out of the men's room, Peter asked if he could do anything for us. He was a friendly, good-looking young man—tall, blonde, and slender—just the type that Bukowski hated. Bukowski had drained five beers in less than an hour, so I was afraid he might get snarly and belligerent with Peter. I prayed he'd remain civil at the very least.

"Is the beer ready?" Bukowski asked.

"It's on stage in a refrigerator," Peter said.

"How much is there?"

"Stocked full."

Bukowski patted Peter on the back, and I relaxed, figuring we were halfway there. As long as Bukowski had a continuous supply of suds, all would be well.

"Can I introduce Hank?" I asked Peter.

Peter turned to Bukowski, who nodded and looked at me.

"Okay with me," he said.

"It's time," Peter said, ushering me toward the front of the house.

I waltzed onto the stage, beer in hand, grabbed the microphone, and looked out over the crowd.

"Ladies and Gentlemen . . . " I began, then paused for effect.

After a few moments, I said, "I regret to tell you that Charles Bukowski could not make it tonight."

The noisy crowd became silent, then started to boo, hiss, and stomp. I was afraid the Bukophiles might jump up and kill the messenger—me.

"Only kidding!" I spurted out. Then I crowed, "Ladies and Gentlemen . . . Charles Bukowskeee."

The audience whooped it up as Bukowski ambled onto the stage, grabbed a beer out of the refrigerator, and meandered over to his chair. He picked up the microphone and told the audience that he had a new gimmick.

He looked at me and said, "They just keep getting younger and younger."

The crowd went crazy. It was like Mardi Gras in July.

Peter escorted me to a table at the front of the room, to the left of the stage.

"Is this all right?" Peter asked, patting the tabletop.

It was the best seat in the house. I nodded and thanked Peter, then turned to see a waitress virtually bowing in front of me. Everyone was treating me like Queen Pamela, and I was feeling flustered by the experience.

"Can I get you something to drink?" the bubbly waitress asked.

With Bukowski safely on stage with nothing but beer to drink, I figured it would be okay for me to switch. All this attention was making me feel exposed, and I needed something to steady my nerves.

"Whiskey Sour, please," I said.

"Be right back," the waitress told me.

As I waited for the drink, I was eager for the waitress to return. All of a sudden, I really needed something strong to drink.

I tipped the waitress, then settled back to sip my drink and listen to Bukowski. Well, I didn't listen that closely to Bukowski—I'd heard these poems before—and I didn't sip my drink. I downed it, then caught the waitress's eye—raising my glass for another round.

While I waited for reinforcements, I watched Bukowski. He was sitting in an easy chair, looking as relaxed as he did in his living room. His voice was strong and steady, and the poems just flowed out at a perfect rhythm. He was really at the top of his game. The audience adored him, and Bukowski didn't seem to hate the crowd. This was starting out well.

Buk at reading at the Troubadour, 1976
(courtesy of Thomas Schmitt)

I slugged down my Sour and ordered another. Bukowski was reading some poems about me. I was beginning to get sloppy drunk, and my normal inhibitions vanished.

"That was about me!" I yelled, after Bukowski finished reading a poem.

"Yes, dear," he replied, unperturbed. "That was you."

I had another drink, and Bukowski read more poems. After each one, I bellowed a comment.

"I love you, Hank."

"Yeah, Baby."

"Read another one about me!"

About an hour or so into Bukowski's performance, I started to get dizzy and nauseated. The room was wobbling and so was my stomach.

I stood up and immediately fell back into my chair. Again, I tried to stand up. I pushed up from my seat, then spotted the exit sign—and tried to keep my eyes fixed on it as I staggered between the tables. I needed some fresh air, or I was going to be really sick.

I was almost out of the room when I heard, "Pam, hey, Pam."

I looked around and saw Jack Nitzsche and Carrie Snodgress sitting at a table in the middle of the room. Jack signaled for me to come over. I took a deep breath and tried to walk a straight line and appear sober.

As I made my way to their table, my façade started to fall apart—I stumbled, and staggered, and bumped into people.

When I finally reached them, I slurred, "Hi, Jack. How are ya?"

"We're having a great time," Jack said. "The old man is killing them," he said, waving his hand toward the crowd.

"Yeah," I said, feeling a wave of nausea.

I prayed I wouldn't embarrass myself by getting sick right in front of them.

As Jack introduced me to Carrie, I felt flushed and covered in cold sweat. Why had I slugged down all those Whiskey Sours?

When I reached out to shake Carrie's hand, I tumbled on top of the table—sending their drinks flying into their laps.

"Oh, sorry, so sorry," I groaned, grabbing some napkins and patting their laps, creating an even bigger mess.

Moving back and forth between them made me even dizzier, and I fell face first onto their table.

"Are you okay, Pam? Would you like to sit down and join us?" Carrie asked in a soothing voice, trying to steady me by holding my arm.

I looked up and could see the concern in her eyes. She was so lovely and gracious. I could see why Jack was crazy about her.

I pushed myself off the side of the table and tried to straighten up and stand tall, but I had the impression that nothing about me was at right angles.

"Oh, no, but thank you," I slurred. "I've got to go."

I took a wobbly step, then turned and said, "I'm so sorry."

"No need to apologize," Carrie said in her honey voice.

"Are you sure you're going to be okay?" Jack asked.

"Yes, yes, I'm fine," I said, trying to make my lips curl into a friendly smile. "I'll see you later."

As I backed away, I staggered into another table. I prayed that I'd reach the ladies' room before totally demolishing the place.

During the trip to the restroom, I felt as if I were in an Olympic-sized stadium, complete with pitfalls and obstacles. Somehow I managed to get to my goal—just as the heaves hit me. As I retched, the whole experience felt like a sick joke—a bookend to Bukowski's pre-reading vomiting session.

After I finished, I splashed cold water on my face, behind my neck, and on my wrists. I needed to get home—and right away. The room was spinning and I felt as if I were going to pass out.

When I left the restroom, Bukowski was still reading. I found a payphone near the exit and dialed my mom.

"Mom, I'm at the Troubadour in West L.A. and I'm really sick. Can you come get me?" I moaned.

"Larry's here. I'll send him over," she said.

"I'm really, really sick . . . tell him to hurry!" I begged.

I told her to have him pick me up out front. She assured me he was on his way.

When I hung up, I found the doorman and asked him to tell Bukowski that I wasn't feeling well and had left with my brother.

While I waited, I sat on the curb with my head on my knees. Within fifteen minutes, Larry was there.

"You idiot," he said as he helped me into the car. "When are you going to learn your limit?"

If I hadn't felt so sick, I would have laughed at the irony. My big brother was telling me to learn my limit. But where alcohol and drugs were concerned, Larry didn't stop until he passed out.

"You owe me, Pam," he said.

During the ride to my mom's, I took a lot of deep breaths, trying to steady my stomach so I didn't throw up. If I vomited in Larry's car, he'd probably pull over and beat the hell out of me.

While he drove, Larry squeezed the steering wheel as if trying to strangle it—or maybe he was picturing his hands around my neck. It seemed that he intentionally ran over every pothole in the street—just to hear me groan and watch me hold my stomach.

As we entered the freeway on-ramp, Larry turned to me and asked, "Do you ever get the urge to drive off the side of the freeway? I do. Sometimes when I'm flying down the highway, I look down over the side and think all I have to do is turn this wheel just a few degrees to the left and it's all over. Don't you ever think about stuff like that?"

"No, Larry, can't say that I do," I groaned. Poor Larry, deep down, he was such a tortured soul.

As we rounded the corner to my mom's apartment, I wondered how Bukowski was doing and hoped he got my message. He would understand. Why not? He was always getting drunk and sick. Unlike Larry, he had some perspective on himself. He wasn't a hypocrite and wouldn't preach about things he couldn't control himself.

"Got any shit?" Larry asked as we were pulling in front of mom's apartment.

I reached into my purse and handed him the last of my uppers. I was ready to dry out again and the thought of them made me sicker.

Good ol' Mom answered the door, and I ran straight to the bathroom. When I emerged, she was in bed and there was a pillow and a blanket on the couch. It was time for another R&R. I wouldn't see Bukowski again for over a week and, of course, he would forgive me.

Buk reading at the Troubadour, his stash of beer at his side.
At one point he banters with an audience member, asking
him to "meet me in the parking lot."
(courtesy of Thomas Schmitt)

THIRTY

". . . get some sleep. And no more screams from the balcony."

$\mathcal{B}y$ September of 1976, my relationship with Bukowski was becoming more strained. Two-thirds of the year was gone and I had no job, no source of income, no pride. My dependency on Bukowski and diet pills was full-blown. He and my mother made it easy for me to continue down my self-destructive path, and I took full advantage. I wasn't sure if they conspired, but I'd soon learn that Bukowski was getting tired of it.

The sex kitten was becoming a wild tiger. The more he did for me, the more elusive my love became. He was losing control—and must have figured it was time for some tough love. I owed rent for August and it was now September. In the past, he would happily advance the rent money for me. I would always attempt to pay him back—at least most of it. This month would be different.

I was on my way to see Georgia and pick up some pills, when I stopped in to see Bukowski. It was a beautiful, warm afternoon. I made sure I was wearing his favorite white dress—the spaghetti-strapped one with the low-cut neckline and tight-fitting bodice that accented all my best features. I walked in without knocking. He was sitting at his typewriter pounding out more poems, I assumed.

"Hi, Hankie," I said in my sweetest, sexiest voice.

He kept typing without looking up from the machine.

"Whatcha writing?" I asked, approaching him from behind.

I put my hands on his shoulders as though I intended to give him a massage. He shrugged me off as if he had a fly on his back.

"Look, Cups, I'm a little busy right now," he said, sounding annoyed.

"Oh, I'm sorry," I said, knowing I had my work cut out for me. "Whatcha writing?" I asked again.

"Look, I don't mean to be rude," he said, attempting to shield the paper in the typewriter with his shoulder. "I'm in the middle of something here, and I promised John I'd get it done by today."

"Okay, I'll come back tonight."

As I approached the door, I decided to let him know what was on my mind.

"Umm, do you think you can loan me a couple hundred until I get my unemployment check? I'm almost two months behind on the rent as of this week. I promise I'll pay you back, one way or another," I said, batting my eyes at him.

"No, Kid, I can't help you this time. I'm broke," he said, turning back to the machine.

"Come on, Hank, just this time. I swear to you, I'll never ask again. Pleeease, I'll pay you back," I begged like a spoiled six-year-old.

"No, don't have it. Please, Cups, I've got to finish this," he said, turning back to his writing.

"Okey-dokey, see ya later, Hank," I said on my way out.

Shit! What was with him? Was I losing my redheaded powers? I decided to try again tomorrow. Maybe he was just a little stressed-out.

When I arrived at Georgia's, her door was wide open. She was sitting on her bed, painting her toes candy-apple red. Summer vacation was over, and our kids were in school. Except for the flies buzzing around, the place looked pretty good. Bill must have cleaned up before he left for work at the Art Mart. Georgia was much more coherent than the last time I'd seen her.

"Hey, look who's here," she said, "the dirty ol' man's muse. What's cookin', Erato?"

"Hey, George, how are ya?" I said.

"I'm livin' the dream, Baby," she said, while painting her big toe. Then she nodded toward the kitchen and said, "There's a couple beers in the fridge."

I walked back to the bed with the beer and handed her one.

"What's the matter with you?" she asked. "You look like you've got a load in your pants. You're not your usual bubbly, prom-queen self."

"It's Hank. I don't know what's got into him. He's acting strange lately," I said, pulling up a chair beside her.

"What are the symptoms?" she asked.

"He's acting like he's mad at me. I asked him for a loan and he refused. He seemed pretty definite about it."

"Jesus on a Ritz, he's a fucking man," she said. "Nothin's definite with a man, except that they're always hungry and horny. Sit on his fucking lap, coo in his ear and give his Wally a couple good strokes. Then make him a sandwich. He'll change his mind."

"Not sure that'll work. He's not himself—something's changed," I said. I snapped out of my daze and then got around to my reason for stopping by. "Got any uppers? My scrip isn't due to refill until next week."

She reached into her purse on the pillow next to her and pulled out a bottle. Into her palm, she poured about ten clear capsules filled with green and white beads.

"I could use a few bucks myself," she said. "I'll give you ten for twenty bucks."

I searched my purse for some cash. I found nine dollars in ones and a couple dollars in change. I handed the money to her, promising to make up the difference when I got my check. I put a pill in my mouth and chased it with a sip of Pabst Blue Ribbon.

"You know, the old fuck called me last week," she said. "I think he was looking for you."

"What did he say?" I asked.

"He wanted to know what I was doing. I told him I was polishing my fuckin' jewels and eating bonbons. What else would I be doing? He thought that was pretty funny. Then he asked if you were here. I told him I hadn't seen you in weeks. Maybe that's what the old bear is pissed about."

"Maybe," I said, not really believing it.

I changed the subject and asked about Bill and the kids. She assured me everything was copasetic. I finished my beer and took off to pick up Stacey.

The next day, I woke up with the rent money still on my mind. Again, I got dolled up—this time in a tight angel blouse and skin-tight, denim peddle-pushers, à la Ann-Margret. Instead of going barefoot, I decided I needed the big guns. I topped off the outfit with my sexiest stilettos. I checked my hair and makeup and went down to visit Bukowski.

It was early in the afternoon. This time I knocked first and then walked in. He was sitting in his favorite chair with a beer in one hand and a hard boiled egg in the other.

"Hi-ee, did you finish your project on time?" I asked.

"Yeah, I got it done," he said.

He took a bite of egg and a swig of beer, then said, "Listen, Red, I'm sorry about the money, but I can't help you anymore. I'm running short myself."

"I don't believe you, Hank. You don't love me anymore!" I said, stomping my right stiletto on the worn-out carpet.

I marched into the kitchen so he could get a good look at me from behind. I grabbed a beer, and then went back into the living room. Instead of sitting on his lap, I stood right in front of him. I took a sip of my beer and looked down at him.

"I don't know what's wrong with you," I said, "but you're not the same. Are you trying to punish me? You've always helped me in the past. Why are you treating me this way now?"

"Hey, settle down," he chuckled. "This is for your own good. Can't you see that? You need to learn how to handle your money better."

"You know I had to go visit my sister last month," I said. "I used the rent money to pay for the trip. She was in a car accident, for God's sake, and she needed me. Come on, just this time, pleeease. I swear I won't ask you ever again."

"Can't help you this time, Cups. Why don't you just move in with me?" he said looking into my eyes.

I finished my beer and slammed the empty bottle on the coffee table.

"You're not making any sense!" I yelled.

I stormed out the front door and went back to my place. I slammed my door, hoping he could hear it. I was seething. I took a diet pill and forgot about it. Later, I picked up Stacey, and we went to Mom's house for dinner.

When we got back to Carlton Way, it was evening. As we headed up the walkway to our place, Stacey automatically walked up to Bukowski's porch. His lights were on and we could hear him typing.

"No, Stace," I said, grabbing her hand. "I'm mad at him. I don't like him anymore. He's being mean to me. Let's go upstairs."

When we got to our place, I looked out the window and saw him sitting at his typewriter. There he was typing away as though nothing was wrong. The longer I watched, the angrier I became toward him and his nonchalant attitude. I was in a terrible place financially, and he didn't seem to care. To calm down, I opened a bottle of champagne and sat out on the balcony drinking it.

"What are you doing out here, Mommy?" Stacey asked.

"Just looking at the moon and the stars," I said, touching her cheek with my hand. "Sit down, Baby."

"I can see Hank, Mommy. See him?" she said pointing to his kitchen window.

"Yes, I do see him," I said, getting angrier by the minute.

After finishing a tall glass of champagne, I grabbed the cork and threw it at his kitchen window.

"Take that, you bastard!" I screamed from the balcony.

"Yeah, take that you busderd!" Stacey mimicked.

"You're a jerk, you know that?" I yelled.

"Yeah, you're a jerk, Hank," Stacey said, laughing.

"You're a Pioneer Chicken," I said, knowing this was getting ridiculous.

"Yeah, you're a, ah, a gizzard," Stacey yelled, enjoying this taunting game.

Bukowski got up, closed the window, then sat back in his chair and continued typing. As he went at the keys, he had a smile on his face and shook his head from side to side. Stacey and I continued to yell at him.

Someone in the courtyard bellowed, "Shut up!"

We were undeterred.

"Your mom's a hamburger and your dad's a dairy queen," I yelled, realizing I was getting sillier and sillier.

"Yeah, and your face looks like mash potat . . . "

Before Stacey could finish her scathing insult, two shots rang out.

What the hell was that, I thought. Then I realized someone had shot a gun. I immediately screamed for Stacey to duck and pushed her inside the house.

"Are you okay, Babe?" I asked, lying low on the floor.

"I'm okay, are you okay, Mommy?" she said with a sob.

"I think so," I said, giving myself the once-over.

I noticed a wet spot on my leg.

"Oh my God," I screamed. "I've been shot! Stay down, Stacey!" I yelled, crawling on the floor to the balcony like a wounded combat soldier on the front lines. "Hank, Hank, come here quick!"

"Hank," Stacey yelled, "come over here, Mommy's hurt! Hurry, hurry!"

Within seconds, Bukowski was in my living room. I was frantic.

"What's wrong, Baby?" he asked coolly.

"I think I've been shot. Look at my leg!"

I couldn't look at it out of fear. I turned my head as he knelt down to examine my legs. He seemed to be enjoying the activity.

"Jeezus, Red, you're fine. You just spilled something on your pants."

He began to laugh. When I had the nerve to look at my leg, I could see that it was only a dark grease spot made wet by spilled champagne. We were all relieved and had a good, nervous laugh.

"You can't make all that noise and not expect someone to want to kill ya," he said. "Not in East Hollywood, Kid."

By this time, Brad and Sam, the Whorehouse Man, showed up. Sam had his shotgun ready to fire at the enemy.

Before either of them could say anything, Bukowski explained what had happened.

"Everything's okay. She just overreacted a little."

Brad told us to keep it down, and then he and Sam left shaking their heads. Bukowski asked if we wanted to stay at his place for the night.

"No, thanks, we'll be fine," I said.

"All right, you two, get some sleep. And no more screams from the balcony."

THIRTY-ONE

I thought about how everyone in my life that I loved and trusted had betrayed me—and now Bukowski had joined the list.

The next day was Saturday. Stacey and I took another trip to Echo Park Lake, then stopped to see my mom. She knew the drill and kept Stacey for the night.

When I arrived back at Carlton Way, I stopped at Bukowski's apartment. He was lying on the bed in his underwear.

"I'll be right back," I said. "I want to get the rest of the champagne."

I walked up to my apartment and saw an eviction notice taped to my door. I couldn't believe it. I peeled it off and rushed back to Bukowski's place.

"Look at this," I said, waving the piece of paper. "It's an eviction notice!"

I expected him to become as indignant as I was. But he didn't even look at the notice. He just walked indifferently to the fridge in his T-shirt and boxer shorts to get another beer.

"Hey, that's what happens when you don't pay your bills," he said, then took a long pull on his beer.

"Hank, did you have anything to do with this?" I asked.

"Of course not, but what did you expect?"

"Goddamn it! I think this is your doing!" I said. "Let me have the landlord's phone number . . . I'm not that far behind in my rent."

"Don't have it, Kid."

"Yes, you do. You told me when I first moved in that you were friends with the guy."

"That was then, this is now. He moved out of town. I don't have his new phone number. Now I just send my payment to a PO Box. That's where Brad sends the checks too."

"YOU'RE LYING, HANK. I HATE YOU!"

I broke into tears and ran out the door. I didn't know what to do next. I walked over to Brad and Tina's place. Brad answered the door. He was distant and didn't invite me inside. He just stood there with his head between the screen and the doorjamb, as though I were a stranger asking to use his phone. When I asked about the eviction, he denied knowing anything and said he couldn't do anything about it. I asked him for the owner's phone number. He gave me a vacant look, shook his head, shrugged his shoulders, and said, "Don't have it," and closed the door.

I walked over to Sam's place. He seemed afraid to talk to me, too, shifting his eyes from side to side. He claimed he had no idea how to contact the owner and then suggested I talk to Brad.

I went back to my place and cried out of frustration. What was happening to me? I was losing control of everything and everybody. I felt like I was in a *Twilight Zone* episode. Everyone was treating me like an alien from another planet. Even my biggest fan, my protector, my hero, had betrayed me. I thought about how everyone in my life that I loved and trusted had betrayed me—and now Bukowski had joined the list. I was having one hell of a pity party. I finished my champagne and sobbed myself to sleep.

I woke up the next morning wondering about my next move. *Okay,* I thought, *just go. No use trying to fight this.* I was convinced Bukowski was in on the conspiracy. My sadness had turned to anger and determination. *I'll show him,* I thought. *I'll leave and never come back. He'll be sorry.* "They can all go to hell!" I mumbled.

I got dressed and headed to Mom's place. I told her what had happened and asked if I could move in with her. She wasn't happy about it, but agreed. I went back to Carlton Way and stuffed a few grocery bags full of our clothes. Bukowski saw me come in and rushed upstairs to see me.

"What are you doing, Cups?"

"What's it look like I'm doing?" I snapped.

"Well, let's see, you've got out your best luggage," he said, referring to the brown paper grocery bags. "Taking a trip to Europe? I know you've always wanted to see the Eiffel Tower."

"FUCK YOU, HANK! YOU KNOW DAMN WELL WHAT I'M DOING AND IT'S ALL YOUR FAULT!"

"Hey, no, Baby, you got it all wrong," he said. "I had nothing to do with that eviction notice. Really, you've got it all wrong."

He almost managed to persuade me.

"Listen," he added, "you've got to learn how to budget your money better."

"Oh, yeah?" I said. "Well, you've got to learn how to budget your life without me! Get out of my way you . . . sanctimonious asshole!"

I stuffed the bags under my arms and pushed him aside as I walked out the door.

"Hey, Red, don't go," he called after me, chuckling.

I ignored him and headed toward my car.

"Red, get back here. Come on, please. Let's talk about this. Maybe I can help," he yelled, following me to the car.

I threw the bags into the back of the Camaro and sped off.

I spent three tense, but sober days at my mother's. Bukowski called several times, but I refused to talk to him. Mom begged me to return his calls. She said she felt sorry for him because he "sounded so sad." She liked Bukowski and felt he was a good influence on me—*ha!* She said he'd told her that he had cleared out most of my belongings from the old apartment and was storing them at his place. *Let him keep them*, I thought.

On the third day, my brother stopped by with his coworker, Norbert. Norbert was a quiet, dark-haired Argentinean, with a used-car salesman mustache that made him look like the Johnny Carson character Art Fern. He was young, about my age, not very tall, but sweet and respectful. I had met him twice before—once when I picked up Larry from work and another time when Larry brought him by Carlton Way to visit Bukowski and me. Larry had mentioned that Norbert was quiet around me because he was in awe. He said he thought I was beautiful and would love to take me out.

Though Larry and Norbert were friends, Norbert was not into drugs at all. He was working at the Art Mart to pay his way through dental school at USC.

I wasn't physically attracted to Norbert, but was charmed by his star-struck gazes. How could I not like someone who found me irresistible?

In my mom's kitchen, we drank coffee and sat around the table talking about nothing in particular. Of course, the conversation eventually turned to drugs.

"Got any shit, Pam?" Larry asked.

"Nope—haven't had anything in a couple of days."

"Why don't you make an appointment with Feelgood? I'll take you and pay for it," Larry suggested.

"I'm feeling pretty good without the pills," I said. "Besides, I need to get a job and get the hell out of here. She's suffocating me," I said, referring to our mother.

"Come on, I just saw the good doctor, or I'd do it myself," Larry said.

"What about Georgia?"

"She doesn't have any good uppers anymore. I just got some bathtub shit from her and she charges too much."

I knew Larry wouldn't stop harping about the drugs until I agreed. I just didn't have the energy to fight with him.

"All right, I'll call the doctor tomorrow," I said.

With that, they said goodbye. A minute later, there was a knock on the door. It was Norbert. He'd left Larry waiting in the car.

"Ah, um, ah, do you think we could go out sometime?" he said, his voice cracking like a junior high school kid's.

He was so shy and nervous. I realized it must have taken an incredible amount of courage to come back and talk to me. How could I say no?

"Sure, I'd like that," I answered.

"How about tomorrow? Are you available?"

"I think so," I said.

"Great!" he said, a big smile lighting up his face. "Pick you up at seven?"

"That'll be fine."

The next day my mother told me she'd found a nice little studio apartment for me. It was located around the corner, about a block from her on Monon Street. She said she'd already paid the first and last month's rent.

Pamela Miller Wood

Even though I'd had no say in the matter, I was delighted. I couldn't wait to get out of her place, and she was just as eager for me to make my exit.

We walked over to the building, and I met my new landlord. He was an aging queen, which brought me some comfort—especially after my last experience with the dirty old landlord on Rodney Drive. He showed me the tiny place and told me I could move in at any time.

Later that evening, Norbert came by to pick me up for our dinner—and even brought flowers for my mother. In the car, he told me we were going to Yamashiro—an elegant restaurant in the Hollywood Hills.

It was an awkward date for many reasons. The restaurant was sophisticated and romantic. I wasn't dressed for it, nor did I have a lot of confidence in my big people manners. Which fork do I use first? What am I supposed to do with the water bowl that has the lemon in it—drink it?

The choice of restaurant also let me know that he was serious about me. This made me uncomfortable, because I had no romantic interest in him. We made small talk, with me doing most of it. After dinner, he suggested we walk around the beautiful Japanese garden court. The surroundings and view were breathtaking and extremely romantic. Too bad it was wasted on me.

I couldn't wait to get home, even if my mom was there. Norbert was just too normal and well-adjusted for me.

Finally, he pulled up to my place and walked me to the door. I thanked him for a lovely dinner and gave him a peck on the cheek. I quickly let myself inside, feeling relieved yet vaguely guilty. The guy was smitten with me. It was the last thing I wanted—and I wondered if it was somehow my fault. I hadn't done anything to lead him on, but here I was in another sticky situation.

The next day, my mom said she was leaving for a few days with a friend of hers. They were going to Las Vegas to see Tom Jones. When I told her I'd be in the new place by the time she got back from Vegas, I could see the relief on her face.

"Better take some extra panties to throw at Tom," I said, as she took off with her middle-aged girlfriend.

They left in a huge Oldsmobile. *Old ladies plus big car equals bad combo*, I thought, as I watched them drive away. I worried about the other drivers, not them.

190

That evening, Stacey and I were watching an episode of "The Bionic Woman" when the phone rang. I thought it might be my mom so I answered it.

"Hey, how are ya, Red?" It was Bukowski.

"I'm doing great, or at least I was up till a minute ago," I said.

"Come on, Baby, be nice," he said. "Don't be mean to me. Please, let's talk. I miss you, little Reds. Don't you miss me?"

Then he broke out into a chorus of "Mean to Me." "Mean to me—why must you be so mean to me?" he crooned.

He was obviously drunk.

"Hank, I'm busy right now, I've got to go," I said, yawning into the phone to show him I was bored.

"When are you going to come back?" he asked. "You left all your stuff in the apartment."

I knew he had most of it so I wasn't in a hurry to retrieve anything.

"Don't worry about it," I said. "It's my stuff, not yours."

"Well I am worried about it, and I'm worried about you," he said. "It's not the same around here without you, Kid."

"I'll get it when I'm ready," I said. "Don't worry about me."

I hung up. The phone immediately rang again.

"Please, Baby," he said. "Can't I come see you tonight? Just for a few minutes? I miss your face."

"No!" I said, hanging up.

I sat there waiting for another ring, but it didn't come.

I put Stacey to bed and settled down on the couch. I was watching the late evening news when I heard a loud bang on the front porch. I sat there petrified, my heart racing. Then there was a knock at the door.

"Cups, are you in there?" Bukowski's voice said. "Open the door. It's me, Blubber Boy."

I ran to the door and opened it a crack, leaving the chain lock on.

"Go home, Hank," I said in a loud whisper. "I'm in bed. You're going to wake up Stacey."

"Just let me in for a minute," he said. "Look, I brought your record player and Stacey's toys. At least open the door and let me bring them in. Someone might steal all this fine merchandise if I leave it out here."

"Good night, Hank," I said, almost shutting the door on his red, bulbous nose.

I turned out all the lights and watched him get back into his car. When he was out of sight, I pulled everything into the apartment. I waited for twenty minutes, and then figured it was safe to go to sleep.

It was around midnight when I heard more rustling out front. *Not again,* I thought. Sure enough, it was him. He had more boxes. This time, he didn't knock. He just left the stuff on the front porch and took off. I wondered how long he would keep this up. I worried the neighbors would complain and my mom would end up getting evicted. Twenty minutes later, the phone rang.

"Hey, Red, I've got a problem," Bukowski said. "I was trying to get your wicker chair into my car, and it got stuck. Half of it's sticking out of the door. It's jammed in there, and I can't get it out. And now the window's broken on the passenger's side. What am I going to do?"

"Call an ambulance," I said and hung up.

I was tired of this game. I took the phone off the hook and fell asleep on the couch.

THIRTY-TWO

Thank goodness, *I thought*. She doesn't have a chance
with the pragmatic Bukowski.

The next day, I called my brother Larry and asked if he and Norbert
could help me move on Saturday.

"Got any shit?" he asked.

"Yeah, I'll give it to you on Saturday," I promised, hoping to ensure his
help.

On Saturday morning, Larry and Norbert showed up early and began to
load all my possessions into their respective cars. They both owned Volks-
wagens, and I had the Camaro, which was now unofficially mine. I had
beaten the poor machine up so badly, Mom bought a used Dodge Dart and
gave me the keys to the embattled Red Bomber.

On the way to my new place, I spotted a garage sale. A vintage Royal
typewriter, similar to the one Bukowski had before his ex-girlfriend Linda
destroyed it, caught my eye. I pulled over to the curb. It was beautiful—
glossy black, with beveled keys, circa 1930—and appeared to be in perfect
condition. I jumped back in the car and met the boys at my new place. We
unloaded and went back to Mom's.

I called Bukowski.

"Hi, it's me," I said. "Thanks for dropping off my stuff."

"Hey, Baby, I was just sitting here thinking about you." He sounded
happy and relieved to finally hear from me. "How are ya, Kid?" he asked.

"I'm doing great," I said. "I'm moving into a new place today, and guess
what? I saw this beautiful vintage typewriter down the street at a garage sale.
I'd love to buy it, but I'm short. It's only twenty dollars and it's perfect."

"Want me to come over now?" he asked.

193

"That would be wonderful. I'll show you my new apartment."

"I'll be right there," he said.

We were loading the last of my belongings when I saw Bukowski driving toward me. I ran out into the middle of the street and lied down on the asphalt, right in front of his car. He stopped inches from me. I jumped up and greeted him on the driver's side window.

"Hi," I said, giving him a peck on the cheek. I ran over to the passenger's side and jumped in.

"Oh—such comedy, Red. I've really missed you," he said.

I was hoping he wouldn't get too sentimental. I just didn't know what to do with his feelings for me at this point. I was more conflicted than ever about the direction of our relationship. I pointed the way to the garage sale.

"There it is!" I said, as he pulled over to the curb. We got out and walked toward the typewriter. "Isn't it a beauty?"

"How much?" he asked the lady in charge.

"Twenty dollars," she said.

"We'll take it!" I whooped.

Bukowski put it in the car, and we drove to my new apartment—a one-room walkup in a nice neighborhood in Silver Lake. The apartment wasn't much—just one room, a small bath with a tub, and a kitchenette—but the architecture of the building was lovely. It was an old Tudor, built around the turn of the century when people were a lot smaller. Bukowski carried the typewriter upstairs and set it on the coffee table. To me, the machine was like a sparkling jewel.

"Isn't it gorgeous?" I asked.

"Yeah, it's real cute," he said. "What are you going to do with it?"

"Write the great American novel," I said.

"Okay, you do that," he said.

Just then, Larry and Norbert arrived with the rest of my stuff.

"I've got to go," Bukowski said. "Will you walk me to my car?"

We squeezed down the narrow steps to the street. As we approached his car, he pulled me to him.

"You know, Kid, you can always come live with me," he said, sounding like Humphrey Bogart.

"It's a little late for that," I said, "and, besides—what about Stacey?"

"We can find a bigger place," he said. "I'm starting to make some dough now. I've got ten thousand dollars in my savings account. I've arrived, Baby. Don't you know that? I'm not some greasy, little pig-shit beanbag with a penciled-in moustache," he said, referring to Norbert.

"I've got too much to do right now. Let me think about it, Hank," I said, moving away from his tight grip.

"Okay, you do that. Call me sometime. I'll give you some tips on how to write that epic novel."

He let go and got in his car.

"I still love ya, Kid," he said, and then drove away.

Was that his scheme all along? Did he think by not helping me with the rent I would move in with him? And how much of a role did he play in my getting evicted? Whatever the original motivation, his plan had backfired. I wasn't certain I could trust him anymore.

I spent the following week getting settled. After a while, the unpacking began to make me stir crazy. I decided to get out for a while and drove over to Carlton Way to surprise Bukowski.

As I approached the porch, his front door swung open. Bukowski stood aside and two attractive women walked out the door. He was saying goodbye to them when he spotted me on the walkway.

The women appeared to be in their late twenties or early thirties. They were both very pretty in a wholesome, debutante sort of way. One was a brunette, the other a blonde. They looked too refined and well-manicured to be interested in Bukowski, and vice-versa. They were dressed simply, yet tastefully. They reminded me of the privileged girls I went to school with. The ones that wore the fancy underpants with a different day of the week embroidered on them; the ones that had their own bedroom complete with a princess-style canopy bed, covered with a pink-laced bedspread with plush, stuffed animals lounging on the pillows.

I felt a twinge of jealousy, which was very uncharacteristic of me. I said hello, as they brushed past, ignoring me.

I was still wondering about the two women when I heard Bukowski say, "Hey, Red, come on in."

He held the door open for me. I looked around, stunned. The apartment sparkled and smelled like Pine-Sol.

"Who were those women, your new cleaning ladies? And where'd you find them—Sorority Sisters maid service?"

"No, just a couple of fans," he said with a chuckle.

"They don't look like your usual fans," I said.

"They love me, Baby," he bragged. "They clean my house. They bring me food and good wine. They think I'm some kind of god creature."

"How nice for you," I said, unimpressed. "Got a beer?"

"How 'bout a glass of wine, instead?"

We drank out of clean glasses, and talked and talked, and drank some more.

Now that I was living around the corner from my mom, Stacey spent a lot more time with her—and I had more freedom to stay out late. I decided to spend the night with him.

We had a very romantic evening and the sex was good and tender. I made sure it was better than usual. I was still supremely confident that he was in love with me, but seeing him with those women made me feel vulnerable.

I realized I could lose him to another woman, but still not certain how I wanted to proceed. I knew I didn't want to give him up completely, but knowing how he felt about me, just friends was not an option. I also knew I wasn't being completely fair to him, but I was confused. The situation was beginning to give me a headache. It was easier not to think about it.

I got up early the next morning to take Stacey to school. Bukowski was still in bed. Before leaving, I washed our glasses from the night before then kissed him goodbye on the cheek.

For the next month, Bukowski would come by my place or I'd visit him. I was now seeing Norbert occasionally and assumed Bukowski was seeing other women too. Norbert lived two blocks from Stacey's elementary school, and I would sometimes stop by after I dropped her off in the morning to romp with him. He was working part-time and going to school, so his schedule was conducive to my whims.

Despite all the romance in my life, the irony was that I was becoming less interested in men. Having a man in love with you was a full-time job—and having two men vying for your attention was downright exhausting. I knew something had to give soon.

It was now November. I stopped by Bukowski's place again, unannounced. I knocked on the door, and he greeted me with a big hug and kiss. I walked in and was hit, again, by the smell of Pine-Sol. The place was spotless. I knew those women had returned.

"Jeez, Hank," I said. "What's got into you? How come it's so clean around here? It's kind of creepy. Did your maids come by again?"

"Her name is Linda and she's not my maid."

"Is that the same one that cleaned this palace last time?"

"Yes, she's one of them."

"Which one is she?" I asked. "The blonde or the brunette?"

"The blonde," he said, "and she's a very nice person. She owns a health food store and wants to take care of me, which is more than I can say for you."

"Don't I take care of you?" I said, snuggling up close to him.

"Yeah, Baby, but not in the same way."

I went to use the bathroom and it, too, was spotless. No whiskers or toothpaste stuck to the sink. The trash wasn't overflowing. The toilet bowl was dazzling.

I walked into the living room and said, "You better watch out for this one, Hank. She's cleaned your thunder bowl. She wants you bad!"

"There are a lot of good women that want me, Baby. Why don't you?"

"I love you, Hank," I said, "but not enough to clean your commode. Now that's true love!"

I was feeling more conflicted than ever. This was at least the blonde's second visit. She was obviously serious about him. And she was smart—she had to be. She knew that Bukowski was looking for somebody to take care of him—and she was playing on his need for a mother. She was also pretty and owned her own business—or, at least, had a job. But worst of all, he was defending her! This would be a challenge.

While Bukowski was sitting in his striped chair in the living room, I walked into the kitchen. I grabbed a beer from the fridge and sat down at his typewriter. I began to type a poem titled "The Housework Whore." As I typed, I said each line out loud in an obnoxious, singsong manner:

The housework whore comes to my door,
    carrying her mop and pail.
She scrubs my brown wall, with a sponge and Pine-Sol,
    while I drink my bottle of ale.

> She dusts my shed, and makes my bed,
>> and cooks for me with honey.
> What could she want, with this dirty haunt,
>> she never asks for money?
> Some might think, her problem is drink,
>> but I state she's just nice.
> Others say, there will come a day,
>> when I will pay the price.

I pulled the paper from the machine and walked over to Bukowski.

"Here's a poem for you and your new friend," I said childishly, flapping the paper in his face then dropping it in his lap. "See, I'm a poet too."

I sat down on the sofa and put my feet on the coffee table. I was marking my territory and feeling possessive.

"So tell me more about your new friend," I said.

I was surprised that he was so willing to discuss her. He said she was a very nice woman he'd met at his last poetry reading. He assured me she was just a friend, though I wasn't convinced. He then went on to tell me that she was a follower of the Meher Baba.

"The who?" I asked.

"She likes them, too," he said.

"Who?" I asked.

"That rock group, the Who," he said. "The head guy is also into Meher Baba."

Bukowski went on to tell me about the Baba. He was a spiritual leader from the Middle East. He had died a few years earlier and had many ardent followers. Linda was one of them. The man didn't speak and frequently didn't eat. His followers believed that he was ordained with divine powers and the best part was that he insisted they refrain from sex, because it interfered with your spiritual connection.

Thank goodness, I thought. *She doesn't have a chance with the pragmatic Bukowski.* A recovering Catholic, he was suspicious of people who followed organized religions or idolized spiritual leaders. Though he and I never actually had a theological debate, I knew enough about his views on the subject to know that he was cynical about anyone who felt the need to belong to a religious order of any kind. Though not devoid of spirituality,

I would label him more of an agnostic than atheist. But no sex—forget about it! I was home free, or so I thought.

Just to be on the safe side, I made sure he was sated in the naughty ways of the flesh before I left.

"I still love you, little Reds," he said, as I was getting dressed to leave.

"We all have our cross to bear," I said, as I kissed him goodbye on the forehead.

THIRTY-THREE

When we got into the car Georgia turned to me and said, "Organic? What the fuck's happening to him?"

$\mathcal{B}y$ December 1976, three months had passed since I'd left Carlton Way. Bukowski and I still spoke on the phone and saw each other, but with less frequency. Though I never asked, I assumed he was spending time with his new friend Linda. I was still seeing Norbert now and then and Bukowski was aware of it.

I was content with the situation the way it was. Though I still had affection for Bukowski, it was liberating to be out from under his watchful eye. Since he had also stopped pressuring me to move in with him, I had the best of both worlds.

One afternoon, Bukowski stopped by my studio apartment for a visit. He brought a couple of six-packs, and I opened up a big bag of potato chips. We sat on my couch drinking our beer and munching on chips. Our conversation was light and relaxed. There was less tension between us, and we talked like a couple of old friends.

By now, he'd resigned himself to brief visits, like this, without the fringe benefits of romance. His melancholia over our separation seemed to be subsiding. We had not been intimate in over a month—and he'd quit pressuring me in that department too. Our relationship had settled into a much more comfortable zone. There was a calm air of respect between us.

We talked for about an hour, catching up on the last couple of weeks. He told me about his recent readings in Santa Cruz and San Francisco. He gloated about the women who fawned all over him after his performances. He said one young woman charged the stage while he was reading, screaming, "I love you, Bukowski! I want to have your baby!" Security had to drag her away. I was never sure how much was braggadocio and how much was true, but I always found these anecdotes amusing—often to his dismay.

He also went on to tell me that he was writing a lot of poetry and was contemplating another novel. I asked what the book would be about. He said he wasn't sure, but it was time for another one. It didn't surprise me that he was reluctant to say much about his work in progress. He never liked to talk about a piece of writing until it was finished. I suspected he didn't want to drain off its energy, or maybe he was a little superstitious.

I told him about my part as an extra in the John Cassavetes movie _Opening Night_ and how I thought Peter Falk had been flirting with me. He asked if I'd written anything on my new typewriter. I showed him the beginning of a short story about a mental patient in an asylum. The patient was delusional and thought he was a psychiatrist. He would counsel the other inmates, often with good results. It was a bunch of rambling crap, but Bukowski was kind to me.

"Not bad, Kid. You've got some glitter there. You just need to focus. Slow down and focus. You're just a little . . . fragmented. Your thought process—your life—too fragmented."

I appreciated his advice and support, I think.

He then asked if I would mind turning on the television. He said the Los Angeles Rams were in the playoffs, and he wanted to see the game.

While Bukowski preferred boxing and the horses, he did enjoy watching football and baseball games whenever they were televised. I, on the other hand, had no interest in either, but happily complied and turned on the game.

After about an hour of pretending to care about the game, I began to get restless. Bukowski was engrossed in the game. He was getting very excited. The Rams were playing the Dallas Cowboys for a spot in the Super Bowl.

"NOT ANOTHER BLOCKED PUNT! JEEZUS! YOU PUSSIES!" he yelled at the television.

I'd never seen him this worked up over a sporting event—not even at the racetrack.

I guess my timing was bad, but I was getting bored and thought it was time for some musical entertainment. I began to sing the "Mr. Touchdown" song.

"You gotta be a football hero
  to get along with the beautiful girls . . .
  you gotta be a touchdown getter, you bet!
  If you wanna get a baby to pet . . .
  you gotta be a football hero to
  get along with the beautiful giiirrls!"

I sang to him while playfully mussing up his hair. He turned and gave me the most mysterious stare, as though he were studying my face for suspicious looking moles.

Then he said in a very serious tone, "Nothing is sacred to you, is it, Red? You don't take anything seriously, do you?"

The intense concern in his voice caught me off-guard.

"Jeez, Hank, it's only a game, but to answer your question . . . no."

"No . . . you don't, do you?" he whispered, locking eyes with mine long enough to make me uncomfortable. Being the absurdist that I thought he was, I figured he would appreciate my answer. His reaction puzzled me.

Within a few minutes of our eerie exchange, Bukowski decided it was time to go.

"But the game's not over yet."

"That's okay—I'll read about it in the paper tomorrow. I've got to finish some poems for John. I promised to mail them tomorrow. See ya later, Kid."

I walked him to the door, and as he was descending the stairs, I yelled, "What are you doing for Christmas? You're welcome to stop by Mom's. It's next Saturday, can you believe it?"

"Thanks, I'll call ya later," he said without committing.

On Christmas Eve, Bukowski called to say he didn't feel like joining in the festivities with the Miller clan. No surprise there. Holidays always made him uncomfortable. We both hated them.

The next day, I took Stacey to visit her girlfriend Nina. Nina's mother, Anna, was also a single parent with one daughter, and we all got along well. We exchanged hugs and gifts. Stacey brought her new sewing machine to show Nina. Anna and I enjoyed a glass of red wine and had a nice chat. But I was in a post-holiday funk and didn't feel like staying long. The kids were having a good time playing with their toys, and Anna suggested Stacey stay for dinner. I kissed them all goodbye and left.

I was feeling restless and lonely, so I decided to pay Bukowski a visit. But first I stopped by Georgia's to see how she was doing. I hadn't seen her in months. My relationship with Georgia was winding down. She was becoming a full-blown junkie.

Since I was no angel myself, I was in no position to counsel anyone about addiction. Still, it was difficult to watch Georgia's downward spiral, especially considering her children.

I stopped at Thrifty Drugs and bought a cheap bottle of champagne for Bill and Georgia and giant Hershey bars for the kids. It was around two in the afternoon when I arrived at her place. The girls greeted me at the door still in their pajamas. They were excited about showing me their new toys. Stephanie, the seven-year-old, had a big baby doll, almost as big as she was. Maureen, who was now eleven, beamed as she showed me her new bike. I handed them the candy bars and gave each girl a hug and kiss. They seemed like happy, normal kids, and I was pleased they'd had a nice Christmas—complete with a little Christmas tree.

"Is your mommy home?" I asked.

Georgia and Bill were still in bed. They slept in an alcove between the living room and the kitchen. It had no door and was actually the dining room. The lack of privacy didn't seem to concern them. This was their command center, and you could sit in the living room and carry on a conversation with them while they sat half naked in bed. Georgia seemed happy to see me.

"Hey, if it isn't 'Kitten with a whip.' How are ya? Where you been hiding out?"

She knew I was no longer living on Carlton Way, because I'd talked to her shortly after I moved out.

"Everything is shiny good. Just getting settled into my new digs around the corner from my mom in Silver Lake," I answered.

"Are you working?" she asked.

"No, and I'm not really looking. I'll wait till after the New Year. Either that or apply for an extension with Unemployment."

"Now you're thinking straight," she said.

Georgia was a master at manipulating the system. She knew every trick when it came to government handouts.

"So what brings you to the urban jungle?" she asked.

"I haven't seen you in a while and just wanted to check in and wish you all a Merry Christmas," I said, handing her the champagne.

"Hey, thanks. You want a glass?" she asked.

"Sure," I said, "why not?"

I was feeling a bit depressed and wasn't certain why—except that I was sober and realized my life was unraveling like a cheap sweater. In the past when I'd dry out, once my batteries were recharged the first thing on my agenda was to find the nearest party. This time felt different—and it was unsettling.

"Billy, would you be a good boy and get us some glasses?" Georgia asked.

Bill hopped out of bed and headed for the kitchen. I was relieved that he was wearing boxer shorts. Of the pair, Bill had the most traditional values, but they both could be very uninhibited, depending on the level of chemicals in their system.

While Bill was in the kitchen, Georgia told me she'd scored some good pharmaceutical uppers.

"I've got some Black Beauties. They're the real deal. Want a couple?"

"Is Santa Claus a socialist?"

She handed me two and wished me Merry Christmas. Bill came back with the glasses. Georgia popped the cork, and I put one of the Beauties in my mouth and washed it down with a sip of champagne.

"Merry fuckin' Christmas," Georgia said, holding up her glass to clink with mine and Bill's.

"Merry fuckin' Christmas and Happy fuckin' New Year!" we all sang.

When the bottle was finished, I told them that I was going to visit Bukowski.

"Hey, I wanna go. I haven't seen the old reprobate in a long time," Georgia said.

It took her a while, but she finally entered the living room fully dressed. She was wearing a pair of low-cut bell-bottom jeans and a tight red sweater that bared her midriff. She topped it off with a green feather boa. She was wearing long, dangly earrings and her signature platforms, which seem to add six inches to her height. For someone who was always stoned, I never understood how she managed to navigate as well as she did on those stilts.

"Well, what do think?" she asked, modeling her outfit for us. "Do I look festive enough for the old bard?"

"You look like a million bucks!" I said.

"Yeah, all green and wrinkly," Bill teased.

"Oh hush, Bill," I said. "You look great. Like a sexy Christmas elf. Let's go."

On our way to Bukowski's, we stopped and bought a six-pack of Pabst Blue Ribbon. It was cheap and, as usual, I was broke. It was late afternoon when we arrived.

Bukowski opened the door and said, "Well, whattaya know? If it isn't the decadent duo. Come on in girls."

He seemed in good spirits. We wished him Merry Christmas and I handed him the beer. I pulled out one for me and handed one to Georgia.

Bukowski put the rest in the refrigerator and came back with a glass of white wine. We parked ourselves on his couch and he settled into his striped throne.

"How ya doing, George? I haven't seen you since our photo shoot."

"Yeah, that was a trip," Georgia said. "Did you ever get the prints?"

"No, I don't give a rat's ass about that shit," Bukowski said. "I don't even remember what they were for. They're probably hanging in the post office," he said.

Georgia and Hank
(© Joan Gannij)

He turned to me and said, "Too bad you weren't here, Red. George and I were hanging out the ham that day. We had some laughs, didn't we, Baby?"

"Yeah, good times, man," Georgia told him. "Christ, Hank, I was so fucked up when I left that day, I don't know how I got home. I think they were shooting for some kind of refrigerator book or something off the wall like that."

"Sorry I missed it," I said, smiling wryly.

I surveyed his place and noticed that it was fairly clean and neat. I figured his new lady friend must have spent time with him recently.

"How was your Christmas, Hank?" I asked.

"I'm glad it's over. Shiiit, I hate these fuckin' holidays. They're nothin' but a damn ploy to bankrupt our wallets and our soul . . . Motherfucks."

Georgia and I made noises in agreement.

Then he asked, "You girls hungry? I've got some turkey in the ice box."

Though we were both buzzed on diet pills, I don't think either of us had eaten all day. It was now late in the afternoon and food sounded good.

"Where'd you get the turkey, Hank?" I asked, following Georgia into the kitchen.

"One of my many admirers cooked it for me."

I was carving up the bird when I heard his answer. It sent a small pang of jealousy through me, but I left it at that. Georgia looked at me to gauge my reaction. I shrugged, as if to say "beats me" and continued to carve.

"Want some, Hank?" I yelled from the kitchen.

"No thanks."

We walked back to the living room and sat on the couch to enjoy our dinner.

I took a bite and said, "Jeez, this is really bland."

I went to the kitchen to get the salt and pepper shakers. While I did find the turkey a little flat, I think, subconsciously, I also wanted to discount the chef's cooking skills.

"Yeah, it is kind of tasteless," Georgia said. "Pass the salt."

"It's organic," Bukowski said.

"Organic?" I said. "What organ did it come from? Or is that some kind of Japanese style of cooking?" I asked, as I bumped Georgia's shoulder with mine.

We both laughed. Bukowski looked to the ceiling and sighed.

We finished our turkey and had one more beer, leaving him with two. Bukowski was in a good mood, but more subdued than usual. Soon it was time to pick up Stacey, so we thanked him for dinner and said our goodbyes.

"Where you two heading now?" he asked.

"We have a dozen hairless dancing boys waiting patiently for us at the Time Motel," Georgia said.

When we got into the car Georgia turned to me and said, "Organic? What the fuck's happening to him?"

"Maybe he's turning into a hippie," I said.

THIRTY-FOUR

"I don't care about your past," he said. "Only today and tomorrow matter."

After finding the turkey in Bukowski's refrigerator, it confirmed my suspicion that he wasn't spending all his time pining over me—and I was surprised at my reaction to that revelation. I felt less guilty and somewhat relieved about what was now a lopsided relationship, with him doing most of the heavy lifting.

Moving out of Carlton Way had changed things. Maybe I was still stinging over Bukowski not helping me with the rent—which I still perceived as a betrayal. But, whatever it was, I was beginning to lose interest. Let him screw anybody he wants, I told myself—confident that he would always be there if I decided to make another go of it.

Getting some distance from Bukowski gave me some perspective on our relationship—and my life in general. Though, at the time, I wasn't aware that's what was happening, but I knew something inside was changing. Yet I still lacked the insight and courage for self-analysis and continued my daily pursuit of chemicals to keep me as far away from both as possible.

I had seen Bukowski and spoken with him a couple of times in the days following the turkey discovery, but I don't recall any discussions between us about spending New Year's Eve together. I do remember where I was at midnight, January 1, 1977. I was celebrating with Norbert at my old place of employment, The Alpine Inn in Hollywood. I hadn't left on bad terms with the owners, Ted and Rita, but I'm not sure why I chose to spend my New Year's Eve there. Maybe I thought I could get my old job back.

The place was packed and "Auld Lang Syne" blared from the jukebox. The crowd swayed to and fro with beer steins raised high, sloshing foam on one and all.

"'Should old acquaintance be forgot and never brought to mind? Should old acquaintance be forgot and days of Auld Lang Syne?'"

It was an appropriate song for me to be singing that night.

I didn't get my old job back, but I did manage to get a six-month extension on my unemployment. I was seeing less of Bukowski and more of Norbert. Though I still had very little interest in him, he treated me like a queen. But, as with Bukowski, my relationship with Norbert was one-sided. I'd see him only when the mood struck and rarely called before I stopped by to visit. I also began seeing Bob, my old boyfriend, the screenwriter. He was no longer romantically involved with Cindy Williams, and we remained good friends. I now had three patient men who were more than happy to subsidize my destructive lifestyle. And, of course, there was always Georgia.

The first few months of 1977 were wasted flitting from one unproductive situation to another. I was like a dog chasing her tail. And though I wasn't working, it seemed I was spending less time with my daughter. Though I was using diet pills and alcohol almost every day, something new was stirring inside. I was beginning to feel emotions that were uncomfortable and foreign. A conscience was trying to emerge, and no matter what I ingested, it was becoming harder and harder to stuff down. I was becoming disgusted with myself and everyone around me.

Georgia was now completely hooked on heroin. She had lost her magnificent ability to communicate. When I stopped by, she was always in bed—stoned and incoherent. She was into self-mutilation and had sores and cuts all over her body. She had track marks on her arms, ankles, and neck. When I could decipher her ramblings, I realized she was hallucinating—often involving conversations with the devil. She complained about Satan following her from room to room—mocking her and threatening violence.

At Georgia's place, a frightening assortment of unsavory characters had replaced the creative, bohemian, avant-garde element that used to fill her home. This new crop was the lowest of the low—they looked like hard-core criminals. Poor Georgia, she clearly had a death wish and was well on her way to fulfilling it.

With the exception of Norbert, it seemed that all the people around me were destroying themselves with drugs or alcohol—usually both. My brother was spending more time doing drugs with Georgia and her crowd. Bob, who had been Hollywood's fair-haired boy just a year before, was now losing writing jobs because of his drinking problem. Even Bukowski was an alcoholic—a high-functioning one, but still an alcoholic, who needed to start everyday with a drink and end it the same way.

Norbert's sobriety is no doubt why I began to spend more time with him. Though I still had no real romantic interest in him and found him a little dull compared to my previous men, he provided some semblance of order and normalcy in my life. He was stable and working hard to make something of his life. While Norbert had a positive attitude and hope for the future, I had neither. He was studying to become a dentist, while I was still badly in need of one.

One morning in May of 1977, I woke up in Norbert's bed, naked with a raging hangover. I looked at the clock on the nightstand, and it read 1:30. If it weren't for the bright sun streaming through the window, I would not have known if it were a.m. or p.m. I was disoriented and couldn't remember anything from the night before. I crawled out of bed with my head in my hands and stumbled to the bathroom.

"Norbert," I managed to squeeze from my voice box, "are you here?"

I waited but heard no response. Norbert was gone, and I was alone.

I shuffled to the bathroom and let out a scream. Someone had broken into the apartment and was standing in the bathroom—staring at me with a hideous face. But then I realized I wasn't looking at an intruder—I was looking at myself in the mirror.

I didn't recognize what I saw. My face and eyes were swollen to the point of distortion. I looked like a blowfish monster. Even my hair, my crowning glory, was dull, dry, and frizzy—"clowning" glory was more like it. I looked like Bozo with a thyroid condition.

I ran a wet washcloth over my face and brushed my teeth with Norbert's toothbrush. I found my underwear on the bedroom floor and slipped them on. Then I made my way to the living room and sat on the couch. I felt nauseated and fragile.

It was a weekday, and I hadn't shown up to take Stacey to school in the morning. Not knowing where to find me, my mother probably dropped off Stacey on her way to work—making them both late.

For a while now, Stacey had stayed with my mom during the week. I'd take her to school in the morning, then pick her up at three and spend the afternoon with her. We'd have dinner together, and I'd either spend the night on Mom's couch or go back to my place to sleep—usually the latter, because I spent most of my nights out carousing. Despite my drug use, I was able to hold up my part of this arrangement.

I knew today probably wasn't the first time I'd left Mom and Stacey hanging, but it was the first time I'd become upset about it. Now it was almost time to pick her up from school. I was suddenly overcome with grief—consumed with guilt and sorrow.

It felt as if a bolt of lightning had come crashing through the ceiling. I was struck with blinding insight and self-awareness. It was as though I had been keeping a scandalous secret from myself. Like the woman who answers a knock at her door and there stands the child she gave away at birth twenty years ago. My reality had finally caught up with me.

I began to confront myself—asking questions out loud.

"What am I doing here? Why am I sitting here in my underwear in the apartment of some guy I don't really like? Why am I living this way? Why am I destroying myself? Why am I neglecting everyone I love and care about? What has happened to me?"

It was painful and overwhelming. I needed answers, and they weren't coming. Though I have always prided myself on being strong and independent, I knew I couldn't handle this challenge on my own. I needed help—professional help.

I looked around Norbert's apartment for a phone book. I found the Yellow Pages in his kitchen drawer and flipped through it until I came to "mental health." Money, or rather my lack of it, was an issue, so anyone with an M.D. or Ph.D. after his or her name was out of the question.

I continued to run my finger down the page and then I found it—"Sunrise Counseling Center, a Non-profit Organization." The name sounded friendly and cheerful, and the place was located nearby at Sunset and Alvarado.

I picked up the phone and dialed the number. A man with a gentle, soothing voice answered.

"Sunrise Counseling, this is John."

I hesitated, not knowing where to begin.

I just blurted it out, "Hi, my name is Pam and I really need help."

"Okay, what do you feel you need help with, Pam?"

"I'm not sure, but I know I need it."

"Okay, what makes you so sure you need it?"

"Well, because I'm sitting here half-naked, alone and hung-over in some guy's house that I don't really like, while my seven-year-old daughter wonders where the hell I am!"

"Okay, now slow down a little. Where is this house? Are you nearby?"

"I'm in Los Feliz, near Hillhurst and Franklin."

"Okay, that's fairly close. I'm at Sunset and Alvarado. Do you have a car?"

"Yes."

"Can you come see me now?"

"No, I have to pick up my daughter from school."

"You can bring her with you. We have a child care facility."

"No, I can't do that."

"Do you want me to come to you?"

"No. Listen, I have to go."

He must have thought he was dealing with a suicide case, because his gentle, measured tone became louder and more adamant.

"NO! PLEASE DON'T HANG UP!"

I was so taken aback with his genuine concern and insistence that I said, "Okay, I won't," as though he were the one who needed help.

His voice mellowed again, and he asked if I could come by the following morning at eleven. I was starting to get caller's remorse and almost hung up, but instead agreed to meet him the next day just to get him off the phone.

I hung up, slipped on my dress, slid my feet into my sandals, and took off to pick up Stacey.

The next day, I dropped Stacey off at school at 8:30 and went back to my place to catch up on some sleep. Lying in bed, I thought about what to do with the rest of the day. I had no intention of keeping my appointment with John at Sunrise Counseling. *I'll be okay*, I thought. The previous day, I'd had a tremendous hangover and had overreacted when I'd made that call. *I'll go see Bukowski today*, I thought. *He'll make me feel better.*

I slept for about an hour then showered and dressed. I headed south on Hyperion toward Sunset. The DJ came on the radio announcing the time. It was 10:50 a.m. when I arrived at Sunset Blvd. I decided it was too early to barge in on Bukowski, so instead of turning right, I turned left. I figured that maybe I'd drive by this Sunrise place and at least see what it looked like.

The address turned out to be a large, old, dilapidated, white, two-story home. The place had a faded beauty and had probably been a showplace over fifty years ago—obviously built for someone with money and power.

In the 1920s, this neighborhood had been filled with beautiful homes occupied by the rich and famous, but now it was a rundown commercial area crammed with Burrito Kings, auto repair shops, and mini-marts. In the middle of it all, this once regal home, after years of neglect, tried to retain its dignity, even though it had been relegated to a free clinic. There was a big banner hanging above the front door that read "Sunrise Counseling Center," with a hand-painted bright yellow sun giving it a little pizzazz.

I thought the place looked kind of funky. I drove around the block a couple of times debating whether or not to go in.

"Oh, what the hell—you're here. What do you have to lose?" I said out loud.

I parked at the curb marked "loading only" and tentatively walked up the steps to the front door. The sign on the front door read "Please ring the bell before entering." It was a rough neighborhood, so the door was kept locked during business hours.

I reluctantly pressed the buzzer. Then the most gorgeous male specimen I had ever seen came to greet me at the door. He was young, tan, and blonde, with beautiful clear blue eyes that sparkled like sapphires. He also had a beard that made him look spiritual. He reminded me of the actor Jeffrey Hunter when he portrayed Jesus in *King of Kings*. Though he was wearing a crisp, white dress shirt with rolled-up sleeves, blue jeans, and Birkenstock sandals, I pictured him in a long, white robe with a gold, braided rope tied around his waist—with cherubs dancing around his head. There was something beatific about him.

"Hi, please come in," he said smiling, flashing his perfect white teeth.

He even sounded the way I expected Jesus to sound—calm and reassuring. I stood there speechless, in awe of his beauty.

I snapped out of my trance and said, "Oh, thank you. I'm here to see John."

"I'm John. Are you Pam?" he asked.

"Yes, yes, I am," I said, still staring at those magnificent eyes.

John, 1976
(courtesy of John Elliot)

He gently put his hand on my shoulder and guided me to one of the many small rooms in the house. The tiny office was unadorned—painted stark white, with nothing more than an old desk and two mismatched chairs inside.

At first, we made mostly small talk, and then he began to ask some penetrating questions about why I'd called the day before.

"Don't you want to know about my childhood traumas first?" I asked in my best wisecracking tone.

"I don't care about your past," he said. "Only today and tomorrow matter."

That was the beginning of our first counseling session. Despite his distracting good looks, I liked talking to him and began to see him at least once a week. Even so, I continued drinking and pill popping—but with less frequency—and would sometimes show up to my appointments while under the influence. He was tolerant and patient with me.

My unemployment compensation was about to end, so I did the last thing I wanted to do—I asked my mom if I could move in with her. The timing was perfect because she had saved enough money to buy a house. It was a small two bedroom, one bath in Glendale on a street named The Midway, across from the community college. By the end of June, the three of us had settled in to our new place.

When July rolled around, I realized I hadn't seen Bukowski for over a month. I was avoiding him. I guess I didn't want him to know about my counseling sessions—afraid that he might discourage or make fun of me.

I continued to see John at Sunrise Counseling. Our objective was to help me get off the pills and get back to work. One day, he suggested I attend one of his group therapy sessions. At first, I was dead-set against it. I still wasn't entirely comfortable with seeing a psychologist on a one-on-one basis, so sitting in a room with a group of neurotics didn't appeal to me in the least. I finally agreed to one session on the following Tuesday evening.

I showed up to the meeting feeling a bit arrogant and reserved—skeptical that this was for me. Eight of us sat on the floor in a circle. It was a relatively young group, and I was surprised at the diversity. There was an attractive gay man, about thirty-five—an executive with a large corporation who was afraid his sexuality would be discovered and he'd lose his job. Besides me, there were two other women. One was a recovering alcoholic with an abusive husband who still drank. The other was a junkie, still addicted and turning tricks, who desperately wanted to quit both.

There was a young man about my age who still lived with his parents. He said they hated him and he hated them. His parents were verbally abusive and disappointed in him because he'd dropped out of college to pursue a career as a musician—unlike his brother who was now in med school. His name was Tommy. He was short, chubby, and had wavy, strawberry blonde hair parted down the middle. Though still in his early twenties, his hairline was already beginning to recede. He wore wire-rimmed glasses and spoke with a thick nasal tone. He was a chronic malcontent and whined incessantly in that annoying voice. His pale face would turn flaming red as he complained about his awful plight. He reminded me of that Flintstone cartoon character "Schleprock," but with a harelip. I imagined he'd been the main prey of many a bully while growing up. I never would have guessed that this troubled, nerdy young man would have such a profound effect on my future.

By August, it had been over two months since I had seen Bukowski. He'd call occasionally, but I was aloof, answering his questions with one-word replies. Because I was changing, I'd grown weary of his lifestyle. On a subconscious level, I knew Bukowski represented the life I was trying to get away from.

When you're an addict, certain people and places pull a trigger within you that causes an impulse to drink or take drugs. Bukowski lived in that self-destructive environment.

There are also certain people you only associate with to feed your addictions—and sadly, I found Bukowski to be one of them. He didn't encourage me to misbehave; it just seemed to work out that way. And, obviously, Georgia was another who fell into this category. Again, it was not a conscious decision on my part to stay away from these people, nor had anyone suggested I do so, it was just becoming too debilitating for me to be around them. My pulling back from Bukowski and Georgia was purely instinctual—and a matter of survival.

THIRTY-FIVE

"I can't take it anymore. Do you hear me? It's over as of today! Okay?"

On August 16, 1977, Bukowski called around noon.

"Hey, Red, how's it swingin', Baby?"

"I'm doing okay, Hank. How are you?"

"Aren't ya gonna wish me Happy Birthday?"

"Oh Jeez, that's right," I said. "Happy birthday, Hank!"

"Listen, I know you've been avoiding me lately, but I would really like to see you today."

"I don't know, Hank . . ." I said.

"Come on, Baby, it's my birthday. Give the old man a treat. All I want for my birthday is to see you. Can't ya find it in your heart to do a favor for a poor old geezer? I may not have too many of these left. At least have lunch with me. It's my birthday, for Christ's sake. I won't keep you long, I promise. Come on. I'll take ya to Musso's."

"Well, okay," I said.

"I'll pick you up in twenty minutes."

He arrived right on time, and we left in his Volks for Musso & Frank.

I was now off the pills, but still drank occasionally. Drinking never was my main problem. It was the pills that were destroying me.

We ordered lunch and a bottle of champagne, then another, and another. The conversation was light and friendly. He didn't drill me this time about other men—and I didn't pry into his personal life.

I complained about living with Mom and how I was looking for a job, but dreaded the thought of going back to waiting tables. He told me he was doing a lot of writing and brought me up to date about the neighbors on Carlton Way. We had a few laughs, and then left a couple hours later with a pleasant buzz.

On the ride home, Bukowski told me he had to stop at his place on Carlton Way. He said he wanted to pick up something. It wasn't out of the way, and I thought nothing of it. When we pulled up in front of his building, he asked me to come in. I was in a pretty good mood, and in no rush to get back to Mom's, so I agreed.

He led me into his apartment holding onto my hand. He walked directly into his bedroom and sat me down on the edge of his bed. He knelt in front of me as though he were about to propose marriage. What the hell is this all about, I wondered. The look on his face suddenly became very serious. He continued to hold my hand.

"Listen, Kid, I can't do this anymore. We've got to end this madness. Do you understand?"

"Huh?" I replied.

"I'm telling you we've got to end this relationship starting today. You're tearing my guts out. I can't think. I can't eat. I can't sleep. This has got to end!"

Just then, there was a knock at the door. Without waiting for Bukowski to open it, in walked a man wearing sunglasses with a camera around his neck. He looked about thirty years old and had long dark hair and a beard.

"Hi, Hank. Well, who do we have here?" he said in a pleasant German accent, referring to me.

The man looked me up and down and said, "Who are you and how do you know Bukowski?"

Just as I began to answer his questions, Bukowski stood up and guided the man toward the living room.

"Never mind, man," Bukowski said. "This is not a good time."

"Okay, I will come back later," the man said.

"Yeah, you do that," Bukowski said, without introducing him and practically pushing him out the front door. I'd later learn that the man was Bukowski's photographer, Michael Montfort.

I was still sitting on the bed when Bukowski resumed his farewell speech.

"Like I said, Cups," he said, and then paused for a moment. "I've allowed you to tear my heart out and wave it on a stick. It's over. I can't take it anymore. Do you hear me? It's over as of today! Okay?"

I stared at him, looking like a felled deer. I had no idea what he was talking about. Though never explicitly stated, in my mind our romantic relationship had been over for several months and I assumed he knew it too. I was stunned and perplexed by the intensity in his voice—and by the urgency of it all. His emotional edict seemed bizarre and inappropriate.

I continued to stare in his eyes, and then whispered, "Okay."

"Good," he said. "Now let's go."

The ride home was awkward and quiet. Still woozy from the champagne, I went straight to bed when I arrived home. I woke up around 8:00 p.m. and turned on the television in my bedroom. There were two doctors holding a press conference over the death of Elvis Presley. I thought I must be dreaming, so I clicked off the TV and fell back to sleep.

I awoke the next morning wondering if the events from the previous day had been a weird dream. I turned on the television, and, sure enough, Elvis was dead. My thoughts then turned to Bukowski.

What was that meeting all about? I had never seen him so intense. He was like a different person—even his voice was different. The signature Bukowski cadence was gone—even his slight lisp had disappeared. It was as though he'd been putting on a façade the entire time I'd known him—until yesterday. That guy was not the Bukowski I knew.

Feeling somewhat dense, I tried to understand why he'd gone through such an elaborate ruse—but I couldn't make any sense of it. I didn't feel I'd been leading him on. Though he'd made it clear that he wanted to be in a one-on-one relationship with me, I let him know that it probably wasn't going to happen—though, admittedly, I never wanted to close the door completely. He seemed to be content with our occasional visits and never let on that he was this tortured over me, or our relationship. Though I knew I would never be happy living with Bukowski, I didn't want to lose him completely as a friend. I now realized this would be impossible.

The word "closure" was not in the pop culture vernacular at that time, but that's what he was attempting to do—find some closure from the grief he felt over my leaving. But unaware of that at the time, I figured his ego had been badly bruised because I had the power in the relationship and it was controlling him.

If it made him feel better to be able to tell himself he'd had the last word in an attempt to regain that control, so be it. I had become his addiction. And just as I was trying to conquer mine, this was his way of attempting to do the same. I felt it was probably the best thing for both of us.

THIRTY-SIX

. . . I applied for the job and was hired. It paid $550 a month, and I was thrilled!

$\mathcal{It}$ was now October 1977. I hadn't seen or spoken to Bukowski since his birthday when he'd delivered his dramatic demand. During this time, I'd been busy learning how to be a good mom and attending my counseling sessions.

I was now actively participating in my group therapy sessions and actually looked forward to seeing my angst-ridden friends. I was becoming much more centered. I hadn't had a pill for months, and I was feeling good about myself.

During one group session, I mentioned that I was proud of myself for getting off the pills, but was bummed that I still hadn't found a job. My nerdy friend Tommy told me he worked in the mailroom for a title insurance company located in the Hall of Records. He said the company was looking for a customer service person.

The job involved taking phone requests from the executives and title officers who were located in the main office. They needed photocopies of documents that weren't available in their computer system. I'd take down the document number, find the book where it was located, copy the document, and send it back to the main office by messenger. That sounded easy enough for even me to learn.

Two days later, I applied for the job and was hired. It paid $550 a month, and I was thrilled!

By November, I was thoroughly enjoying my new entry-level position at Stewart Title Company. I was working in the Hall of Records building, located in the heart of downtown Los Angeles at Temple and Hill. I loved the job—and didn't even mind getting up every morning at five a.m. to catch the 6:15 bus on Glendale Avenue.

While I enjoyed my new job, getting to work was another story. In the middle of October 1977, the city was gripped with fear over reports of young women found brutally raped and murdered. Their bodies had been dumped near my neighborhood in Glendale. I was afraid and no longer wanted to walk to the bus stop alone, so Mom would drive me to the stop. I would sit on the bench at dawn clutching a can of Dow oven cleaner as my weapon, petrified when a stranger approached.

It seemed like every week there was a new victim, with each young woman's body being discovered closer to where I lived. One body was found near City Hall, right down the street from where I worked. It was frightening, and it felt eerily personal. The media referred to the murderer as the "Hillside Strangler."

Kenneth Bianchi, one of "The Hillside Stranglers," worked at the same company where I was employed and killed in close proximity to where I lived.

Two years later, the police would finally arrest the murderers. They were two men who were cousins: Angelo Buono and Kenneth Bianchi. Buono owned an auto repair shop in Glendale, three blocks away from my bus stop, and Bianchi worked as a title officer in the main office for Stewart Title Company. The same company where I was employed, during the same time!

A few years later, my brother sent me a copy of an old Stewart Title Company Christmas list. My last name was Brandes at that time. Kenneth Bianchi's name was right above mine. Larry's message read, "You had a much better Christmas than you thought!"

Larry had access to the company Christmas list because shortly after I was hired at Stewart, he hounded me to find him a job with my company. All the title companies in Los Angeles rented space at the Hall of Records on the 7th floor. They were situated side-by-side each other, separated only by partitions, so most of the employees from the other title companies knew each other. I knew all the managers and would ask them periodically if they had any openings for my brother. One day, the manager of Chicago Title told me he had an opening in the mailroom. Larry inter-

221

viewed and got the job. Though we were working for different companies, I'd see him in the halls every day.

One day, a searcher from my brother's company approached me. His name was Walden "Monty" Muns. He said Larry had told him I knew Charles Bukowski. I was trying to put my past behind me, but did confess to knowing him—feeling as if I were admitting to a crime. Monty told me that he, too, was a poet and had been published in small literary magazines. Monty was a former English teacher who'd taken early retirement. He was a nice man and I liked him very much. He and my brother would become good friends. The three of us would occasionally have lunch together.

One day, Monty asked if I could arrange a meeting with "The Great One." I promised to see what I could do.

The following day, I called Bukowski from work. I hadn't spoken to him in four months—since August 16, 1977—and wasn't sure how he'd react to my call. I was surprised at how friendly he sounded. I told him about my new job and the coworker who wanted to meet him. I expected Bukowski to hang up on me, or, at the very least, tell me to give him a break and not bother him with such things (I knew how he hated meeting fans). Instead, he was gracious and agreed to meet us that evening after work at his place on Carlton Way.

Monty drove, and on the way we stopped to pick up a six-pack. Bukowski greeted us at the door and even shook Monty's hand. Monty seemed a little intimidated by him and didn't say much. Bukowski was also very subdued, so I did most of the talking. It was obvious he hadn't had much to drink prior to our visit and seemed a little tired. I, too, was sober, and was acutely aware of how awkward everyone felt, but I was grateful for Bukowski's hospitality. It wasn't an unpleasant meeting, just slightly uncomfortable. We shared a couple beers, and then Monty and I left about an hour later.

As we walked back to Monty's car, he turned to me and said, "He's not at all what I expected. He's so . . . polite!"

That would be the last time I saw or spoke to Charles Bukowski.

THIRTY-SEVEN

She had killed herself with a drug overdose.

Within six months of being employed, I had saved enough money for Stacey and me to move out of my mom's house and into our own place. Within eight months, I was promoted to the main office as a title officer's assistant making three times the pay. Within two years, I was promoted to title officer and had my own office with two assistants. Finally, I had my cherrywood desk and leather chair. I was now well-ensconced in the nine-to-five corporate world and loved every minute of it.

Life was good for Stacey and me. We lived in a nice little home in Los Feliz on the corner of Tracy Street and Claremont Avenue. By 1981, it had been four years since I'd seen or spoken to Bukowski or Georgia.

I had a new life, complete with a new set of friends. I was no longer dependent on drugs and never volunteered information about my past, including my affiliation with Bukowski. I still enjoyed a drink occasionally, but tried to stay away from anyone who used drugs. Not that I had become a judgmental anti-drug campaigner, I just wanted to steer clear of those circles.

In February 1981, my sister Tracey came to visit. She was now living in Seattle and working as a newscaster for KING radio. She wanted me to take her to a Country and Western bar, which were all the rage at the time thanks to *Urban Cowboy*, the movie starring John Travolta. While a C&W bar wasn't my idea of a good time, I was happy to oblige Tracey. Since I rarely saw her, I wanted her to have a good time during her brief visit.

We went to the Landmark, a bar in Glendale complete with cowboys and line dancing. That night, I met my next husband, David Wood—a

David
(Photo courtesy of Pamela Wood)

stockbroker who had custody of his three sons, Jeffrey, 19, Eric, 14, and David, Jr., 10. He lived in La Canada-Flintridge, a prestigious rural suburb east of Pasadena. David was ten years older than me—and much more conservative, but a lot of fun. He was smart and witty, and, though our politics and backgrounds were diametrically opposed, we enjoyed many stimulating debates, with good humor and respect. We dated for five months before we became engaged. The wedding was set for August 1, 1981.

One night during our engagement, we went out for dinner and then stopped at my place for a nightcap. David scanned the reading material in my bookcase. He was an avid reader. He would read three or four books a month. He pulled out a book from the bottom shelf. It was *Scarlet*.

"You read Bukowski?" he asked.

"Well . . . not really," I answered.

I went on to briefly disclose my relationship with Bukowski and thought that was that.

A week later, we were having dinner at the Nite Watch in Pasadena.

After a couple drinks, David said, "I've got to come clean about something. I read Bukowski's last book, *Women*, and almost called off our wedding."

"What are you talking about?" I asked. "What's the name of the book?"

That was the first time I'd heard of the novel. David proceeded to tell me that my relationship with Bukowski, and his portrayal of it in the book, caused him great distress. He'd been so upset that he'd had to seek advice from friends and even consulted with a psychologist. I told him I couldn't defend myself without first reading the book.

The next day, I purchased a copy of *Women*. When I came to the fanciful "Tammie," it was obvious by the physical description that this character was based on me, but that's where the similarities ended. I found the book very funny and couldn't help laughing out loud at many of the fantastic scenes. Some of the situations were so ridiculous that I couldn't imagine anyone believing this was anything but fiction. I loved Bukowski's writing style and sardonic wit and thoroughly enjoyed the book. This would be the first time I'd read one of Bukowski's novels.

Bukowski was a great comedic writer. Distort and embellish is what a good writer does with a work of fiction—even if it's based on real characters. I wasn't angry with Bukowski for his less than flattering portrayal of me in _Women_. But I did wonder how a smart man like David would consider Bukowski's fictional work as anything closely resembling reality. David knew me well enough to realize this character had no basis in fact. He was also astute enough to understand the concept of "poetic license."

After some assurances from me that Tammie was not my alter-ego, David relaxed. We proceeded to get married, as scheduled, on August 1st.

After the wedding ceremony, Stacey and I moved into David's home in La Canada. My

The portrayal of me in the book Women _nearly derailed my upcoming marriage to David_

brother Larry loved my little house on Tracy Street and offered to sublet it. Unbeknownst to me, I left a few things behind.

About a year after my marriage, I received a call from my ex-boyfriend Bob, the screenplay writer. He and Larry were still friends and he told me that Larry had found a box of Bukowski's letters and paintings in a cabinet high above the hall closet in the house he sublet from me and had sold them. I'd taken a box of books that Bukowski had inscribed to me, but the remaining box must have been pushed back too far in the tall deep cabinet for me to see. I hadn't noticed they were missing. I must have assumed they were among the many boxes stored in the garage of my new home with David.

Given how upset David was about my affiliation with Bukowski, I decided not to pursue the matter with Larry. After all, Bukowski was an ex-boyfriend, not a commodity, and one that had almost ruined my relationship with my new husband. Still, I was angry and upset, but mostly at

Larry's larceny, and lack of respect for me or my possessions, but I never did confront him about it.

Larry had disappointed me my entire life. He never had that big brother protective instinct toward me and it never failed to hurt me. But I felt more pity than anger toward him. I loved my brother, but he had become a self-centered drug addict—what was the point?

Years later, I read a book titled *Literary Los Angeles*. In it, the author, Lionel Rolfe, interviews Monty Munns (the coworker I introduced to Bukowski in December, 1977). In the book Monty shows a Bukowski painting to the author. He goes on to say that the painting was given to him by my brother Larry. It was one that used to belong to me. I've also been led to believe that most of the letters ended up being sold to a bookstore owner in Hollywood, named Red Stodolsky, who is no longer alive. I had obtained the paintings through questionable means, so I chalked them up to Karma—but losing the letters, notes and poems really hurt.

The day I moved in with David, and long before I was aware of the missing box, I'd spent it unpacking my belongings. When I came to the box that contained Bukowski's inscribed books and the journal I kept while with him, I stored the books, but decided to do away with the journal. I didn't want to take the chance of David finding it.

I was a newlywed and wanted to do everything I could to make the relationship work. Getting rid of the diary was a way for me to symbolically obliterate my unwholesome past. I put the notebook full of incriminating evidence of passion and mayhem in the fireplace and turned on the gas starter. I'd give anything to read it today. Ah, foolish youth. We can never imagine when we're young that a day will come when documented memories like these would mean so much.

Stacey and I settled into our new life in the pristine, upper-class suburb of La Canada with David and his sons. Stacey loved David, and he was a wonderful father to her. She was also delighted to have three adorable brothers. We had our challenges, as most blended families do, but the house was filled with comedians, and there was never a dull moment.

During our first year together, David suggested we have Thanksgiving at our house. David loved to entertain and was a gourmet cook—a true blessing, since I had zero culinary skills.

We invited both our families. Larry arrived with Georgia's ex-boyfriend Bill. I asked him how she was. He told me she had passed away four months earlier. He and Georgia had split a couple years prior. She had remarried and moved to East Los Angeles with her new husband. According to Bill, the husband came home and found her lifeless body on the living room floor. She had killed herself with a drug overdose. He wasn't certain if it was an accident, but assumed it was.

Poor Georgia. She had so much potential to do something exceptional with her life. She had a brilliant, creative mind and a magnificent wit. Though she clearly had a death wish, evidenced by her out of control drug use, she also had a funny, skewed view of the world and seemed to enjoy life. She rarely discussed her past and I wondered where her demons came from.

Georgia had told me that she considered herself a misfit growing up in her provincial small town. She said that as a young girl she admired the town hussy named Tullah.

According to Georgia, Tullah was an exotic dancer at the local nightclub. She was a flamboyant, unabashed sexpot. The priggish, moralistic town's women were jealous of Tullah because all the men lusted after her. The women would often conspire to have Tullah run out of town on trumped up censorship charges, but never succeeded.

Georgia was self-conscious about her appearance from a very young age. Her features were sharp and unrefined, but not what you'd call ugly—just different. She knew she would never be referred to as a delicate flower. She wanted to be pretty like the other girls and desperately craved attention from the opposite sex.

Tullah Hanley (above) inspired the "Georgia" look and style.

She would often see Tullah strolling confidently through town dressed like a Vegas showgirl, unapologetically flaunting her physical gifts. Georgia watched with longing while the men drooled and tripped all over themselves trying to catch a glimpse of the charming sex symbol. There was something magical about her, Georgia thought, and she wanted to be just like her.

Idolizing the local harlot didn't sit well with her conservative staunch Catholic parents. According to Georgia, they were religious zealots who sent her and her younger brother to Catholic school from the time they could walk until they graduated from high school. Her pious mother was especially disappointed in the immoral direction her daughter was heading and would perform mini-exorcisms on her wayward spawn by quoting scripture from the Bible on a daily basis while praying out loud to God like an evangelical preacher—begging the good Lord to save her misguided child from the path to Hell.

Once Georgia turned eighteen, she rebelled against her deity-devoted parents by doing a 180 degree spiritual about-face, completely liberating herself from all the tenets of her intense religious upbringing—giving the finger to her bible-beating parents, the sacred scriptures and the self-righteous townspeople. I wondered how large a role religion played in her hedonistic, self-destructive lifestyle. After all, the last time I saw her she was being chased by the devil.

Though I was saddened by the news, it didn't come as a big shock. She'd been in such bad shape the last time I saw her. I knew it wasn't a matter of "if," but "when" the drugs would do her in. She'd emulated her idol, Janis Joplin, in life and now in death. Georgia was thirty-seven years old.

THIRTY-EIGHT

He allowed me into his closely guarded inner sanctum . . .

$\mathcal{M}eanwhile,$ life was going smoothly for me and my new brood. We all transitioned nicely into a comfortable, predictable routine. The only drama in my life was refereeing an occasional quarrel between siblings. I had finally achieved a sense of purpose and stabilty that I had been longing for since childhood.

A couple years into our marriage, David suggested I change jobs. He encouraged me to become a sales representative. "After all, that's where the real money is."

I was reluctant to make a career change, because it didn't seem like a good fit for me and I was basically a shy person. I was also less than impressed with the sales people I came in contact with at the office. Most of them seemed like smarmy, glad-handers and were much too aggressive for my taste. I truly didn't feel I could succeed in that side of the business. I wasn't unhappy with my position, but I enjoyed challenging myself and thought it may be time to shake things up. With David's support I figured I had nothing to lose. I decided to give it a try.

I interviewed for a sales position with another title company and got the job. Within a few years, I was the top producing sales rep for my company in Los Angeles County. I would hold that title for several consecutive years, collecting many awards along the way. I'd eventually become assistant vice president of sales for a large Fortune 500 company.

During this time, I thought about Bukowski now and then and hoped he was doing well. Once in awhile, David and I would spend the day at

Santa Anita racetrack. I would fantasize about seeing Bukowski seated in the Club House, or standing in the betting line, and wondered how he would react to me. I would picture myself running up to him and giving him a big hug. He would be so proud of how far I'd come, I thought. Maybe we would share a beer and laugh about our salad days. Then in 1987, his movie *Barfly* was released. That same year, I read an article featuring him in the November issue of *People Magazine*. I was pleased that he was finally being recognized by the mainstream media and achieving some commercial success. The article also mentioned that he and his *wife* Linda lived in a home located in San Pedro, California. I smiled at the irony of how we two nonconformists had ended up in middle-class suburbia.

After seven years of marriage, David and I divorced in 1988, but remained good friends. We never lost affection for each other, and in 1994 decided to make another go of it. Our children were now grown and on their own. Maybe without all the distractions, we could make it work.

I was still enjoying a successful career in sales, while David was on the board of directors of a popular infomercial company.

On March 9, 1994, I was driving to a client meeting, with the radio tuned to the all-news station, KFWB.

"Pornographic poet, Charles Bukowski died today of leukemia in San Pedro, California," the announcer said. "The self-proclaimed dirty old man was seventy-three."

A wave of sorrow washed over me, and my eyes began to well up. Then I became angry with the announcer.

"Pornographic poet? That's it? Pornographic poet? That's what you've reduced him to? Over thirty years of prose, poetry, even a screenplay, and that's the best you can do?!" I yelled at the radio.

I had made the same mistake when I'd met Bukowski at twenty-three—almost twenty years before. I now realized how wrong I'd been. Who is writing this copy, I wondered—some nineteen-year-old intern?

Then I thought about the man. I couldn't believe he was gone. It didn't seem possible. Men like him didn't die. He seemed larger than life, and the thought of him leaving this earth one day had never occurred to me.

I became filled with sadness. I'd never taken the time to let him know how much I appreciated him and all the things he'd taught me. He had been my friend, my lover, my mentor. He had been so patient and caring toward my daughter and me. Somewhere in the back of my mind I always felt certain I would see him again. Now that would never happen.

Memories came flooding. I thought about the time he bought a dress for Stacey so she'd have something to wear to her friend's birthday party. She had outgrown her only party dress, and I was too broke to buy her a new one. Bukowski quietly took it upon himself to go shopping and bought a beautiful, frilly yellow dress for her. He took the dress to my mom's house, where Stacey was staying that day, dropped it off, and left without saying a word. I would have never known if my mother hadn't told me about it.

I thought about the way he was always there to help, no matter where I was, or what trouble I found myself in—without delivering a lecture or passing judgment.

I thought about how he loved to cuddle, like no man I'd ever met. He could be so tender and gentle. He was a very sentimental man—*just a rough, tough, creampuff*, I thought to myself.

I also thought about the tears in his sad eyes and the tortured look on his face that night he begged me to stay, but I left anyway—an image that will always haunt me.

It would be years after his death before I knew the extent of the grief he suffered over me. It wasn't until I was contacted by John Dullaghan, the film-maker who produced the Bukowski documentary *Born into This*, and at the same time, contacted by Howard Sounes, the author of the Bukowski biography *Locked in the Arms of a Crazy Life*, that I would be made aware of the deep emotional impact I had on him—a revelation I would find stunning.

I do regret any pain I may have caused Bukowski due to my lack of grace and sensitivity, but not my decision to leave. I could have taken the path of least resistance and stayed. I'm sure he would have been happy to continue caring for me while I merrily proceeded down my road of self-destruction. Life would certainly never be dull. But dull is exactly what I needed. Though I loved him, I loved my daughter more. She needed a stable, predictable mother and environment—not the miasmic lifestyle I had created with Bukowski. We both possessed too many deep insecurities and unresolved trust issues—it would have been a disastrous situation for all of us. I am convinced we would have gone from "Arthur and Marilyn" to "Sid and Nancy," resulting in a tragic ending. I'm also convinced I never would have achieved the personal satisfaction and feelings of self-worth I now possess. He deserved someone more mature and sensitive to his needs—and by all accounts he found that someone in his widow, Linda Lee.

I loved Charles Bukowski as much as I could love any man at that time in my life. Though I may have been immature and thoughtless at times, I always knew I was in the presence of an extraordinary man. Some call him a genius and I would agree. He was a uniquely complicated, beautiful eccentric. He lived life full of white-hot passion—often motivated by love and rage—with a special gift for "laying down the word" with clarity and ease. Unafraid to bare his soul, he wrote with a raw intensity about subjects many considered too intimate or taboo to address. What set him apart was his ability to expose life's obscenities with humor, dignity and an underlying elegance, while touching millions in a very deep place—including me.

Our romance lasted less than two years, but it is an experience I will always cherish. At times bordering on insanity—like guns, alcohol and politics—we were a combustible combination. But for all the madness and turbulence in our relationship, we shared many tender and poignant moments. He allowed me into his closely guarded inner sanctum and trusted me with a rare glimpse of his vulnerable heart and soul—a privilege reserved for a chosen few. I now realize what a special gift it was for me to have been given the opportunity to love and to be loved by Charles Bukowski—and for that I will always be grateful.

Maybe he didn't give a damn, but I do hope he left this earth aware of how much I did love and appreciate him. I can see him now, sitting on a brown and mustard striped throne in his celestial kingdom, surrounded by adoring cherubs, with a beer in one hand and a cigarette in the other, having a marvelous time regaling the gods with his wildly entertaining stories about the beautiful (but) crazy fallen angels he left behind.

© Joan Gannij

SPECIAL ACKNOWLEDGEMENTS

Norman Mailer once said, "Writing a book is the closest men will ever get to giving birth." Having accomplished both, I couldn't agree more. The parallels between the two are uncanny.

Much like parenthood, writing this book was the most monumental challenge I have ever voluntarily subjected myself to without benefit of anesthesia. Though ultimately a labor of love, it was at times frustrating, emotionally painful and just plain hard work. Many assume writing is purely a solo exercise; yes, the end product is my responsibility—with my name and literary DNA on the final manuscript, but during its gestation I enlisted the expertise of many intellectual superiors, most of whom I'm privileged to refer to as friends and feel it would be disingenuous to take full credit.

Writing this memoir was also one of the most humbling experiences of my life; had I known how little I know about English composition and the creative writing process, this book would not exist. Fortunately, arrogance is bliss, and I had access, directly and indirectly, to many good minds who contributed significantly to the creation of this baby. They are as follows:

Special thanks and affection go to my family, friends and clients who have trusted me both personally and professionally with their business and confidences. Your unwavering loyalty and support made it possible for me to take the necessary time away to write this book. I love you all.

There are five dear (and patient) friends in particular that I called (imposed) upon for literary advice when I felt "stuck." Though I'm certain they would have preferred a top-lip hot wax, they graciously took time from their busy schedules, when solicited, to offer their unvarnished opinions and constructive criticism, which helped tremendously. They are: Dan Jordinelli, Patty Barr, Alice Hartwell, Angela and Barbara Cardinal. Thank you, friends.

Much appreciation goes to wordsmith Jeff Menell, copyeditor extraordinaire. This book would not have moved past a publisher's mailroom clerk without assistance from this gentleman. Thank you for your obsession with the English language.

Many thanks to filmmaker, John Dullaghan and author, Howard Sounes—both of whom included me in their masterful projects. John for his tour de force documentary titled, *Born into This*; and Howard for his fascinating and amazingly well researched biography titled, *Charles Bukowski: Locked in the Arms of a Crazy Life*; two finely crafted works of art based on the life of Charles Bukowski. During our respective interviews, each shared astounding personal revelations about my relationship with Buk, prompting me to revisit that closed chapter of my life, which became the motivation for writing this book.

I'm thankful to Michael Phillips, creator of Bukowski.net, a valuable source of all things "Bukowski." Without this website, it's likely I would not have been introduced to Roni Braun, founder of the German based *Bukowski Society*—Bukowski-Gesellschaft.de. I owe an overwhelming debt of gratitude to Roni for reuniting me with copies of priceless long lost letters and poems written to me from Buk during our affair. (Copies were found among Michael Montfort's vast Bukowski collection.) Thank you both for keeping his voice and true spirit alive on a daily basis.

Immeasurable gratitude goes to my friend, mentor and "polisher," Melanie Villines. I could not have written this book without the benefit of your extraordinary talents, saintlike patience, and remarkable insights. You've taught me more about writing and courage in the one year it took to complete this book, than all the academicians preceding you. There for me every step of the way—offering everything from spiritual and professional guidance and encouragement to diplomatic literary advice—you helped make my words shine brightly (and readable); your participation in the creation of this book was invaluable—I can't thank you enough.

A special thank you to photographer Joan Gannij for providing a newly-discovered photo of Charles Bukowski as seen on page 232.

I would be terribly remiss if I did not thank the cutting-edge German filmmaker and Renaissance man, Thomas Schmitt for his generosity in allowing me to use footage from the first of three penetrating Bukowski documentaries, "Charles Bukowski—East Hollywood 1976." Your contribution has helped my story come alive, as well as preserving precious personal memories, and for that I will be eternally grateful (I hope).

Finally, my deep affection and appreciation go to Al and Judy Berlinski of Sun Dog Press. Reminiscent of the legendary publishing duo, John and Barbara Martin of Black Sparrow Press, your numerous combined gifts, warm hearts and good humor have made my first publishing experience an absolute delight. The professional dedication you've invested in this book and the personal kindness you've shown mean more than you'll ever know. Thanks for taking a chance on me.

BOOKS BY SUN DOG PRESS

Steve Richmond, *Santa Monica Poems*

Steve Richmond, *Hitler Painted Roses*
(Foreword by Charles Bukowski and afterword by Mike Daily)

Steve Richmond, *Spinning Off Bukowski*

Neeli Cherkovski, *Elegy for Bob Kaufman*

Randall Garrison, *Lust in America*

Billy Childish, *Notebooks of a Naked Youth*

Dan Fante, *Chump Change*

Robert Steven Rhine, *My Brain Escapes Me*

Fernanda Pivano, *Charles Bukowski: Laughing With the Gods*

Howard Bone with Daniel Waldron, *Side Show: My Life with Geeks,
Freaks & Vagabonds in the Carny Trade*

Jean-François Duval, *Bukowski and the Beats*

Dan Fante, *A gin-pissing-raw-meat-dual-carburetor-
V8-son-of-a-bitch from Los Angeles*

David Calonne, Editor, *Charles Bukowski, Sunlight Here I Am:
Interviews and Encounters, 1963-1993*

Ben Pleasants, *Visceral Bukowski, Inside the Sniper
Landscape of L.A. Writers*

Chandler Brossard, *Over the Rainbow? Hardly*
(Introduced and edited by Steven Moore)

Dan Fante, *Short Dog*

Dan Fante, *Kissed By A Fat Waitress*

ABOUT PAMELA MILLER WOOD TODAY

A native Californian, Pamela Miller Wood has lived in the Los Angeles area most of her life. For over 30 years she has enjoyed a successful career in the Southern California real estate industry, garnering many awards for outstanding achievement along the way, including "Top Producer" in Los Angeles County for ten consecutive years.

This is Ms. Wood's first full-length book—a true tour de force!